W9-BKW-738

Welles-Turner Memorial Library

2407 Main Street
Glastonbury, Connecticut 06033

In memory of

George Sanford

DEATH MARCH ESCAPE

DEATH MARCH ESCAPE

THE REMARKABLE STORY *of a* MAN WHO TWICE ESCAPED THE NAZI HOLOCAUST

JACK J. HERSCH

Frontline Books, London

First published in Great Britain in 2018 by
FRONTLINE BOOKS
An imprint of
Pen & Sword Books Ltd
Yorkshire - Philadelphia
Copyright © Jack J. Hersch
ISBN 978 1 52674 022 9
The right of Jack J. Hersch to be identified as
Author of this work has been asserted by him in accordance
with the Copyright, Designs and Patents Act 1988.

A CIP catalogue record for this book is
available from the British Library

Typeset in India by Versatile PreMedia Services. www.versatilepremedia.com
Printed and bound by TJ International

Pen & Sword Books Ltd incorporates the imprints of Pen & Sword
Archaeology, Atlas, Aviation, Battleground, Discovery,
Family History, History, Maritime, Military, Naval, Politics,
Social History, Transport, True Crime, Claymore Press,
Frontline Books, Praetorian Press,
Seaforth Publishing and White Owl

For a complete list of Pen & Sword titles please contact
PEN & SWORD BOOKS LTD
47 Church Street, Barnsley, South Yorkshire, S70 2AS, England
E-mail: enquiries@pen-and-sword.co.uk
Website: www.pen-and-sword.co.uk
Or
PEN AND SWORD BOOKS
1950 Lawrence Rd, Havertown, PA 19083, USA
E-mail: Uspen-and-sword@casematepublishers.com
Website: www.penandswordbooks.com

Contents

CONTENTS

CONTENTS

Part III. ENNS

List of Plates

FAMILY PHOTOGRAPHS

1. The photo of my father that I saw on the KZ Mauthausen website in 2007. (Author)
2. My father with his brother, Villi, in the rear storage area of their father's small soap factory in Dej, 1938. (Author)
3. My father with his sister, Rosie, in an undated photo inside their home. (Author)
4. My father, second from left, in an undated photo. He is assembled with his Hungarian Labor Service battalion. (Author)
5. My father and two of his friends in 1942 or 1943, when he was around seventeen. (Author)
6. My mother. The picture is dated July 30, 1951. (Author)
7. My mother in 1944, when she was fourteen, with her younger sister, Renee, and their uncle, David Grossman, a medic with the 16th Regiment of the US Army's 1st Division. (Author)
8. Ignaz Friedmann, in his World War I Austro-Hungarian Army uniform. (Mauthausen Memorial)
9. Barbara Friedmann, in an undated image.
10. My father's Prisoner Personnel Card. (Author)
11. The photo my father's siblings mailed him in 1946, during his recuperation in the Kohlbruck Klinik. (Author)
12. My father among unidentified fellow patients – all 'survivors' – in the Kohlbruck Klinik in 1945. (Author)
13. My father in a hospital bed in the Kohlbruck Klinik in Passau, in 1946.
14. This portrait in camp uniform was taken in 1945, while my father was recuperating in the Kohlbruck Klinik. (Author)
15. My father on an Israeli beach in an undated photo. (Author)

ON THE GROUND

Foreword

One day a few years ago, while at my job working for the Mauthausen Memorial Archives, I received an email from the USA: 'On your website, in the section "death marches," I came across a photograph of my late father in his teens. Can you tell me how your institution came into possession of this photograph?'

Following up, I learned the photo was part of a manuscript that had been completed in the 1970s by a local historian, Peter Kammerstätter. Kammerstätter had conducted interviews with people who lived along the route of the death marches from the Mauthausen Concentration Camp to one of its sub-camps, Gunskirchen, and who still remembered those events of April 1945. One of these people had given Kammerstätter a photograph of a young man who had escaped from the march and had been hidden in their house until the end of the war. The young man in the photograph was David Hersch. The sender of the email was his son Jack.

Researching the answer to the question posed in Jack's email, I had the distinct sensation something important was happening; that, like a puzzle, the pieces of a fragmented history were about to be put back together, resulting in something particularly significant. Some days later, I had Jack Hersch on the phone. From two completely different spots in the world thousands of miles apart, two people who apparently had almost nothing in common were talking to each other. Jack, a US citizen, is the son of a Jewish survivor of Mauthausen, a man born in Transylvania, formerly part of the Austro-Hungarian Empire. I, an Austrian, am a descendant of a society that bears responsibility for what Jack's father had to endure. Our origins could hardly be more divergent. But there was one thing we did share: a common history of which both of us only knew tiny pieces, stemming from the stories and investigations of others; a history which we both hadn't experienced ourselves but which, to a large extent, was certainly ours.

Jack continued digging deeper into his father's history. Now, years later, I have read the complete results of his research in the pages of *Death March Escape*. This book has given me insight into the thoughts and emotions of the author and I realize that my first, distinct sensation back then was right: the story told in these pages is indeed of enormous importance – for Jack, for myself, and especially for the world we live in.

At one point in the book, Jack talks about his visit to Mauthausen, what we now call the Mauthausen Memorial. He describes how he was walking through the preserved rooms and buildings of the former concentration camp, reading the short texts which we designed some years ago in order to give visitors comprehensive historic information on the site. 'I can understand each word I read,' Jack writes, 'but I cannot fully comprehend its meaning.' Now as I read Jack's words, I ask myself: did we, a team of historians, museum curators, and educators, comprehend their full meaning when writing these texts, however historically accurate and well-founded they may be? Or is there possibly a deeper meaning which the texts obscure, rather than reveal?

National Socialism and the *Shoah*, the Holocaust, succeeded in violently destroying communities and their common histories, fragmenting them and scattering their pieces all over the world. Isn't it, therefore, absolutely necessary to collect stories like the one in this book, to gather them and bring them back together, to link them to each other, and in doing so, make history "whole" again? Isn't that precisely what the work of remembrance is all about? Jack Hersch's book makes an extraordinary contribution to this effort.

Christian Dürr
Curator, Mauthausen Memorial
Vienna, Austria, March 2018

PART I
DEJ

Chapter 1

Lufthansa

I'm traveling light as I step aboard the Lufthansa 747 jumbo jet at Los Angeles International Airport's Bradley Terminal. It's Friday evening, the start of the Labor Day holiday weekend, but I'm not going on vacation and I won't be gone long, so I don't need much. I'm on my way to northern Austria to walk the grounds of the concentration camps where the Nazis tortured and enslaved my father, and to find precisely where he hid after he'd escaped. It is a journey that beckoned to me from the moment my cousin Vivian telephoned from Israel a few years earlier with astonishing news about him.

In June 1944 my father entered KZ Mauthausen as a 160-pound, eighteen-year-old youth.[1] By the Nazi's own rating system, KZ Mauthausen and its nearby sub-camp, KZ Gusen I, were the harshest, cruelest labor concentration camps in the entire Third Reich. After ten brutal months in both camps, my father had been whittled down to 80 pounds. And then, because he was still alive five weeks before the war ended, he was forced onto a Nazi death march with the expectation that he would finally collapse and die somewhere on the road between KZ Mauthausen and KZ Gunskirchen, a concentration camp thirty-four unfathomable miles away.

My father came close to dying many times that year, but he didn't die in those concentration camps, and he didn't die on that death march. Nor did he die on a second death march ten days later.

Instead, he escaped from the death marches. Twice. Once was unheard of. Twice was thought to be impossible.

---

1 KZ stands for the German word, *Konzentrationslager*, literally 'concentration camp.' Camps were usually named for nearby towns, and the letters KZ were put ahead of the camp's name. Sometimes KL (L for *Lager*, German for 'camp') was used instead of KZ. I will use KZ.

3

Chapter 2

Cousin Vivi

Early on a warm May morning in 2007, I was sitting at my desk in a Los Angeles office high-rise, facing computer screens showing stock and bond prices and world news, talking heads chirping away on the wall-mounted television, volume set on low. I work in the financial field and was just beginning my day. The rising sun threw long shadows off the tall buildings visible from my window.

As I was reading the morning's headlines, my cell phone rang. Caller ID revealed it was my cousin Vivian Tobias, my father's sister's daughter. She's my age, forty-eight at the time, and lives in Netanya, Israel, a pleasant coastal resort town twenty miles north of Tel Aviv, with her husband David. Though it was already mid-afternoon in Israel, she usually didn't call me this early. I answered my phone.

Normally we would begin by comparing notes on our children, my three teenagers and her two boys who were doing their compulsory Israeli Army service. Not this time. Vivi, as I called her, got right to the point.

'I was on the computer looking for something for my mother, and I saw your father's picture,' she said in her melodious voice. She had learned English in Israeli schools. 'Did you know he's on the internet?'

'My dad?' I asked incredulously. 'No, I had no idea. Where did you see him?' Why, I wondered, would he be on the internet six years after his death? Maybe she'd made a mistake.

'He is on the Mauthausen Concentration Camp website,' Vivi replied. 'It says he escaped from a death march.'

'It's true, he did,' I confirmed. I had no idea Mauthausen even had a website. I'd never bothered looking.

'Jackie,' she said, addressing me by the childhood name my relatives still use, 'you make it sound like it's nothing, but it seems

5

your father is special. I've read about the death marches. Hundreds of thousands of Jews were forced to march thirty, forty, even one hundred miles to get away from the Russians and Americans who were coming near to their concentration camps. Almost no one escaped from the marches. But your father did.'

'Well, he actually escaped twice,' I said. 'He told me the story many times over the years.' I stole a peek at my computer screens.

'I think you don't understand.' Now I heard a distinct note of irritation in her voice. 'His is the *only* story on the Mauthausen website about escaping from the death march. No one else is there, only your father. I don't think you know the whole story. Please, type Mauthausen and his name into Google. You will see.'

I did as she said, and my father's name appeared atop a full screen of search results.

'Huh, I had no idea,' I said, more to myself than to Vivi.

Clicking on the first link took me to KZ Mauthausen's website. I was instantly drawn to my father's name in the menu on the top of the webpage, in a section called *Death Marches*. Sitting straighter in my chair, I clicked on it, and after a beat, a black-and-white picture unfurled onto my screen. It was a head shot, a brilliantly clear photo from the shoulders up.

A young man who looked remarkably like my seventeen-year-old son, Sam, was staring at me. I stared back, frozen.

It was my father, as a teenager.

I had never before seen this photo, or any like it, of my father in his youth. I kept all my parents' old photographs. I had only a few of my father from before the war, and all were taken at a distance. None let me see so clearly the angular planes of his young face, and the impish eyes that belied a man with a monumental determination to survive. My father told me that before being sent to a concentration camp he had done modeling work for his town's photographer. The professional-looking head shot now on my screen must have been one of those pictures. His hair was wavy and thick. He was wearing a light colored, pin-striped, open collared shirt and a stylish, peak-lapel blazer. He looked like he was about to tell one of his unlimited supply of jokes.

How had the people at the Mauthausen website gotten this photo?

I noticed the English caption underneath. I read it aloud:

In April 1945 Ignaz and Barbara Friedmann from Enns Kristein rescued the completely exhausted David Hersch from the death march from Mauthausen and Gunskirchen and hid him until the end of the war.

6

I knew about the Friedmanns. I knew the story of how they'd found my father the day after his second escape and had hidden him, at great risk to themselves, until American soldiers liberated Enns, their town. How did the Mauthausen website people know his story? Why had they singled him out? Why was his story the only one here?

My world had gone silent.

I had often heard and read that survivors of the 'Holocaust,' Hitler's nearly successful attempt to destroy the Jews of Europe, are reticent about recounting their experiences in 'the camps' (survivors, I knew from growing up with many of them, referred to concentration camps as, 'the camps').[1] Supposedly many survivors have gone their entire lives without breathing a word of what they'd endured. I had even heard many of them had not cracked a smile or told a joke since the day they were crammed aboard a cattle car bound for places like Auschwitz and Treblinka.

My father was *nothing* like those survivors. He told me often about his time under Nazi occupation in Hungary, his year in the camps, and his escapes. He told his story lightly, almost breezily, and without hesitation.

He particularly liked to tell his survival story on Passover. After all, the holiday commemorates the Jews' breakout in the dead of night from Egyptian bondage under the command of Moses and presumably with supernatural help. The first night of Passover is marked by a traditional family meal, the Seder, where it is customary to recount that ancient midnight adventure. Since the Passover meal is, at its core, a celebration of escape and deliverance, at every Seder my father recounted to my brother and me his own adventures of escape, capture, near-death, and escape again.

As readily as my father told his tale, I sensed a hidden darkness within him, pain he never shared with me. The only hints he ever gave of it was when he'd tell me he hadn't slept well, or he'd had a nightmare about the camps. But then he would quickly toss it off with a casual wave of his hand, saying it was, 'no big deal,' just an off night.

'You have this picture, yes?' Vivi snapped me back to the present.

I took a deep breath. 'No,' I confessed, 'I don't. Does your mother?'

Vivi's mother, Rosie, and my father were two of eight children in their family. Four of them – my father, Rosie, and two uncles –

---

1 'Survivor' is a label given to anyone who'd emerged from any Nazi concentration camp. It is also sometimes used more broadly, denoting European Jews who'd survived the Nazi era.

had survived the Holocaust. The other four had been murdered by the Nazis.

'No, but she remembers it. She said it was taken when your father was seventeen. A local photographer used it as an advertisement for his studio.'

As I'd suspected. 'Interesting,' I said. 'But I can't imagine how the people at Mauthausen got it.'

'Do you think maybe he gave the picture to them when he visited to there?'

'What?' Now alarm bells rang in my head. 'My dad never visited Mauthausen,' I said firmly. 'He never went back there, he hated that place. He nearly died there.'

'Yes, he did,' Vivi replied with absolute conviction. 'He went back in 1997. He told this to my mother. He didn't tell you?'

I was utterly stunned. Until that moment I believed my father had told me everything going on in his life. 'No,' I managed to say. 'No, he didn't. Are you sure he went back?'

'Yes, one hundred percent I am sure. I asked my mother again just today, and she said he went alone, on his way to Israel.'

Vivi's mother and the two other surviving Hersch brothers all lived near each other in Natanya. My father had lived in Long Beach, New York, and visited his sister and brothers at least twice a year. I always knew when, and where, he was going. Or so I thought.

Vivi continued, 'My mother asked him about it when he came to her house and he told her he went, but he said that it was no big deal. He didn't say anything more about it.' 'No big deal' was one of my father's favorite phrases. I easily imagined him saying that to his sister.

'This makes no sense,' I said. 'I just can't understand why he didn't tell me.'

'I'm sure he had a very good reason,' Vivi said definitively. 'I think you should try to find out what his reason was. I would want to know if I were you.'

Vivi and I sent our love to each other's families and hung up, leaving me alone with the photo of my father filling my computer screen while the rising sun's rays streamed through my office window.

Chapter 3

Dad

David Arieh Hersch, my father, was 5ft 10in tall, and slim but deceptively strong. He wore his salt-and-pepper hair combed back, had a fantastic smile that lit up his face, and owned a thin line of a scar under his left eye from a seltzer bottle that had exploded in his hands. After the war he'd worked for a short while in a seltzer bottling plant in Haifa, Israel, owned by his girlfriend's father (she was not my mother, Mom hadn't come along yet).

My father was a fun, light-hearted guy who laughed easily, spoke nine languages fluently, followed the New York Jets football team closely, loved reading non-fiction, and had a twinkle in his eye. It was in his left eye, and when he told you a story I swear it sparkled. He remembered jokes and told them like a stand-up comic, in any of his languages. When he told them, he had a knack of bursting out laughing just as he delivered the punch line, and that always brought you right into the joke with him.

He was born on July 13, 1925, in the semi-rural town of Dej, Romania ('Dej' rhymes with 'beige'). In the years before World War II, Dej was a community of 15,000 in the Transylvania region, thirty-seven miles north of Cluj, Romania's second biggest city.

Transylvania is home to verdant hills, shimmering farm fields, and salt, gold, copper and iron mines. Its mountains are also the home of Count Dracula, if you believe in those things. The Austro-Hungarian Empire controlled the region from the mid-1800s until its defeat in World War I, when the empire was broken apart. The Kingdom of Hungary and the Austrian Republic became distinct sovereign nations, while Transylvania was cleaved off and given to Romania.

Typical of communities in the region, the Dej my father knew was populated by farmers, merchants, professionals, and tradesmen.

The homes on its rolling hills were of sturdy cement construction, painted white or in light pastels of tan, green and blue, with red tile roofs and tidy back yards. Like other European towns as old as Dej, its streets were narrow, serpentine, and mostly unpaved, running haphazardly out from the main town square, which was then (and is still today) dominated by a sixteenth-century Calvinist church boasting a 230ft tall spire. Horse-drawn-cart was the dominant means of transportation in my father's time, and even now horses can be heard clopping around the town.

My grandfather, Jozsefne Jacob, was born in Dej in 1886. In the Jewish tradition of naming children after deceased relatives, I'm named after him, though I've been given the inverse of his name, and thankfully a few letters were left off, so legally I'm Jacob Josef. Everyone now calls me Jack, but growing up I was Jackie because my mother liked the name.

My grandfather was of average height and thin, with a tightly trimmed beard and innate but unexploited talent as a writer and artist, but he made his living as the owner of a small soap factory. In 1908 he married my grandmother, Malvina, who was five years younger, a sweet and charitable woman who was better known by her Hebrew name, Malka.

The eight Hersch siblings were born in two bunches. Two girls and two boys arrived before my grandfather went off to fight in World War I as a corporal of cavalry in the Austro-Hungarian army. Lazar was the oldest, born in 1909. In quick succession came two girls, Hanna-Leah, and Blina, and finally Adolph in 1914. He was Uncle Villi to me, a name he assumed in his twenties, since 'Adolph' was an unappealing name for a Jew by then.

My grandfather was captured by the Russians early in the Great War and spent four years as their prisoner. When he returned home to Dej, he and Malka had four more children, again two boys and two girls. Chaya-Sarah was born in 1919, followed by Vivi's mother Rosie in 1921, Isadore in 1923, and finally my father in 1925.

Chapter 4

Realization

After hanging up with Vivi, I leaned in close to my computer screens. Carefully inspecting the photograph of my teenaged father, I could see a crease along the upper left corner, like it had been dog-eared and then smoothed over. Had it been in his wallet? Had it been inadvertently folded when he'd slipped it into his pocket? Instead of being folded, was the crease the result of a paper clip crimping the picture when it was attached to a file? If so, whose file?

Where did this picture come from?

Then much larger questions loomed up before me. Why am I only now, this morning, seeing the KZ Mauthausen website, the site belonging to the concentration camp that nearly killed my father? Shouldn't I have known about it? Shouldn't I have seen this long ago?

Vivi was right. For my father to be the only person in the *Death Marches* section of Mauthausen's website must mean the story of his escape and being hidden by the Friedmanns was far more unusual and unique than I had ever considered. I had thought it was common. Apparently it wasn't.

Clearly, as she said, I didn't know the whole story.

Then there's that trip my father took to KZ Mauthausen in 1997. The more I thought about it, the more bothered I became that he had gone back there without telling me. What was there? What was in KZ Gusen I, or in KZ Mauthausen, or in the town of Enns that he didn't want me to know about? Why wouldn't he have invited me along? What was it he didn't want me to see?

What was he afraid of?

I suddenly, unexpectedly, felt intensely as though I'd failed my father. Could that be why he went back without telling me, without inviting me along? Had I shown such a lack of interest in what he'd gone through, in the suffering, starvation and brutality he'd experienced at the hands of the Nazis? Had he thought it wasn't important to me?

I found myself wishing I'd taken a trip there myself while he was still alive. I'd had plenty of opportunity. That way I could have seen the places he had been and then asked him questions. It would have given life to his story of that year, made it more vivid. I could have asked *him* to come with *me*.

But I hadn't gone. Until that morning, it hadn't even occurred to me to go. Why not? Why had I been so uninterested?

What was *I* afraid of?

Chapter 5

Mauthausen Memorial

After recovering from the twin shocks of seeing my father so prominently displayed on the Mauthausen website and learning of his secret 1997 trip back there, I decided to take action. I was unquestionably missing a large part of his past. Though I knew the story as he told it, there was clearly much more to it, details he'd never talked about, specifics I obviously didn't know.

I had the time. While my job kept me very busy during the day, the rest of my work week was clear. My twenty-year marriage had just ended. My seventeen-year-old son, Sam, and his sixteen-year-old identical twin sisters, Rachel and Lauren, were in high school and living with their mother, my ex-wife, in a San Francisco suburb. Weekdays my work kept me in LA, but I flew north every weekend to be with them. So when the business day ended, I had no place I had to be. I had no excuse for not learning all I could about my father's time under the Nazis.

The KZ Mauthausen website was part of *The Mauthausen Memorial*, an organization that maintains the concentration camp in nearly its original form and runs its internationally-known museum, housed in a few of the camp's original buildings. After work I emailed its General Information mailbox, asking how they had come across that photo of my father, and offering details about him in return. I had no expectations, figuring I'd get a standard reply thanking me for my interest. But it would be a start.

Instead, surprisingly, a day later I heard back from one of the historians at Mauthausen Memorial, expressing great interest in anything I was willing to share about my father. That first email quickly expanded into a dialogue with a number of the staff. I described to them my father's story in brief, from his deportation to Auschwitz through his liberation, and they guided me as I discovered details of the camps he'd never told me.

I quickly realized that if I had done even a minimal amount of research, I would have discovered Mauthausen's website years earlier. But I never did. I knew the story my father told me, and that had been sufficient. I never dug further. After Vivi's phone call, besides emailing Mauthausen Memorial, I searched the internet for information on the death marches, and especially for stories of death marchers who'd escaped. I found precious few, none at all from KZ Mauthausen, and not one anywhere of a death marcher who'd escaped, been recaptured, and escaped a second time.[1]

Early on, I asked the Mauthausen Memorial staff how they'd heard of my father's escape, and in particular, how they'd gotten that photograph. They told me in the early 1970s a local electrician named Peter Kammerstätter had set out to write a book about the death marches. Kammerstätter was not just an electrician. He was also a senior, life-long member of the *Kommunistische Partei Österreichs*, the KPO, Austria's communist party.

Born in 1911, Kammerstätter's communist leanings got him imprisoned by the Nazis in Buchenwald Concentration Camp. Released in 1940, he kept out of trouble for the remainder of the war, but once it ended he again became active in the KPO. After retiring, he set out to research anti-Nazi resistance in Austria. That led him to the death marches, and to a search for Austrians who'd helped the marchers, a narrow but important form of resistance. Walking the Mauthausen death march routes, he knocked on doors, interviewed people, and collected stories which he put into a manuscript he hoped to publish.

Kammerstätter never found a publisher, but the manuscript exists today and is held in high regard by concentration camp historians. While researching his book, he came across Ignaz and Barbara Friedmann. He doesn't say exactly how he'd uncovered them, and he died in 1993, so it will remain a mystery. But he wrote the story Barbara Friedmann told him, of finding my father after a death

---

1 Though in 2007 I found no stories of Mauthausen death march escapes, long after I learned that in addition to my father, three other marchers are *believed* to have successfully escaped from Mauthausen death marches. Two had no further corroborating information, not even their names. A third, last-name Engel, cut out of a death march on April 19, 1945, during a rest break as they passed near the town of St. Marien, and was hidden by a local family until liberated on May 7. He moved to Israel after the war, but nothing further is known about him. No one escaped from a death march twice – no one except my father.

14

march had passed by and sheltering him until the end of the war (it seems Ignaz did not participate in the interview). And Barbara gave him that picture, which he included in his manuscript.

But how did Barbara get it?

Chapter 6

That Picture

The story Peter Kammerstätter didn't write, the story he didn't know, was the one behind the photo of my father, him with the subtle grin and peaked lapel blazer, the photo that was on the Mauthausen Memorial website. Here's what happened.

One typically cold morning in the first week of April, 1945, my father woke in his KZ Mauthausen barracks and started his day the way he'd started every miserable day since arriving there the prior June: by standing for roll call, then getting in line for breakfast, a single thin slice of bread. Not long after, the prisoners were ordered to stand for a second roll call, and the Nazi guards announced a 'transport' of around 1,000 Jewish prisoners. They were to march to KZ Gunskirchen, a sub-camp thirty-four miles southwest of KZ Mauthausen.

No one used the words 'death march' in those days. It wasn't even called a 'march.' Instead, marches, train trips, movements of any sort from one place to another were called 'transports,' a word in both German and English my father used often when talking about his experiences under the Nazis. He wouldn't say, 'I was on a "train" from …' or, 'I "marched" from …' Instead, he would say, 'I was on a "transport" from …' This 'transport' turned out to be a death march, one of the first out of KZ Mauthausen and away from the advancing Russian Army, which was ninety miles to the east.[1]

My father was selected to be on this 'transport.' Also selected were his good friends Izsak and Chaim Mozes, brothers from his home town. Slight and bespectacled, Izsak was a couple of years

---

1 During World War II the combatant army belonged to the Soviet Union rather than to Russia. But as the Soviet Union no longer exists, I will refer to it as the 'Russian' army.

younger than my father. They had been together since their very first days in the camps, ten months earlier. Chaim, tall and powerfully built, was two years older than my father. Rather than being sent to a concentration camp, in 1941 he had been put into a Hungarian Labor Service battalion building and repairing roads and bridges throughout Hungary. With the war nearing an end, the Jews in the labor battalions were 'transported' to concentration camps. Chaim had just survived a one hundred mile forced-march to KZ Mauthausen, but he had been fed well enough through the war, and so was still in relatively good shape. That day, the three young men from Dej intended to help each other along.

The 'transport' began. For three miles, a downhill trek until reaching the Danube River, my father, Izsak, and Chaim kept pace. But once across the river the road flattened and Dad began faltering. Before the march, he had been extraordinarily weak, weighing only 80 pounds, and suffering from tuberculosis, pneumonia, and probably typhus. Chaim took my father's arm and supported him as they walked. They continued this way for another couple of miles, until my father told Chaim to leave him and tend to his brother Izsak, who was nearly, but not quite, as frail. My father felt like he had fought hard enough, long enough. It was time.

Chaim hesitated, but my father insisted. He told Chaim to save his strength for his brother. Family first. Reluctantly, Chaim let go.

My father started slipping back among the slower marchers. Chaim turned around to look back at Dad one last time, the expression on his face a plea for him to stay with them. My father saw it and felt the pull of Chaim's healthy body language urging him on, but he didn't have the horses to keep up. It wasn't in him. He was drifting back in a sea of slowly trudging marchers the way an overboard passenger drifts behind the ocean liner he'd fallen from.

A few minutes more, and my father was totally spent. He went to the side of the road. To go to the side of the road meant death. Any time a prisoner on these 'transports,' these death marches, went to the side of the road and sat down, one of the SS soldiers guarding the Jews along the route would put a gun in the back of the prisoner's neck and shoot them dead. Sometimes, as a courtesy, the SS man would ask if the prisoner would prefer to die, or keep walking. The answer was usually unspoken.

My father sat down on a small boulder, took off his Nazi-issued wooden shoes, and rubbed his aching feet while waiting to die. He looked up to meet the eyes of an SS trooper who was stepping purposefully straight towards him, his pistol already in his hand, index finger on the trigger. My father was ready, his mind clear. The Nazi glanced down at my father's shoeless feet, then back to his face, and their eyes met again. Without a word, the Nazi veered away, stepping past Dad and continuing down the road.

What the ...? My father was stunned.

He looked over his shoulder at the trooper, at his executioner, moving away. The Nazi must have thought my father had a pebble in his shoe, or that he needed a break for a minute. Actually, my father had absolutely no idea what the man thought, because the unassailable rule was, if you went to the side of the road, you died. You didn't get to take a pebble out of your shoe, or rub your feet, or take a break for a minute. But the rule apparently didn't apply to my father that morning.

His heart racing, the near-miss jarred him and the blood coursing through his veins energized him. Those few seconds sitting on the boulder regenerated just enough strength for my father to stand and resume marching. But he was struggling to move now, lost in a fog. Soon the road pitched up steeply for a few hundred yards. At the end of the uphill, the route flattened as my father and the other marchers reached a major intersection. From their left, streams of soldiers and refugees were moving directly across their path.

SS guards attempted to keep order in the dust-choked and chaotic crossroads, trying to shepherd their Jewish charges through gaps in the flow of soldiers on foot and horseback, and civilians with their luggage carts and children. My father stepped into the junction moving like he was under water: slowly, exhausted from the steep uphill. A particularly large group of refugees was waiting impatiently to go and could barely be held in check. Recognizing this, the Nazi guards halted the line of death marchers immediately behind Dad.

My father worked his way across the intersection alone, his steps agonizingly short, every breath a struggle for air. Suddenly, the stream of civilian humanity surged forward, unable to wait for him to cross. They hit him like a tidal wave, nearly knocking him over, refugees crossing in front and behind him, from his left to his right.

My father couldn't believe it. He lost sight of the far end of the intersection. He was completely swallowed up within the middle of the refugee column.

Fear began overtaking him. But then a switch went on. He became hyper-alert. His fog dissipating instantly, he grasped that it wouldn't take much to become a refugee, to become one of them, to disappear in plain sight. Just a quick turn to the right was all it would take.

My father made that turn, and no one saw him do it. He was free. He was completely on his own. By this point Izsak and Chaim were far ahead, so all they knew when they'd finally arrived at their destination was my father was one of the hundreds of marchers on their 'transport' who had not made it. They were technically right, but in the most important way imaginable, they were completely wrong.

Dad *had* made it. He had escaped back at that busy intersection, though he was recaptured an hour later and returned to KZ Mauthausen. One week or so later he was selected for another 'transport.' Again he escaped. This time the Friedmanns found him and hid him until the Americans rolled through Enns.

After being liberated, my father spent eighteen months in an American-run hospital, the Kohlbruck Klinik in Passau, a small German city straddling the Danube River fifty-five miles west of the Friedmann home. He was not expected to live, as he not only needed to regain the 80 pounds he'd lost starving in KZ Mauthausen, but he was now fighting simultaneous cases of tuberculosis, pneumonia, typhus, and most dangerously, peritonitis.

While fighting for his life in Passau, his surviving siblings Rosie, Villi, and Isadore were living back in Dej and running the family soap factory again. All three had relatively easier – *relatively* being the key word – courses through the Holocaust than my father, and soon after the end of hostilities they had returned home to resume their lives.

Uncle Isadore spent the war in a Hungarian Labor Service battalion. Like Chaim Mozes, who'd reluctantly let go of my father on their death march, Isadore moved around Hungary with his battalion, fixing roads and bridges. His war ended in December 1944 when he escaped as his Labor Service battalion worked near the Russian front lines. As soon as he could, he made his way back to Dej, which the Russians had liberated by then.

Uncle Villi's path through the war was more difficult. Like all the Hersch siblings (except Isadore), in June 1944 he, his 24-year-old wife Dora, and their one-year-old son Tibor were deported to Birkenau, a death camp within the Auschwitz concentration camp system in Poland. Tibor and Dora were killed in one of the death camp's giant gas chambers almost immediately. Villi remained in the Auschwitz system as a slave laborer until, as the Russians neared, the camp was liquidated by death-marching its prisoners deep into Germany. He ended up in Buchenwald Concentration Camp, where he was freed by American soldiers in April 1945. He, too, quickly returned to Dej.

Aunt Rosie was also sent to Birkenau in June 1944. Shuttled among a handful of concentration camps, one of her jobs was riding Nazi ammunition trains. The Nazis believed partisans wouldn't blow up a train with women aboard. At least in Aunt Rosie's case, that was true. She ended the war in KZ Kaiserwald, in Latvia, where she worked as a cook, or whatever passed for a cook there. After being liberated, she returned to Dej, meeting up with her brothers.

My father was unaware of his siblings' post-war life. He had assumed everyone in his family was dead, because he knew first-hand how low the odds of survival had been. Still, he didn't know for sure, so in February 1946, after pulling through the worst effects of his illnesses, he wrote a letter saying he was alive, addressing it to 'the Jewish Community of Dej.' A letter to that general mailbox was the best way to find out if he was the only Hersch survivor.

While my father was recuperating in Passau, Chaim Mozes had returned alone to Dej. His younger brother, Izsak, had not survived. The death march to KZ Gunskirchen had been one exertion too many for him, and though the march itself didn't kill him, he died a few days later. Chaim connected with my uncles and aunt and told them how Dad had tried valiantly to keep up with the march but had eventually succumbed.

Death was not something the three living Hersch siblings had grown accustomed to. Though the Nazis had killed their mother, four other brothers and sisters with their families, and Villi had lost his young wife and child, learning they'd now lost a fifth sibling, the baby of the family, crushed them all over again. For Villi, his only consolation was there was no one else to take from him. Though he would eventually remarry, he would never again have a child. Isadore and Rosie, too, were wounded by the announcement of my father's death. They were much closer to him in age than Villi, and until they'd talked to Chaim they had held on to hope that he might be alive. Losing that hope was a body blow.

A daily reminder to the family of my father's death was his head shot photograph, the one on the Mauthausen website. Dej's best professional photographer had taken it, and posted large billboards of the photo around town to advertise his studio. He'd kept the billboards up even after the town's Jews were deported to concentration camps, and they remained up after the Nazis were defeated. Upon hearing from Chaim Mozes of my father's apparent death, Villi asked the photographer to finally take down the ads, saying, 'I don't want to see my dead brother every day.'

Then my father's letter arrived.

The joy in the Hersch family that day was breathtaking, like welcoming a newborn brother to the household. After believing they were the only survivors of an extended family of twenty-four parents, siblings, spouses, nieces and nephews, this was joyously remarkable news. My father's happiness, too, was electric when he received their letter back, always describing it as 'the happiest day of my life till then.'

Much as they wanted to, Rosie, Villi and Isadore couldn't travel to Passau. They couldn't secure the necessary travel permits in that precarious time when the global superpowers were staking out their territory and the Cold War was first igniting. Dej was under Russian occupation, while Passau was within the American Zone, and movement between the superpower sectors was tightly controlled, if there was any at all.[1]

Instead, they all corresponded regularly. In their first letter back, my father's sister and brothers sent him a recent color photo of themselves, taken by the same photographer who had used Dad as a model (and Villi happily allowed him to again post his billboards with Dad's picture). In the photo, my two uncles and aunt glow radiantly, like they were hoping the picture alone would heal my father. Meanwhile, in one of his letters my father asked for a few copies of that head shot. He was clearly recovering nicely.

In late 1946, fully mended, the Kohlberg Klinik discharged him. To return home, he boarded a train heading east that would stop near Dej. In a lucky coincidence, the train was required to halt for a few hours in Enns for inspection, as it was on the border between the post-war American and Russian Zones.[2] While in Enns, passengers were not allowed to leave the train platform. The Friedmanns did not own a telephone, but the station was only a mile and a half from the Friedmann home. So my father asked the stationmaster to alert the Friedmanns that he was in town, and request that they come meet

---

1 After the war, both Germany and Austria were divided into American, British French and Russian (Soviet) 'zones.' During World War II countries to their east – Czechoslovakia, Hungary and Romania – had been overrun by Russia as it fought to defeat Germany. Russia remained in those countries after the war ended, retaining significant influence in their governments.

2 Enns was just on the American side of the American-Russian Zone border in Austria.

him so he could thank them again for risking their lives to save him. The stationmaster complied, and Ignaz Friedmann came, meeting my father for what Dad said was only a few minutes.

That seemed not long enough to me, too short a time to thank a man for saving your life, but my father said Ignaz was subdued that afternoon, and didn't have much to say. My father thought he'd detected a subtle hint of regret, that perhaps Ignaz had decided rescuing my father had been a mistake.

Why would Ignaz Friedmann have had any regret? Had neighbors or family learned of what he and Barbara had done and ostracized them for it, for saving the life of a Jew? Did they have a change of heart and wished now they had not saved my father? Ignaz was a respected and successful brick mason in town. He and his employees were exceedingly busy constructing homes and small factories in post-war Austria, yet he had taken the time to appear that afternoon to meet my father. What greater proof could there have been of the Friedmanns' continued desire to wish, and think, well of my father?

Barbara Friedmann died in 1973, and Ignaz two years later. But I've met a few of their neighbors, as well as their lone grandson (their son, their only child, was no longer alive). Through them I have come to know the couple a bit, and I have decided it was just Ignaz's way, just his demeanor. That afternoon Ignaz was fifty-five years old, making my father, at twenty-one, easily young enough to have been his son. My father was outgoing and high-energy, and probably overflowing with nervous anticipation, as he was finally going home to see his brothers and sister for the first time in over two years.

Ignaz, meanwhile, was sensitive but taciturn, not uncommon for men of his community and his generation. He was a solid guy who'd done a solid thing and didn't need or want to be thanked for it. My father's survival was thank-you enough. And yet, with no advanced notice he came to the station to see my father again, to see him healthy and well fed, gaining closure on the story of a young man he'd met as an emaciated and deathly ill boy. When Barbara Friedmann spoke with Peter Kammerstätter, she told him she and Ignaz even thought of my father, 'like a second son.'

No question in my mind, my father had misread Ignaz.

Dad gave Ignaz the photo while they'd chatted on the train platform. Two decades later Barbara Friedmann gave the photo to Peter Kammerstätter, and he, in turn, put it in the manuscript now in the possession of Mauthausen Memorial.

And that's how it came to the Mauthausen website.

If I had been a better son to my father, if I had shown him that I'd cared more, I would have known all this while he was still alive. I could have talked to him in detail about those minutes at the train station, when the man who'd risked his life to save my father's showed up but had little to say. At some point he would have probably told me about giving Ignaz the photo. But at least I had now solved one mystery, that of the photo, and I took some comfort from the fact that if I kept working at it, I could learn much more.

I could probably even discover why my father didn't tell me about his trip in 1997.

Chapter 7

Me

In the early 1950s, after surviving the camps and that list of deadly medical issues, my father was living in Haifa, Israel. He had an enormous collection of friends, who called him 'Dah-VID' (David in Hebrew), Dave, or Dudie (sounds like 'cookie'), depending on what language they were speaking. Among them, he was particularly close to three: Nat Rosenwasser, a childhood pal from Dej, Chaim Lichtenstein, a redhead everyone called Gingie, and Yishai Lovinger, whose trim mustache lent him a debonair air. They had dreams of one day coming to the United States and they knew they'd need to speak English to make their way. So they chipped in to hire a beautiful Israeli girl who had offered to teach them.

In 1954 that girl, Miriam Rachel Zeilingold, was twenty-four years old, slender and light skinned, with a patrician nose, a serious air, and a soft London accent. Born in Jerusalem in 1930, at the age of four she moved with her parents to London, England, so her father could join his brother in a bookstore business. By the early 1950s Rachel – she went by her middle name, and sometimes by the anglicized Rita – was back in Israel with a teaching certificate in her pocket and doing her compulsory military service in the Israeli Air Force.

Not long after she started teaching the four men English, Rachel and Dave – as she preferred calling my father – fell in love. They were married in 1955, and I was born three years later, their first child. With Israel's economy struggling, when I was exactly two months old we immigrated to the U.S. so my parents could start over again. It was my first plane flight, and might explain my obsessive attraction to airplanes and flying.

We settled in Long Beach, New York, a sedate beach town on the south shore of Long Island that had become a mecca for residential senior citizen hotels, where the elderly got three meals a day, bingo, movies or music in the evenings, and camaraderie all the time. The business attracted concentration camp survivors because it required hard work, compassion, and business savvy, but little education. During the next seven years my father worked hard and spent carefully, climbing from busboy to waiter to manager to, in 1965, owning a piece of a hotel. In exactly twenty years he'd gone from inhabiting Hitler's nightmare to possessing a slice of the American Dream.

My father spent long hours in his hotel but took off Saturdays for the Sabbath and Wednesdays because it was the slowest day of the workweek. My mother, on the other hand, battled for her life from the day I was born, never getting a day off. She'd had rheumatic fever as a child in London, which had scarred her heart's mitral valve. The scarring went undetected until she became pregnant with me. The bodily stress of bearing me caused her weakened valve to nearly fail, and only surgery in 1959 saved her.

Three years later, and against her doctor's orders, she became pregnant again. In April, 1962 my brother Elliott was born, a miracle baby considering the further damage the pregnancy did to my mother's heart. For the next seven years, Mom struggled. Running out of breath easily, she could only walk short distances. She could barely climb a flight of stairs. She was still slender, still beautiful, and she even taught Sunday Hebrew School in a local temple, but she wasn't living the way she wanted to.

My parents kept a 'modern orthodox' Jewish home. That means we ate only kosher food, didn't travel or spend money on Saturday, and prayed in temple on Friday nights and Saturday mornings. My brother and I attended 'Hebrew day school,' the Jewish version of parochial school, with the mornings dedicated to religion, the afternoons to everything else. I was a pretty good student, never the smartest kid in class but always close to the top. Except in science, where I beat all comers.

Until third grade I was an easy mark for class bullies. Many days I would come home crying, and my father would implore me to hit back. 'Give 'em a *zets* in the face,' he'd say, using the Yiddish word for 'hit,' while demonstrating his right cross. My mother, tougher than all of us, would purse her lips while nodding in agreement. Finally, in the middle of third grade I got the courage to hit one of my tormentors, and he never bothered me again. But that didn't end it. Once a year, for reasons I never figured out, someone would start with me. But after third grade I felt if my father could survive the Nazis, I, his son, should be able to handle a mere classmate.

So I would be taunted or pushed, we'd face off, and in one *zets* I'd finish it.

In the spring of 1969 my mother underwent open-heart surgery, replacing her damaged mitral valve with an artificial one made of silicon and metal, among the first of its kind. For the next two years Mom lived life again. She traveled on vacation with my father, took my brother and me to Israel for the first time since we'd moved to the U.S., and planned and celebrated my bar mitzvah. But on November 7, 1971, the man-made valve suddenly failed, and she died. She was forty-one years old.

I'm sure I still carry the emotional residue of her ill health and too-early death. But what I remember most after she'd died is considering that my father had lost his parents, half his siblings, and all his nieces and nephews when he was eighteen – only five years older than I was – and he seemed to be doing well. I, who'd only lost a single parent, determined I would do well, too. If he could do it, I could do it.

Besides, I still had him. To me, he was strong as an I-beam, confident and handsome, and he still laughed more in a day than most people laughed in a week. But the load he carried was just so great, and I sensed the burden on him. He didn't smile quite as much. He appeared weary after work, something I had not detected before. Me, my brother, his job. It seemed to me an immense set of responsibilities, beyond possible.

And then, one day it was. He had his first heart attack in June 1972. It was three weeks before my fourteenth birthday.

Chapter 8

Pre-war Dej

In the 1930s, the Hersch family lived in a two-story, four-bedroom home on a steeply-sloped street on the north side of Dej. Most of the town's nearly 4,000 Jews lived close by. My grandfather's soap factory produced enough income to afford the family a solidly middle-class lifestyle. At one time or another all the kids helped out in the soap business, but Uncle Villi managed the plant by the time he was in his late teens.

Religiously my father was raised about the same as we had been in Long Beach. He even attended a Hebrew day school not unlike the one my brother and I went to. He spent half his day on secular subjects – Romanian, Hungarian,[1] history, math and science – and the other half on Hebrew, Yiddish, and bible studies. The Jews of Dej mostly spoke Yiddish among themselves, though my father had a phenomenal ear for languages. Before he was twelve he could fluently speak Romanian, Hungarian, Yiddish, Hebrew, and German. Later, in the melting pot of the concentration camps, he learned Polish, Spanish and Czech just from being around those prisoners (add in English, which my mother taught him, and that's the nine languages). People in Dej in those years saw little need for education, so by the end of fifth grade my father was done with school, and helping around the house and in the soap factory.

He always described his youth as happy and unremarkable. He played soccer in the local park, worked in his father's factory, rode his bicycle around town to friends, and hung with his older siblings and their own families, where he was a very young uncle who knew

---

1 Though Transylvania was then under Romanian rule (until 1940), it had been part of the Austro-Hungarian Empire since 1867. Hungarian language and culture dominated.

how to make his nieces and nephews laugh. He belonged to a Zionist youth group, Bnei Akiva, which was popular among Jewish kids in the area, and he would occasionally travel to nearby towns to meet kids in other chapters. Mostly he stayed out of trouble. I'd always felt that except for the size of his family and that he left school so young, his early upbringing sounded not very different from my own.

But then it became very different.

In the late 1930s, the ground beneath his family's comfortable existence grew unstable. Hungarian internal politics began leaning to the right, which in those days meant it also became more anti-Semitic. Worse, in November 1940 Hungary officially joined the Axis Powers, made up of Germany, Italy and Japan. As a reward for signing up, Germany gave Transylvania back to Hungary. For my father, that meant Hungary's laws and policies, and not Romania's, governed life in Dej from that day forward.

Official, government-sponsored anti-Semitism was encoded in Hungarian life. Two years earlier Hungary had established a series of anti-Jewish laws which defined, among other things, who was a Jew, how many Jews could be employed by a single company, and how many Jews could participate in certain professions. It wasn't a complete duplication of the German Nuremberg Laws restricting Jewish life in the Third Reich, but it was a strong echo and a harbinger of worse to come.

That was the bad news. The good news was – and it certainly was good considering the alternative – Hungary's Jews were not being sent to concentration camps, unlike the Jews of every other country under Nazi influence or control except Romania. Hungary's Regent, Miklos Horthy, a former naval admiral who had ruled the country from soon after it was separated from the Austro-Hungarian Empire in 1920, purposely kept its 860,000 Jews under his control and out of the camps, though for reasons he never explicitly gave and to this day are not known for certain (there are many theories, but no one knows for sure why). What is known for certain is the delay saved thousands of Jewish lives.

Though Hungary's Jews – like my father and his family – in the early years of World War II weren't sent to the camps, the regime had other plans for them. Hungarian Jewish men, as well as non-Jews considered political enemies, were conscripted into what was officially called the 'Labor Service.' In 1941, when the first Labor Service battalions were formed, Uncle Isadore and Chaim Mozes, both over eighteen years old, were assigned to battalions that traveled throughout Hungary.

My father, only sixteen, was detailed to a battalion that assembled once a week, performing what he called 'city work.' While living at home, he and his battalion cleaned streets, raked leaves, filled potholes, and maintained Dej's public spaces. Unlike Jews in the rest of the German-occupied countries, Hungarian Jews were not yet required to wear the distinct yellow star that marked them as different. The exception was Jews in the Labor Service, who wore a yellow armband while they worked. After work, they could remove their armbands and stick them in their pockets.

The armbands would not remain in their pockets much longer.

Chapter 9

Passover 2001

Four years after my mother died, Dad married Rika, an attractive Austrian woman a few years younger than him. Her husband had died, leaving her with a daughter, Michaela, two years younger than my brother. Eli and I had grown up in a small two-bedroom home with a single bathroom. After getting married, my father and Rika moved to a larger home to accommodate her daughter (and, I suppose, because we could now afford it). Their marriage coincided with my freshman year of college at Columbia University in Manhattan, where I lived in the dormitories while studying computer science and electrical engineering. At the same time Eli began attending an orthodox Jewish high school in Manhattan where he dormed as well, so neither of us lived at home any more, and we had little interaction with Rika, which was fine with us. From our distance it seemed they had a decent marriage, though Dad never stopped telling my brother and me that Mom had been the love of his life. Obviously Rika didn't match up to our mother.

I met Karen in graduate school. Brilliant, attractive, and athletic, we married in 1987. In 1990 she gave birth to Sam, and fifteen months later our identical twins, Rachel and Lauren were born. Bright, and in our opinion very handsome, Sam had been diagnosed with cerebral palsy before he'd turned one, and was never going to walk. So in 1998 we moved to San Diego. Karen and I had decided its warm, dry weather and slower pace made for a better environment to raise Sam than New York City, where we'd been living and working. It turned out to be a great place for all of us and our three kids thrived, in school and out.

Once a year, my father flew west to visit us. Picking him up at the airport one February afternoon to begin his 2001 trip, he was still vibrant and fit at seventy-five years old, and excited to be with us.

On the drive from the airport, he asked me, 'Do you know the best thing about being seventy-five?' He loved jokes almost as much as he loved his sons and his grandkids. His voice was firm and with a mid-ranged resonance to it. Defying easy description, his accent was a stew of the nine languages he spoke. I've never heard another like it.

'No, Dad, I don't. What's the best thing about turning seventy-five?' I took my eyes off the road for an instant to catch his face at the punch line.

'You can't die young anymore!' And then he let out his infectious laugh.

It was a memorably fun week of family meals, sight-seeing, and watching his granddaughters play soccer. My kids' faces were luminous when they spent time with their *saba*, grandfather in Hebrew. And so was my father's.

For all we did that week, my children's most prominent memory is of the time at dinner my father accidentally knocked his fork off the table while telling us a story. His hands were always quick as lightning, and he somehow caught the utensil before it hit the ground. But one of the tines penetrated the thin skin between his thumb and index finger. While continuing to tell his story, he brought his hand up to the table, pulled the tine out of his skin, covered the slight bleeding with his napkin, and kept on like nothing had happened. To my kids, that was all one needed to know about their *saba*. When asked to describe him, they are as likely to tell that episode as they are to mention that he was a survivor.

Later that month my father's doctor discovered the mitral valve in his heart was weakening slowly, but steadily. Eerily it was the same mitral valve that led to my mother's death. Only open-heart surgery could halt the decline before it killed him. But surgery was monumentally risky. Statistically he had one chance in four of dying on the operating table solely because of his age. Possible complications from the complex operation made his odds even worse. But my father was adamant that he would not slowly wilt. He wanted to either be better, or have it over with. He wasn't being fatalistic, he was being confident. He enjoyed life immensely, and he presumed he'd survive this, just like he'd survived everything else life had thrown at him.

He scheduled the operation for July. His doctor believed his heart wouldn't weaken much by then, and using the time effectively might even improve his odds. He went to work strengthening his body with long daily walks and light weight lifting at a local gym.

Then in late March he phoned me with a request.

'Hi Jeckeleh,' he started. He'd been calling me that my entire life. It's 'Jack' pronounced his unique way, with a Yiddish endearing ending.

After a minute of catching up, my father said, 'I'd like you to come this year for the Seder.'

I hadn't been to a Passover Seder at my father's house in at least ten years. While Seders were important religious events, for us they were never the culturally must-have-everyone-together gatherings characterizing them in many Jewish families. My wife and I spent the Seders in Florida with her family, until we'd moved to San Diego. There, we had been having Seders with friends' families, either in our house or theirs.

But I'd heard something in his voice. 'Sure Dad,' I said immediately, and then added, 'It will just be me, though. The kids have plans through that week.'

I knew he wouldn't ask my brother Eli to come, so I didn't even inquire. While I had drifted far from my orthodox Jewish upbringing, Eli remained very observant. He lived with his wife and four children only eight miles away from Long Beach, but he would never violate the holy day by driving to our father's house for a Seder, and my father would never ask him to.

Checking the calendar, I saw Passover was two weeks away, with the first Seder on Saturday night, April 7. My father held two Seders, but in San Diego we only did one. It would work perfectly.[1]

'Dad, I'll do the first Seder here with Karen and the kids, then take the early flight Sunday and do the second night with you.'

'Good, thank you.'

I heard my father smiling. But the suddenness of the request worried me. 'Is everything alright? Is this about the operation?' I held my breath and concentrated on the tone of my father's reply.

'No, Jeckeleh, everything is alright,' was his quick and automatic response. 'Everything is alright' was another of his go-to phrases. We spoke by phone four or five times a week, the conversations often lasting barely a few sentences: 'How are you?' I'd ask, and

---

1 Orthodox Jews celebrate the first two days of Passover with two Seders. Reform Jews have only one Seder night. The two-day routine came about because in ancient times Jews living outside of Israel relied on communication from the Holy Land to pinpoint the first night of Passover. Fearing those communications might not arrive in a timely manner, the two Seders provided a margin for error. Modern communications obviates this reason, hence many non-orthodox Jews consider the second Seder unnecessary.

he'd usually say, 'Everything is alright.' Only this time, I didn't believe him.

On Passover Sunday I was at my father's before sundown. Dressed in suits and ties, we went to temple together to welcome the second night of Passover, as we did when I'd lived in his house. Watching him pray, he seemed much fitter than when he'd visited me in San Diego. He was always thin, but that evening he was trimmer around the waist, and his cheeks were rosy. Year round he loved walking Long Beach's two-mile-long boardwalk that ran along the town's white-sand Atlantic Ocean beach. He told me he'd recently been going further and faster than he used to.

Returning to the house after services, I sat at the dining room table at my customary seat to my father's right. I'd slipped my suit jacket onto the back of an empty chair, though Dad kept his on. The room had white walls, gold and white drapes across the windows, imitation Louis XV table and chairs with matching sideboard and breakfront, and a crystal chandelier hanging just out of reach. It wasn't my taste, but it had an old-world feel that was comfortable for my father.

A Seder can take anywhere from a few minutes, to a few hours. In the longer ones, participants read aloud every word of the *haggadah*, the ancient text detailing the foods to be eaten and the stories to be told that night. Dinner – the meal itself – comes after most of the *haggadah* has been read. My father always hewed closely to the text, but tonight he picked up the pace slightly, and we were ready for dinner ninety minutes after sitting down.

After eating and before resuming reading the *haggadah* was the point when my father would normally tell his concentration camp survival-and-escape story. I was getting ready to ask him about it when he said, 'You know I'm going for the surgery in three months.' It was a statement.

'Yes, of course. Are you worried about it?'

'No no,' he said, shaking his head for emphasis.

That may or may not have been true, but his answer was not surprising. 'So then what is it, Dad? Why the invitation for the Seder this year?'

There was a long pause. 'Jeckeleh, the surgery is not guaranteed. I don't know what will be. What will be will be, but I want you to hear my story again.'

'The story about the camps?'

'Yes. You haven't heard it from me in many years. What they did to me, and what I had to do to survive.' He leaned closer. 'The Nazis couldn't kill me, and the surgeon won't kill me, either.'

So that's why I was here. My father was getting himself ready, psyching himself up for the operation. He was using this Seder to remind his body – no, to *tell* his body – that it was not time yet. Together they had one more big battle ahead.

We pushed our chairs away from the table, angling them to face each other. My father loosened his tie, and I did the same. I determined I would be the best listener I could be, acting like I was hearing this story for the first time. 'Where do you want to begin?'

My father took a sip of his club soda and licked his lips. 'I'll start when the Nazis first came to Dej. That's when things started to change for the worst.'

I was ready.

Chapter 10

The Nazis Arrive

In November 1943,' my father began, 'A regiment of German soldiers moved into Dej.'

'There hadn't been any Germans in the town before?'

'We saw a few on the streets, but that was all. Horthy, the Regent who ran my country, didn't want too many.'

'What changed?'

'The Russians were pushing back the German Army. They were almost in Kiev, in the Ukraine, which was less than 400 miles from my town. Hitler must have been known Hungary would be next.' My father never perfected when 'been' belonged in a sentence.

He said the German regiment's soldiers were logistics troops, with non-combat roles in the towns and villages dotting Transylvania's hills and valleys. They were being housed in private homes, and his parents were required to participate. Four German soldiers were ordered billeted in two bedrooms. The house had the room, as by that time all but the three youngest Hersch children were married.

My father said the soldiers were somewhat older, had been on the Russian front, and had a deep weariness to them. They may have once served on the front lines, but they were now burned out and no longer of that caliber. He said they kept to themselves, were generally neat and polite, and allowed my father's family to lead their lives uninterrupted. All that was required was that they be fed, which my grandmother dutifully did.

'Wasn't it strange having Nazis living in the house with you?' It has always seemed to me incredibly incongruous, an orthodox Jewish family housing Nazi soldiers.

'They weren't Nazis, they were just ordinary Germans,' my father said sincerely, 'and I could feel that these soldiers, these young guys, were tired of war.'

My father had every reason to remember this period of his life with bitterness, but he insisted there was a normalcy to it that was uneasy, but real. He pointed out that, while he and his family were aware of the anti-Semitic views of Hitler and the Nazis, there had been plenty of anti-Semitism under Romanian and Hungarian rule, so there was nothing new there. And they were wholly unaware of how extreme the Nazi version of anti-Semitism would turn out to be.

Plus my father sensed that the soldiers in their house did not care that they were living with Jews. They had seen enough death and wanted nothing more to do with it. He thought they didn't hate Jews, or anyone else.

'Not every German was an anti-Semite,' he said to me. 'The soldiers in our home minded their own business and stayed out of ours. One of them became very friendly with me.'

'Do you remember his name? Or any of their names?'

'No,' he said with a slightly embarrassed smile. 'This one, the one I was friendly with, he tried to warn us about the future. He was very honest, I remember, and he said that bad things were coming to the Jews of Hungary. He told us that if we could, we should get out. His exact words to me were, "I'm worried for you," and "I've seen what happens."'

'Why do you think he warned you?'

'He liked us, we could tell. He acted like he was at home. I guess his conscience bothered him.' A pause, and then my father shrugged. 'We should have listened to him.' Another pause. 'That, Jeckeleh, was a tremendous mistake.'

Amazingly, my father, his family, and all their friends were oblivious to the future just six months ahead, of cattle car 'transports' and gas chambers and labor camps and death. None of them had ever heard of Auschwitz or Mauthausen. No one in Dej had ever heard of 'The Final Solution.'

The Final Solution was the Nazi High Command's name for their plan to exterminate the Jews of Europe. Hitler wanted every Jew in Europe dead, though he was content working to death the more robust of them. The best way for the Final Solution to succeed was for it to remain secret until thrust upon the Jews in the cities and towns the Nazis steamrolled over. That no one knew was, to me, the Final Solution's second most incredible feature. The first, of course, was its magnitude – the murder of six million Jews (as well as the murder of many millions more – gays, gypsies, communists, the disabled, and a horrendously long list of other human beings). Even after being herded into ghettos and shoved aboard cattle cars, most of Europe's Jews believed what the Nazis told them: the trains were taking them to resettlement camps elsewhere in the Reich.

A prime reason no one knew was that *almost* no Jews who'd entered the camps got out to warn others. *Almost*, because there was a small number of revolts and mass escapes in the camps during the Nazi reign, but nearly everyone who'd escaped was recaptured and killed. The few who got away went underground and were in no position to spread the word of what they witnessed behind the camps' high walls and electrified fences. Jews in the United States and the United Kingdom had learned of the Final Solution as early as August 1942, but they lacked the means to convincingly transmit what they knew to European Jews who had not yet boarded cattle cars.[1]

Besides, Hungarian Jews who *had* been warned – like my father and his family – refused to believe the worst. Though they knew of the more famous pre-war anti-Semitic atrocities in Germany, this was Hungary, where they assumed Miklos Horthy would protect them. They figured that if the Nazis, Hungary's ally, had planned a nationwide extermination of the Jews, it would have happened already. But it hadn't. For the Jews of Dej, except for the oddity of German soldiers living in their houses, life was still pretty much the same as it had been before the war.

That was certainly true of the Hersch family. My father was working part time in the local Labor Service battalion and part time in the soap factory. My grandfather and Uncle Villi were keeping the factory humming. As soap was considered a necessary part of the war effort and a vital need of the population, they'd received government contracts paying well enough to enable them to afford food and clothing, and for there to be money left over to help others in the community who were less fortunate. Plus, with the German Army on the defensive, there was a sense in the Hersch home the war wouldn't last much longer.

Finally, and perhaps most importantly, there was this: even *if* they had heard what was really happening to the Jews of Europe, why would they believe the existence of facilities built for the sole purpose of killing hundreds of people at a time, thousands of people

---

1 On August 8, 1942, Dr. Gerhart Riegner, the Swiss representative to the World Jewish Congress, sent a telegram that is believed to be the first credible alert to the world that the Nazis planned to exterminate the Jews of Europe. His source was an anti-Nazi German industrialist who employed many high-ranking Nazis in his businesses.

a day, millions in total? The idea that structures of this kind could be created by modern men was beyond comprehension.

So when the friendly German soldier who'd seen too much war warned my father and his family of dire things to come, it simply didn't compute. They had been told they would eventually be resettled elsewhere in the Reich. It sounded reasonable. They would make a new life in their new home, wherever that would turn out to be.

Chapter 11

The Ghetto

On March 18, 1944, Miklos Horthy was urgently summoned to Berlin to meet with Hitler. One week earlier, Nazi internal-security spies had discovered Horthy and his Prime Minister, Miklos Kallay, secretly negotiating an armistice with the Allies. Until now Hitler had barely tolerated Horthy's harboring of Hungary's Jews, but this perfidy was unacceptable. So he ordered his generals to prepare to implement Operation Margarethe, the long-planned total military takeover of Hungary he'd been waiting for an excuse to initiate. Then he called Horthy to Berlin for a little chat.

In Berlin, Horthy listened as Hitler demanded Hungary's political leaders govern their people in line with the Nazi state's own rules. But while Hitler was seemingly making a request, Horthy was never given a chance to respond. The meeting had been a sham. Operation Margarethe had been launched that day. German tanks and troops were at that moment moving into key buildings in Hungary's capital city of Budapest. Having no choice, Horthy removed his prime minister, Kallay, and installed a government fully in line with Hitler's policies. At that moment Horthy's nominal control over the country ended.

Less than one month later, Adolf Eichmann, one of the chief architects of the Final Solution, ordered all of Hungary's Jews deported to concentration camps. For my father and his family, the Holocaust in its purest form had now begun.

'The exact date was April 14, 1944,' My father said. 'On that day they made us wear a yellow star all the time.' He had sat up taller, proud.

Forcing all of Hungary's Jews to wear the yellow Star of David was the first step in carrying out Eichmann's order. Until that day, they had not had to identify themselves overtly, though my father had been required to wear a yellow armband while at work in the Labor Service for the past three years. Now they were forced to conform to the laws governing the rest of Europe's Jews since the Nazis had risen to power.

My father continued. 'I remember the date exactly, because five days later, on April 19, 1944, your *saba*, my father *olov-hasholom*,[1] died of a heart attack. From the minute those four German soldiers moved into our house, your *saba* sensed in his bones that our lives in Dej would never go back to the way it was, where we got along with our neighbors. My father had been a soldier, a cavalry soldier, and he knew how these things worked. Unfortunately, when the order came to wear the Star of David, his health took a bad turn.'

Because he'd been gassed in the war, my grandfather's health had been delicate since returning from a Russian prison camp in 1919. He'd ignored it, thriving in post-war Transylvania. But the specter of wearing a yellow six-pointed star had been too much for him. He was the last person buried in the Jewish cemetery in Dej.

Dad picked up the story. 'I'll never forget what happened next. My father must have been known it was coming. On May the third, all of the Jews in Dej were forced to move to the ghetto. We were there for four weeks.'

My father never gave any details about the Dej ghetto, and I never asked. Telling his story, he'd just say exactly what he said that Seder night in 2001, that the Jews of Dej were forced into a ghetto for a month. I never asked for particulars because I thought I knew what a ghetto looked like. And I had not yet suspected my father was avoiding sharing the worst details of his time under the Nazis. But now that I was finally delving deeply into that year, I looked into the Dej ghetto.

What I found shocked me.

Whenever I heard my father use the word, 'ghetto,' a very distinct image always came to mind, that of the Warsaw Ghetto, whose story is well known. In late 1940, 400,000 Jews from Warsaw, Poland, and its surrounding communities were moved into a 1.3 square mile walled-off section of that great city. To me, *that* was a ghetto. The Warsaw Ghetto's great fame came from what is popularly known as 'The Uprising,' the 1942 revolt by its more militant inhabitants against their Nazi overseers. Using homemade and stolen guns and bombs, Jewish fighters battled for nearly a month against elite SS

---

1 Hebrew for 'may he rest in peace.'

storm troopers before they were wiped out. Very soon after, the remaining Jews in the ghetto were shipped to death camps.[1]

That distinct image in my mind was dead wrong. There was absolutely no visual relationship between the ghetto my father and his family were forced to live in, and the ghetto I had always pictured when I'd heard his story. Dej's ghetto was a cordoned-off section of a forest, the Bungur Forest two miles north of town. Not a single structure stood anywhere near the land allocated to the Jews of Dej. No buildings or homes. No sidewalks or streets or paths. No kitchens, no bathrooms, no showers, no toilets, no nothing. It was just a field in the forest, studded with trees, surrounded by barbed wire, and guarded by the Royal Hungarian Gendarmerie, who famously wore a rooster-feather in their uniform hat.[2] They were Hungary's national police force.

The town elders had considered moving the Jews into homes in a small corner of Dej. But the homes belonged to non-Jews, and evicting them was asking too much. Instead, the elders concluded it was much better to move the Jews to the local forest. After all, nobody lived there. And so that's what was ordered and carried out between May 3 and May 10, 1944. Thanks to efficient German record-keeping, the tally of Jews from Dej and its nearby small communities forced into the ghetto was 7,674 men, women, and children.

The town elders provided the Jews with straw to sleep on while they got settled, though the gesture was tainted. The straw was wet and infested with lice. Later that first week, the Jews were given wooden planks which they could use to fashion rudimentary streets and footpaths, and for flooring in their shelters. They were also given canvas, to make their tent-homes at least partially water-resistant. My father said it rained that first week, so regardless of how they tried to stay dry, everyone got soaked and stayed that way.

Now I understood why my father never gave any details about the ghetto. It was inconceivable that twentieth-century Europeans would be asked to leave their homes and reestablish their lives in a forest, yet that's exactly what happened to the Jews of Dej. Dad's few weeks in the Dej Ghetto must have ranked as one of the most

---

1 The word, 'ghetto,' is Italian, first used in 1516 to name Venice's Jewish Ghetto. Though ghetto's exact etymology is not known, there are two likely sources. The Venice Ghetto was situated on the site of an iron foundry, and a byproduct of foundries is slag. The Italian word for slag is 'ghetto.' That's one. Or 'ghetto' might be a shortening of the Italian word *borghetto*, which means 'borough.'

2 The force is called *gendarmerie*, while an individual within it is a *gendarme*.

intensely demeaning aspects of his life in wartime Hungary. He's probably glad I'd never asked him to describe it.

But I *should* have.

Chapter 12

The Friedmann Home

One thing the historians at Mauthausen Memorial knew for sure, thanks to Peter Kammerstätter, was the Friedmanns' address: 57 *Kristein Strasse, Enns Kristein, Austria.*[1] Curious about how it looked, I asked one of the Mauthausen Memorial historians if she could photograph the home. One cloudy afternoon she did, snapping a couple of pictures of the outside, and emailing them to me. When they arrived, I put aside the work I was doing and brought the pictures up on my computer screen.

They were mesmerizing.

The sturdy, block-like, two-story house looked formidable and safe, with a facade of light-brown stucco and a red tiled roof. It had small square windows with white frames and white guards on the ground floor, larger rectangular windows, without guards, on the second floor. A front door of a dark but indistinguishable color was cut into the facade near one end of the house, and two smaller, brownish-looking doors were close to the other end. Its style, if it had any at all, was Tuscan.

My father always said the Friedmanns had put him in the attic of the barn next to their house, on a bed of hay and straw. But where was the barn? These pictures showed only the front of the house itself. An idea occurred to me. On my second computer screen I brought up Google Earth, typed in the Friedmanns' address, and held my breath. The picture that came up was immediately recognizable. The Friedmanns' house, with its dull-red tile roof, was clearly visible in the brightly sun-lit and slightly offset high-altitude photo. It was as if my father was leaning over my shoulder pointing it out to me. My heart was pounding.

---

1 The home was no longer in the Friedmann family.

Centering the house on my screen, I saw it was surrounded by expansive farm fields of green and brown and gold. It sat just south of a tiny cluster of homes and streets – the hamlet of Kristein. The larger town of Enns was one mile to the east.

Kristein Strasse, Kristein Street, ran roughly north-south by the Freidmanns' front door. On my screen it seemed like a narrow, black-topped country lane. Fifty yards to the south of the house, the *Strasse* ended in a T-intersection, really more like a broadly-shaped Y. A small stream, the *Kristeinerbach*, paralleled *Kristein Strasse*. The stream appeared to be bordered on both banks by thick green brush or small trees. At the Y-intersection the stream turned west, meandering away from the Friedmanns' home. A stream near the Friedmann home figured importantly in my father's story. Seeing no others nearby, I figured it must be that one.

The house was shaped exactly like a lowercase-h. The long vertical section fronted *Kristein Strasse* and was the main house the historian had photographed. I supposed the rest of the lowercase-h was an extension, and maybe the barn. But I couldn't be certain.

If it was the barn – the barn my father had been in – I wondered what it looked like from ground level. All the structures in the 'h' appeared to share a roof, so were all three of similar construction, as well? Were they all covered in that light-brown stucco? What animals were inside? Was it warm inside in the winter? What did it smell like?

I could see the roof had no windows, so the attic would have been dark. Was there an air vent, or space between the tiles my father could peer through? I hoped so. If he could see out, would he have seen the hamlet to the north? The fields? Trees? People? The barn's attic was certainly the safest place to put him. It would have been too dangerous to give him a room in their house, particularly one with a window overlooking the street where he might be spotted. Even in the barn, without a window, without a proper room, even without a bed, my father must have felt like royalty. Or hopefully he felt just a little bit like a human again.

I kept staring. Until this instant, until this exact moment in my life, every image I ever had of my father and his wartime story was invented in my mind's eye. Until now I could only imagine how things looked to him as he described on that Passover evening in 2001 – and every other Passover Seder I'd had with him – what he'd been through.

No more. Now I knew exactly how some of the things he had seen looked. I could not take my eyes off my screens. I needed to go there. I needed to walk on *Kristein Strasse*, see the inside of the house, dip my fingers in the *Kristeinerbach* stream, and step into the attic I know helped save my father's life.

Chapter 13

65th Infantry Division: 5,217 Miles Away

When U.S. Army troops overran and liberated the town of Enns in May 1945, my father didn't know the unit details of the American men he'd encountered that day. And frankly, at the time he didn't care. He was just glad he was finally in safe hands, that his war was over.

But I researched it, and learned the soldiers he'd encountered were attached to the U.S. Third Army, commanded by General George S. Patton Jr. Specifically they were men of the 261st Regiment of the 65th Infantry Division of the Third Army.

Patton, born in 1885, was one of the most famous generals in the long history of the U.S. Army. He was a brilliant tank leader who helped formulate American armored doctrine in the early days of tank warfare. He was also a barrel-chested former U.S. Olympian equally famous for his ivory-handled revolvers, for his lightning tank assault across France and Germany, and for his mishandling and manhandling of soldiers who'd cracked under the strain of combat.

When the Japanese bombed Pearl Harbor on December 7, 1941, Third Army was a training command, responsible for turning Stateside soldiers and tankers into combat-ready warriors. But in late 1943, it was shifted to the fighting role it was meant for. Moving to the United Kingdom, it was ordered to prepare for combat in Western Europe. To lead its tanks and troops into battle, on January 26, 1944 General Patton was put in command.

Earlier in the war he had distinguished himself as a combat leader in North Africa. Then, in Sicily in 1943, he famously slapped and verbally abused two shell-shocked soldiers (they were suffering from what we now call combat post-traumatic stress syndrome). Punished for a time by being denied further front-line commands, Third Army would be Patton's opportunity to right his record.

Meanwhile, on August 6, 1943, the 65th Infantry Division was officially formed at Camp Shelby, a gigantic army training base just south of Hattiesburg, Mississippi. The 65th had the distinction of being the last infantry division created in the U.S. Army during the war. The division's commanding officer was 49-year-old Major General Stanley Reinhart, a 1916 graduate of West Point who had commanded artillery during World War I. Between August 16, 1943 and the end of that year, more than 12,000 men filed into Camp Shelby, and training formally got under way in January 1944.

It would take nearly fifteen months, until March 1945, before the division was a cohesive and capable fighting unit, ready to meet the German Army. Though late in the war, its soldiers would eventually see plenty of combat.

Part II
KZ MAUTHAUSEN

Chapter 14

Arrival

My flight touches down in Munich on schedule, a little after eight local time Saturday morning. We are the only international flight landing just then, so I quickly exit passport control and customs and pick up my rental car, a black Audi A3 wagon with GPS and twenty-seven kilometers on the odometer. It still has that new-car smell. I am bound for Enns, where I will meet Angelika Schlackl, a guide and historian at Mauthausen Memorial who had recently become my prime contact in Austria. Tonight and tomorrow night I have a reservation in the Hotel Romer, an inexpensive but comfortable-looking inn judging by its website, not far from the Enns town square. I'll check in later. Angelika and I have things to see first.

Enns, a town of 11,000 people seven miles by car southwest and across the Danube from KZ Mauthausen (three miles on a direct line), is best known – if it's known at all – as the oldest town in Austria. It was first inhabited by Roman legionnaires in the second century AD, who called it Lauriacum, and its land has been occupied, farmed, and fought over continuously ever since. Like most medieval towns, Enns' dominant feature is its central square. The square's four borders are delineated by buildings dating from the sixteenth century, around the same time as the Calvinist church in my father's hometown of Dej. In its center sits a 190-foot tall belfry, a combination clock-, watch-, and bell-tower, also built in the 1500s.

The car's GPS shows the drive to Enns is 277 kilometers, 172 miles, and will take two hours and forty minutes. But the GPS isn't accounting for how excited I am to get there. After ten minutes heading in the wrong direction, I'm making good progress. This morning the highway is empty, the weather sunny, the road dry, and the car feels good in my hands. I slept a bit on the plane so I am alert, and do my when-in-Rome best on the *Autobahn*, hitting

120 miles per hour for long stretches, and holding 130 a couple of times. I can get used to this.

But I'm bothered by that first directional mistake – I rarely make them. I'm a licensed pilot and usually have a reliable sense of direction. I don't attribute it to jet-lag. Instead, I conclude it's a sign I'm not only excited, but nervous and anxious as well.

Much of the scenery on the drive is gently rolling hills, lush green meadows, and farmland stretching to the horizon. I enjoy reading military history and I recognize this to be classic tank country, the sort of terrain where mechanized warfare dominated during World War II. To me, tanks mean Patton's Third Army and my father's liberation, and that leads to thoughts of what I might see, and how I might feel on this trip.

I assume I will see things that shock me. After all, I am going to a concentration camp, *my father's* concentration camp, a place I know defies description, a place I know my father didn't invite me along to see. I will be walking the same earth he walked, seeing the same things he saw so many years earlier. Will the visit pierce the bullet-proof shell I've built around myself in the years since my mother died? Will my self-reliant foundation be somehow shaken by the things I see, or by the things I learn about my father, perhaps by unanticipated things that surprise me? Will I learn things that change my view of myself, of my tiny world? Will I find one big thing that reveals why my father never told me about his return trip back? I grip the wheel a bit more tightly as I motor on.

Following my GPS, I pull off the highway at an intersection leading to a Chinese restaurant where Angelika is having Saturday brunch with her family. We have agreed to meet there. Though I've never seen a photo of her, I don't anticipate having trouble finding her. Nor do I expect having trouble finding something to eat. I'm famished, as I haven't eaten since dinner on the plane the evening before.

Chapter 15

Deportation

In a surprisingly short amount of time the Jews of Dej established a semblance of order in the forest. Families jury-rigged tents from the canvas they'd been given and from blankets they'd brought with them. A few of the more well-to-do put their money and local contacts to use building small wood-framed barracks-like structures to live in. Latrines were dug and cordoned off, wood paths were laid down into a semblance of streets and intersections, and eventually a tiny sense of civility and humanity came to the site. The joyous shouts of children playing could be heard during the day, while at night the sweet smells of cooking wafted through the air as candles flickered, families caught up, and, I assume, sometimes love was made between couples full of hope.

During this time, luck came my father's way.

'It was our fifth day in the ghetto,' he said, then paused to drain his glass of club soda. I reached across to refill it while he continued. 'The German army came to the ghetto and said they needed a baker. The family of one of my best friends owned a bakery in town, so I knew a little about baking.'

Dad smiled at me, and that twinkle in his eye sparkled. I doubt he knew much more than how to light the oven, but he was confident he could fake it. He volunteered, saying that in fact he was an expert baker. He was selected, and assigned to oversee three German soldiers baking bread for their fellow troops stationed in the area. Amazingly, he quickly proved himself capable, and so was given a place to live in town, meaning that unlike the rest of his family, he avoided the worst of the ghetto experience. He had gotten off easy.

On May 28, 1944, the semblance of peacefulness and order that had been established in the ghetto, however primitive the conditions, evaporated. With absolutely no warning, on that morning one third of the ghetto's Jews were ordered into trains for shipment, for 'transport,' to Birkenau. One instant, families were planning their day, and the next they were being herded by the Hungarian Gendarmerie to the local railway depot and into railroad box cars. It took a total of three 'transports' to empty Dej's forest ghetto of its nearly 8,000 Jews. After the May 28 'transport,' the other two, which were scheduled and families assigned, were on June 6 and June 8. My father and most of his family went on June 6.

Even now, six months after the first German troops had moved into Dej, the town's Jews were unaware that their steps towards the local train depot were, for most, steps towards doom. Not only did they not know it, they didn't even *suspect* it. They still believed what they'd been told by the Royal Hungarian Gendarmerie and the town elders, that they were going to Germany to be resettled in new camps.

Even my father, with his teenager's ear for rumor and daily contact with German soldiers, believed the resettlement talk. The warning of the German soldier he'd befriended had receded far into the background. But after the May 28 'transport,' he arranged with a Christian family he'd known for years to hide him in their attic. He, and they, figured the war would be over before the end of the year and the family was willing to take the risk.[1]

'But Dad, wait.' There was a contradiction in here. 'Why would you arrange with a family to hide you if you believed the Nazis were simply moving the Jews to new camps where everyone would be safe?'

'Why? Because it was the difference between being free, and not free. In the attic maybe I couldn't walk outside, but that was my choice. And also I knew the Russians would soon be coming. The deportation was different. We thought the deportation was taking us to a place where we might be under the thumb of the Nazis for a long time.'

My father had clearly weighed his options. But in the end, he was uncomfortable letting his mother go on the trip without him. He felt responsible for her. His father had just died. His five oldest brothers and sisters were already married and with families of their own. Of the other two siblings, Rosie was scheduled for the third 'transport,' two days later, and Isadore was in a Labor Service

---

1 I never learned the name of the family, or anything about them, but they had figured it right – by December the Russian Army was in Dej.

battalion working hundreds of miles away. His mother would have no one watching out for her.

'Besides,' he said with a shrug, 'I assumed I would get a job as a baker at the new place.'

Each time I heard my father say this, it would stagger me all over again. It did that Seder night. Though he could have avoided the 'transport,' though he could have spent a few months in an attic in Dej counting the days till the Russians arrived, though he could have entirely missed the horrors of his concentration camp experience, when my father told the story he always made the decision to go with his mother sound simple, as easy as that shrug.

But it couldn't have been. He was giving up certainty – safekeeping in an attic – for the uncertainty of the 'transport.' He was surrendering freedom of a sort, for the unknown deep inside the Third Reich. My father was an intelligent young man. He had to have assumed the train trip wasn't leading to any place fun. Yet he went because he believed his mother needed him.

Perhaps he needed her as well? He never put it this way, but maybe he needed his mother's presence more than he needed the comfort of the Christian family's attic?

I bet climbing aboard that train was gut-wrenching. Could I have done this? Could I have gone with my mother, if I'd been in my father's shoes? I should have asked him about this. I should have explored with him how truly hard it must have been to make that call.

But I didn't.

Leaving the bakery the morning of the 'transport,' my father grabbed two big loaves of bread for the family to eat on the trip. Arriving in the ghetto, his mother instructed him to return to town to buy cured pork. The request shocked him, as orthodox Jews were forbidden to eat it. But my grandmother explained that cured pork was the only meat that would last during a long, hot journey without spoiling, and God would forgive them their desire to remain properly nourished. So Dad purchased pork in town.

The 'transport' to Birkenau was a train of boxcars, each suitable for cattle, or for hobos making their way through the American West. They were absolutely not suitable for the fifty to sixty Jews crammed into each one.

'I hopped onto the boarding step and up into the car,' my father said. 'Then I helped my mother, and my young nieces and nephews and my sisters. There were no seats, nowhere to sit. We sat on the dirty floor, like sardines.'

Dad was in a boxcar with his mother, his sister Hanna-Leah with her husband Bernát Weingertner and their four children, his sister Chaya-Sarah with her two children (her husband was doing Labor Service on the Russian front and would die there), and his oldest brother Lazar with his wife and two children. That made eight cousins in total, ranging in age from four to twelve (Villi, Blina, their families, and Rosie, went two days later).

The sliding door was flung shut and the lock clanked into place, plunging them into nearly total darkness. A few people screamed, some moaned, but my father just observed.

'What else should I do?' he said to me. 'There was nothing else to do. My spirits were good. I was fine, so I talked to the little ones to keep their spirits up. I still wasn't so worried about anything.'

There was barely room to sit. Everyone was touching those around them. Feet crossed, hands at their sides or on their laps, they could only escape by losing themselves in conversation or thought. Sleep, when it came, came while sitting. There was no place to lie down. There were no bathroom facilities, resulting in a smell people were never meant to be acquainted with. In every car, people who had already been humiliated by being forced to live like animals in the forest that was the Dej ghetto now surrendered whatever dignity they had left. There was no choice. A few, older and weaker, died on the journey.

'We were in this cattle car, this way, for two days,' my father said. 'The time was like one long, miserable night. I talked all the time to my nieces and nephews and my mother.'

One particular memory from that long night stayed with my father throughout his life. It is a memory that actually *gave* him life, that he said sustained him during the worst times in his year in the camps.

My father explained. 'Near the end of the trip, my mother leaned into my ear so I could hear her over the noise of the train, and she said, "Dave, the next time you take this journey, you will take it in a luxury way."'

He paused briefly, and I was about to ask him to clarify that, but then he went on.

'Jeckeleh, I didn't know what she meant. So I asked her to say it again, and she did. She said, "The next time you are on this trip, it will be in a luxury way." I stared at my mother, I couldn't see her very well in the dark car, it was almost black inside there even though I knew it was already the next day, and I thought to myself, 'The next time? There can only be a next time, if I survive whatever is at the end of this journey.' I didn't know where we were going, and I never could imagine how terrible it would be, but when I heard my mother say this, suddenly I felt sure, I felt confident, that no matter where we were going, I would survive.'

My father said that when his life in concentration camp became especially difficult and dangerous, when his weight dropped, when his strength waned, when his store of luck dissipated, his mother's words came back to him. He would say to himself, 'My mother somehow knows I am going to survive. She somehow knows I am going have a good life after this is over. She somehow knows a train trip in a *luxury way* is in my future.'

The words my father used that Seder night were the exact words his mother had used. They were Yiddish, and translate directly into 'luxury way.' It's an awkward idiom for an English speaker, but I never asked him to clarify it, such as, 'You mean "first class," don't you?' I didn't ask him because he spoke English fluently, and he obviously knew first class railcars existed, so I have no doubt his mother had used precisely those words.

Now when I think about it, I realize my grandmother was trying to convey something extremely important to my father. She was trying to tell her son of the bright future she saw for him. Traveling in a 'luxury way' is more than just 'first class' train travel. It's being well dressed, well fed, and – especially given the circumstances of this particular train trip – well treated. It's where everything is the best available.

My grandmother was telling her son, my father, she foresaw not only would he have a life after the war, but that his life would be great, his would be a life of luxury. She didn't mean it literally, because that had never been their lives in Dej. But she meant it figuratively, and comparatively. Compared to that boxcar, compared to his life as a baker for the German army, compared to his life since the Nazis had come to Hungary, his life would be one of luxury. She knew this.

Suddenly my father came alert as he felt the train slow, and then halt. He heard voices outside. The boxcar's lock was unclicked and the door slid violently open, bathing him in harsh midafternoon light. He squinted to see through the bright glare as his heart beat wildly.

He had arrived in KZ Birkenau.

Chapter 16

Angelika

A ngelika told me she has short dark hair, would be wearing a black sweater, and would be dining with her husband and grown children. As the woman sitting in a booth along one wall fits that description, I walk over and introduce myself. She stands to shake my hand as she confirms that she is, indeed Angelika Schlackl. She is attractive, of medium height and with a friendly air about her. I guess that she is in her late forties. Smiling warmly, she introduces me to her husband, Kurt, and their three kids, and I instantly feel I am in good hands.

My own hands, I notice, are shaking.

'Do you live far from here?' I ask as an opener as I sit and fill a proffered plate with food.

'No,' she says. 'We live in St. Marien. It is not far. It is thirty kilometers for me and Kurt to drive this morning.'

We'd never spoken on the phone, only communicating by email, but Angelika's accent is what I expect, Germanic, with *vee's* and *zee's*. I then notice a small gold Jewish star on a chain around her neck.

'You're Jewish?' I could have been more tactful, but I'm taken by surprise. I'd thought she'd told me otherwise.

She smiles while fingering the star. 'We are Evangelical Christian. Jesus was a Jew, you know, and we feel close in our life to Judaism. This helps for me to remember that every day.'

I consider for a moment the obvious strength of her faith. In an email she told me she grew up Catholic in Linz, Austria, and worked as a school teacher until the first of their three kids came along. A few years ago, with the children nearly grown, she went back to school to study history. She recently joined the Mauthausen Memorial team, though only part-time. She wrote me she feels she has found her calling in working with survivors of KZ Mauthausen and KZ Gusen, both Jews and non-Jews, and getting their stories recorded in the Mauthausen archives. She was doing it so they, and what they went through, would never be forgotten.

I was initially surprised to learn most of the people working at Mauthausen Memorial – historians, curators, archivists, interns and others – were not Jewish. I had naively figured most of the prisoners in KZ Mauthausen had been Jews, and so the people staffing Mauthausen Memorial would be, as well.

I was wrong on both counts.

The vast majority of the men and women murdered by the Nazis in KZ Mauthausen and in its sub-camps were *not* Jewish. Hitler had many concentration camps for gassing Jews or working them to death, but until the late spring of 1944 Mauthausen was not one of them. Of the 190,000 persons incarcerated in KZ Mauthausen and its sub-camps during the war, less than 32,000 of them were Jews, and half of that total arrived by death marches in the last few months of the war.[1]

Instead, most of Mauthausen's prisoners were non-Jewish communists, socialists, intellectuals, politicians, resistance fighters, gays, gypsies, common criminals, prisoners of war, and others deemed unfit to live under the Nazi flag. People who might spread unrest, who by their presence alone might remind the populace there are more palatable political systems than Nazism, found themselves in Mauthausen. They came first from Germany, Austria, and Czechoslovakia, and then later from every country touched by the Nazi war machine.

So strictly for its horribleness, and not to memorialize the attempted genocide of the Jews, these Mauthausen Memorial employees had zealously accepted the mission of preventing KZ Mauthausen and its sub-camps from disappearing into history.

---

1 The Mauthausen Memorial website states *'around* 190,000' people were in KZ Mauthausen and its sub-camps during the war, and *'at least* 90,000' of them died there (emphasis added). But other sources claim the prison population totaled as many as 360,000, and that up to 320,000 were killed. The truth will never be known with certainty because, as the war neared its end, the Nazis both stopped keeping records and destroyed most of their old records. My guess is the total population was probably in the 200,000s, and between 100,000 and 150,000 of them were murdered by the Nazis. I say that because the staff at Mauthausen Memorial has worked hard to be accurate, but that rightly implies a degree of conservatism, so I assume their numbers are somewhat shy of the true tally. Therefore, Jews may have totaled as little as five percent of the total Mauthausen system population.

Even though Jews were not the Mauthausen camp system's dominant residents, *mostly* Jews were on the camp's death marches. The primary purpose of these 'transports' at the end of the war was to move Jews away from the Allied armies rapidly closing in on central Germany, and they originated at many concentration camps.

Their death toll was appalling. After surviving, sometimes for years, in concentration camps and labor battalions, and barely weeks away from the war's end, half of the more than 20,000 Jews who left KZ Mauthausen in a series of death marches in April 1945 didn't make it to liberation. At least 6,000 died on the road, before reaching their destinations thirty or more miles away. Many dropped dead of exhaustion, some died of a bullet to the base of the neck because they could go no further, and still others were outright murdered by Nazi guards shepherding the march. Over 4,000 more died at their destinations, camps with little or no food, no water, and inadequate shelter.

The death marches were aptly named.

Chapter 17

Roadside

Breakfast finished, I bid good-bye to Angelika's family and we head to our cars. We decide I will follow her small red Citroen, keeping my cell phone handy should I lose her. We are bound for our first stop of the afternoon, KZ Mauthausen.

Driving the local roads, I am surprised by how pretty everything is, colorful farm fields and immaculate houses all around me, the September sun's rays filtering through trees lining the road and glinting off the Danube River as I cross. I wasn't expecting such a pretty landscape. The truth is, I can't fathom anything *pretty* given why I'm here today, but I have to admit it seems pleasing enough.

Now on the north side of the Danube, I am on a narrow two-lane road climbing the hill topped by KZ Mauthausen. It dawns on me that I am driving on the same road my father had walked on at least three times before – once going uphill to KZ Mauthausen, and twice on death marches headed downhill. I know this from all the research I'd done before today.

I call Angelika's cell phone to tell her I want to stop, then pull over and get out. I am not sure why. Dad never described the early goings of his marches. I can't point to any specific spot along this road and associate it with him. But I feel compelled to stand on the roadside.

The sky is cloudless. The early September air feels light and comfortable, warm but not hot, and lacking in humidity. It reminds me of summer days in Los Angeles. 'My dad was here,' I say to Angelika, who has parked her car and come beside me. 'He walked on this road.'

'Yes, at least three times,' she says, nodding her head as if understanding better than me why I'd stopped. Through our emails she knows my father's story almost as well as I.

Standing on the roadside, it feels like, well, like the side of a road. There is nothing unique about it, no sensations coming through the soles of my feet, nothing in the air to induce thoughts or images. Not surprisingly, I guess I need a direct connection between my father's story and the geography, a connection that doesn't exist right here. In fact, the area looks a lot like upstate New York or New England, a narrow road bordered by leafy trees, now a BMW driving by going up, now a Ford pickup coming down. A gust of wind kicks up leaves lining the shoulders, reminding me summer is ending. Strung along the road are houses painted white, peach, and light-green. They aren't new. They were here during the war.

Eyeing a home across the road from me, I say, 'I wonder what it would have been like to look out of your living room window and see prisoners marching past on their way to or from Mauthausen.'

'Perhaps the families of these houses were warned to not look,' Angelika replies.

'Perhaps,' I acknowledge, but I wonder even more what my father thought as he passed by. Did he make eye contact with anyone behind the windows? Or was he so consumed with merely trying to move forward, that he wasn't thinking at all? Whether going uphill or down, my father was probably so wrapped up in the precariousness of his life as a Jew caught in the teeth of the Nazi death machine, he might not have been thinking of anything except the next step, and the next, and the one after that. It would have been nice to be able to ask him now, ask him what he'd thought back then. Alas. We get back in our cars and drive on.

Near the top of the hill the trees suddenly end, and on my left I see a large grass field. A few yards further up on my right is a parking lot. It appears nearly full. A short distance in front of me is an ancient castle, with dark, nearly black stone walls two stories high. I stare at the walls as I drive closer. They are so ominous-looking, so foreboding, I imagine helmeted men with crossbows and shields are watching me. The castle seems gigantic and out of place.

Then I realize it is no castle at all. It is KZ Mauthausen.

Chapter 18

The Mauthausen Camp System

The Nazis didn't coin the term 'concentration camp.' It was originally used in the late 1800s, referring to refugee camps in which people were 'concentrated' during Spain's Ten Year War with Cuba. Though those concentration camps were overcrowded and unhealthy places, the Nazis' use of the same term for their infamous slave-labor and death camps gave it its sinister connotation.

KZ Mauthausen is situated on a hilltop 1,130ft above sea level, three miles north of the eponymous municipality of Mauthausen, a sleepy town on a bend in the Danube River. The concentration camp was purposely sited 200 yards from a massive granite quarry, called Wiener-Graben because it was owned by the city of Vienna (Wien in German) and, before the war, most of its granite had been bound for there. It was easy to get granite from the Wiener-Graben quarry to Vienna via barge on the Danube, where the one hundred mile trip eastward took one day on the water.

Two-and-a-half miles west and downhill of KZ Mauthausen was the small village of Gusen, and three more granite quarries, Oberbruch Kastenhof, Unterbruch Kastenhof (Upper Kastenhof and Lower Kastenhof), and Gusen. The three were adjacent to each other and were collectively known as the Kastenhof Quarry. Like Wiener-Graben, Kastenhof was close to the Danube and so could easily ship its granite throughout Europe.

Mauthausen and Gusen – in fact every one of the Reich's concentration camps – were managed and guarded exclusively by the notorious SS. Run by bespectacled Hitler crony Heinrich Himmler, the _Schutzstaffel_ ('protective squadron' in English) was the most powerful organization in Germany, with military and state-security branches that reached into every aspect of life in Germany and occupied Europe.

More than an elite combat and internal-security organization, the SS was also an immensely profitable criminal enterprise, with a corporate structure that would have been familiar to any Wall Street analyst. It was as if the mafia had been an official branch of the government. The main, top-level corporate organization – the 'holding company,' in the parlance of modern finance – went by the unwieldy name of *SS-Wirtschafts und Verwaltungshauptamt,* the SS Main Economic and Administrative Office, SS-WVHA for short.

The SS-WVHA subsidiary I cared about was DEST, *Deutsche Erd- und Steinwerke GmbH,* the German Earth and Stone Company Inc. DEST mined, manufactured and sold building materials for use throughout Germany and the occupied countries. A subsidiary of DEST, *Granitwerke Mauthausen,* operated the Mauthausen and Gusen granite quarries. Other DEST subsidiaries, as well as legitimate, long-established German corporations, used KZ Mauthausen slave labor for plants producing steel, cement, rockets, tanks, airplane wings and fuselages, and pharmaceuticals. By the end of the war, DEST was as big as any conglomerate trading on the New York Stock Exchange.

In addition to civilian job titles, men in the SS-WVHA, the 'corporate' side of the SS, held paramilitary rank similar to ranks in the Wehrmacht, Germany's regular army. The four most senior men in *Granitwerke Mauthausen* were each an SS-Hauptsturmführer, equal to an army captain. They were Otto Walther, Managing Director and the man in overall charge of the business; Alfred Grau, directly under Walther; Paul Wolfram, the general manager of the three quarries at KZ Gusen I and II; and Johannes Grimm, the general manager of the quarry at KZ Mauthausen.

Mauthausen's commandant from 1939 till the end of the war, SS-Standartenführer Franz Ziereis, had the civilian title of Director of Operations at DEST. His Wehrmacht rank of colonel officially put him above the other four.[1]

DEST leased the Wiener-Graben quarry in 1938, and acquired Kastenhof the next year. They were to provide granite for Hitler's

---

1 After the war, in 1948 Paul Wolfram was tried by a U.S. Military Tribunal in Nuremberg and sentenced to life in prison (though by 1960 he was free). Johannes Grimm was sentenced to death by the U.S. Military Tribunal and executed in 1947. Franz Ziereis tried to escape by hiding in his hunting lodge with his wife, but was found and shot by American troops soon after KZ Mauthausen was liberated in 1945. He died of his wounds a few days later. Alfred Grau was Argentinian. He disappeared after the war and is believed to have escaped back there. Otto Walther was interviewed by a U.S. Military Tribunal but never charged.

plans to rebuild Nazi Germany to conform to his grandiose image of the country he assumed would rule Europe for the next thousand years. Over a few short years Hitler wanted to build sports stadiums, apartment and office buildings, municipal facilities, and railway terminals, all partially or mostly from granite. Crushed granite was also needed to build the country's expanding network of highways and railroads.

KZ Mauthausen began operating in 1938, taking in political prisoners and criminals to work as slave labor in the quarries. Within a single year, the camp's prisoner population outgrew its capacity to house and feed them. The solution was to open 'sub-camps,' some nearby, some further away, but all run by KZ Mauthausen's commandant, Ziereis.

In 1940, the first Mauthausen sub-camp was opened, near the Kastenhof mines in the village of Gusen, and was formally known as KZ Gusen I. Gusen I was built not only to alleviate KZ Mauthausen's overcrowded barracks two-and-a-half miles up the hill, but also to save the prisoners from the daily five-mile round-trip hike. This was *not* a humanitarian gesture by a suddenly compassionate SS. DEST's brain trust had been seeking a way to reduce the death toll the daily march down the hill and back up was taking on the prisoners, to say nothing of the number of prisoners killed while working in the quarries. They were dying faster than they could be replaced. Opening a sub-camp near Gusen was the obvious solution.

In March 1944, KZ Gusen II was opened next door to Gusen I. It was primarily built to house slave labor to construct, and then staff, manufacturing plants being tunneled into the local mountains so they would be shielded from allied aerial bombing. It also served to alleviate overcrowding in Gusen I. Gusen II was known as a particularly depraved and horrific concentration camp. In June, 1944, my father was sent there, experiencing for himself the camp's incredible barbarity.

Eventually, the Mauthausen network of sub-camps grew to more than forty. Though most of the sub-camps were in Austria, a few were in German towns near the border. Their names are unfamiliar to most people, even to me. But prisoners there worked just as hard, were treated just as miserably, and died just as surely, as in any of the more famous camps.

The Nazis ranked their labor concentration camps by *stufe*, which translates into level, or grade, or rating, from *stufe I* to *stufe III*: the higher the number, the more difficult the conditions in the camp, and the lower the survival rate.[1] Auschwitz I, perhaps the most well-known of all the labor camps, was a *stufe I*. Most camps, in fact, were accorded the *stufe I* grade, while a few were rated *stufe II*. The great distinction accorded KZ Mauthausen and its Gusen I sub-camp was they were the only *stufe III* concentration camps, confirming they were the most abominable work camps in the entire Nazi concentration camp universe. They were built to be unsurvivable. If the *stufe III* rating wasn't warning enough of the mortal danger of being sent to KZ Mauthausen, its nickname eliminated all doubt: *knochenmühle* – 'the bone grinder.'

Although its stated mission was to provide slave labor for its granite quarries, and later for its manufacturing plants, KZ Mauthausen's true *raison d'être* was to slowly murder its prisoners. They were worked to death, starved to death, beaten to death, shot, drowned, exposed to freezing cold till they died in winter, and to sweltering heat till they died in summer. Many arrived with their *Häftlings-Personal-Karte*, their Prisoner Personnel Card labeled *rûckkehr unerwünscht* (return not desired).[2] Given the backbreaking labor in the stone quarries, the sadism of the guards, and the minimal food fed the prisoners, whoever stamped those Prisoner Personnel Cards had little to worry about: return was extremely unlikely. Assignment to KZ Mauthausen was an unofficial death sentence.

---

1 Death camps, such as Birkenau, had no need for a rating – people were sent there only to be killed, or selected for 'transport' to labor concentration camps, with a small few remaining behind to work as slave labor in that particular camp.

2 I have my father's *Häftlings-Personal-Karte*. It does not have any labeling like this. He was sent to KZ Mauthausen solely because he was in good shape and the camp needed him for labor.

Chapter 19

Not So Terrible

I park my rental car in one of the few available spots in the KZ Mauthausen parking lot. Walking towards Angelika's car, my gaze is drawn to the large grass field I saw driving up as I reached the top of the hill. Now in front of me, it is the size of three football fields side by side, and is sunken. It was dug into a shallow hillside and then leveled to be usable. A single long set of steps sinks down into it. The field is bordered by trees on two sides – the side to my left, and the side opposite me. Bare patches of brown dirt are scattered haphazardly here and there.

From Google Earth, I know the Wiener-Graben granite quarry is just beyond this field, past the trees opposite me at the far edge. To my right and looming over the field is the massive granite south wall of the concentration camp itself. Looking like it was built in 1238, rather than in 1938, it is straight out of medieval construction school. The camp within the walls encompasses thirty-seven acres, not including the quarry or this sunken field. I will be there soon.

But it will not be soon enough. My hands are shaking again. I waited too long to come here. I should have come in 2007, right after seeing my father's photo on the Mauthausen website. But I didn't. Why the delay? Ambivalence? Fear? I was going through my divorce right then, and I was immensely busy at work as the global economy began its precipitous decline into the Great Recession of 2008. But those are really just excuses. I don't know why I didn't come until today. Whatever the reason, I realize more importantly, I should have come while my father was alive. I consider that he would probably still be alive, if not for the significant damage done to his heart by that first heart attack.

One morning in early June, 1972, my brother and I were getting dressed for school. Dad came into the bedroom we shared to tell us he felt pain in his upper chest and left arm. He said we shouldn't worry, because the pain was 'not so terrible,' but he was going to the doctor after we left the house. Maybe because he wasn't a native English speaker, my father had phrases he loved to deploy that summed things up. Phrases like 'no big deal,' 'everything is alright,' and 'not so terrible.'

A story about my brother typified my father's 'not so terrible.' I was ten or eleven years old, Eli six or seven. One evening after dinner, we were horsing around in our bedroom when Eli fell, slamming his head on the sharp corner of a dresser. Blood pouring from a cut on his scalp like water out of a tap, he tore out of the room screaming, me right behind him. Dad, who had been reading a newspaper at the kitchen table, intercepted him. By the time I'd caught up, Eli's T-shirt was soaked with blood. I watched my father calmly guide Eli to our house's bathroom, turn on the tap, and stick Eli's head under it. Then he grabbed a bath towel off the rack and held it over the wound. Mom, the Israeli Air Force veteran, stepped past me, slid off Eli's shirt and washed the blood off his chest and back.

A few minutes later my father lifted his hand off the cut. It had stopped bleeding and Eli had stopped crying. So, what did my father say when he inspected the cut? 'It's not so terrible,' followed by, 'by the time you get married, you won't even have a bump there.' Eli giggled. We felt safe when Dad had his hands on us.

Though the pain in my father's chest and arm that June morning was 'not so terrible,' it had grabbed his attention. Standing in our bedroom, he told us definitively 'everything would be alright,' and we'd see him that evening. We believed him, because he was invincible. But when we arrived home after school late that afternoon, my Uncle Villi told us the pain Dad had felt that morning was actually a heart attack, and he had been admitted to Long Beach Memorial Hospital.

Villi and his wife, Mary, had been staying with us since our mother had died seven months earlier. A few years after the war ended, Villi had shut the family soap factory in Dej and partnered with a Turkish businessman, opening what became a successful chemical plant in Turkey. While there, he met and married Mary, a sweet and tall Jewish woman who'd been raised in Ankara. When Mom died in November 1971, Villi sold his share of the company, retired, and moved with Mary to our house in Long Beach to help my father manage. Mary cooked, Villi entertained us with impossible yoga feats, and my father, Eli, and I had a semblance of normalcy in our lives.

My father's admission to Long Beach Memorial was only a bit disturbing to me because I had an unshakable belief in his ability to survive anything. I figured a heart attack was nothing compared with KZ Mauthausen. He rolled with life events that would, I was sure, paralyze others. My mother's death was an example. I saw him cry about it only once, briefly, when Yishai Lovinger, the mustachioed friend from his days in Israel, who now lived in Brazil, called to express his sorrow. Even at the funeral, my father was a rock. Of course, that's what I saw. I have no idea whether, or how much, he cried when he was alone, and now, looking back, I can't imagine the pain he must have endured so silently. But I modeled myself on what I could see. So I believed his heart attack was just a small bump in the road.

My father came home after four weeks in the hospital. Helped by Villi and Mary's cooking and companionship, he slowly regained his strength, and by the end of the summer it was as if nothing had happened.

Israel figured prominently in my parents' lives. My mother had been born there in 1930, or more accurately in Palestine, and most of her relatives still lived there. My father's brothers and sister lived there, in Natanya, where my cousin Vivi and her husband David now live. Isadore emigrated in the late 1940s, around the time my father went to Haifa, Rosie moved there with her family in the early 1960s, and Villi and Mary moved to Natanya soon after my father recovered from his heart attack. And, of course, I was born in Haifa.

After recovering from his heart attack, my father went to Israel at least once a year to see his brothers and sister. I went a few times as well, although we never went together because I went during summer breaks, while summer was my father's busiest season at work. By 1980, with Eli and me in college and beyond, he picked up the pace. Some years, he went three times. He went so often that I lost track.

And that was my mistake. Because in 1997, on one of those visits to Israel, my father made that side trip to KZ Mauthausen, and never told me.

Since hanging up from that phone call with Vivi, I've tried conjuring up a reason why he'd kept it from me. Was he embarrassed by what we might see together? There would have been no reason I could think of to be embarrassed by anything we'd see or do.

It could be he assumed I didn't care. It's possible that, to my father, I never showed enough interest in his story, never asked enough questions, never probed for enough details during all those Seder tellings.

Maybe the fact that I never expressed a desire to see the camps had him assuming I wouldn't want to come along. He could have asked me, but maybe he didn't want to be rejected, didn't want to hear me say, 'Thanks Dad, but why don't you go on your own, and tell me about it when you get back.'

I would *never* have said that, but how would he have known?

Now, as Angelika and I walk out of the parking lot, the reason for my father's choice not to tell me he'd returned here is a painful mystery. As is what he did when he came here. I desperately wonder what he saw and what he felt as he walked the grounds of the camps. I wonder what he thought to himself as he looked at these fields now in front of me. I wonder if he stood in the rock quarry where he once slaved, if he walked the death march routes where he nearly died. Did he relive his escapes? Did he find the Friedmann home, and visit the attic where he hid? I have so many questions.

Without a single answer to contemplate, I wedge my hands deep into my jeans pockets.

Chapter 20

Birkenau Selection

My father's *Häftlings-Personal-Karte*, his Prisoner Personnel Card, which survived the war, is date-stamped showing he was admitted to KZ Auschwitz on Wednesday, June 7, 1944. The train actually took him to KZ Birkenau, two miles away.

Also known as Auschwitz II, Birkenau was originally opened in 1941 to alleviate overcrowding in Auschwitz I, but by the time my father got there it had been turned into the penultimate Nazi killing factory, with multiple gigantic gas chambers, some of which could murder one thousand people at a time. More than ninety percent of those who disembarked there were killed there, usually within hours of arrival. Of those remaining, some were assigned to work in Birkenau, Auschwitz I, or one of its sub-camps, like my Uncle Villi. Others were held in Birkenau for a few days until being shipped to concentration camps elsewhere, to be worked until they died. My father was in this latter group. By the end of the war, not less than two million and perhaps as many as four million people were killed in Birkenau, most of them in those massive gas chambers.

My father's train pulled into Birkenau that Wednesday afternoon, rolling past the concentration camp's often-photographed brick main gatehouse, and halting just yards from the gas chambers and crematoria, though the Nazis had effectively disguised the true purpose of those buildings near the railhead. The SS tried to maintain a sense of calm at Birkenau's unloading platform, and from what my father described, they succeeded.

My father continued. 'The train stopped, they opened up the doors, and I took a breath fresh air,' he said, taking a deep breath in through his nose. 'Jeckeleh, it felt so good, after being in that car for two days.' The irony was not lost on me.

Kapos, prisoners who had been entrusted with a small degree of responsibility and authority, ordered everyone out of the cars sternly, but coolly, issuing the German orders, *Raus!* (get out), *Runter!* (get down) and *Los!* (get going, get moving), and commanding my father and the others from Dej to leave their belongings behind on the trains. Those still alive in the boxcars stepped down into the bright afternoon sunlight. German troops and dogs walked slowly and unmenacingly among them, or as unmenacingly as jack-booted SS storm troopers with Dobermans at their heels could make themselves. The *kapos*, along with *KZlers*, regular prisoners assigned to work at the railhead, guided the new arrivals into long lines to be processed.[1]

This initial introduction to Birkenau was, according to my father, remarkably benign. It didn't fill him with dread, with the threat of imminent extinction, as I had expected it would. It's possible he didn't remember it well. It was certainly an overwhelming experience. Maybe his description is how he *chose* to remember it. As the years passed, perhaps he subconsciously softened his memory of those life-altering minutes when he'd first arrived, so that he could accept the terrible results better. Or perhaps his description is really the way it happened.

'Men and women were separated,' he said at the Seder table. 'Children went with their mothers. Walking among the men, some of the *kapos* and *KZlers* hissed, in every language in Europe, "Idiots, why did you come here? Why didn't you run when you could? Don't you know what this is?" I heard them as I stood in the line and I thought to myself, "No, I don't know what this is."'

Astonishingly, my father still assumed they were entering a resettlement camp of some sort. Even the separation of men and women hadn't alarmed him. He still figured everything was going to work out.

The process my father, his mother, and his family stood in line waiting for was the dreaded 'selection,' where incoming Jews were sorted like widgets in a factory, good from bad, functional from defective, most to be killed immediately in gas chambers, the rest to be worked to death in concentration camps. Similar to English, the word in German is *selektion*, and it was a process feared by every prisoner, every *KZler*. 'Selections' took place not only at the Birkenau

---

1 *KZler*, pronounced ka-tset'-ler – enunciating the German 'K' and 'Z' and then adding 'ler' – comes from the KZ prefix shorthand for *Konzentrationslager*, the German word for 'concentration camp,' and was used interchangeably with 'prisoner.'

railhead. They were done regularly in every concentration camp barracks to weed out those who had become too weak to work. My father eventually learned that in the nomenclature of the camps, being 'selected' was always bad. If you were 'selected,' you lost. You died. But neither my father, nor his family, nor anyone else in his boxcar had ever heard of *selektion*, so they took what was about to happen as part of some kind of induction process.

They couldn't have been more wrong.

My father said the 'selection' itself seemed simple and inconsequential while it was taking place. He recalled a slight man wearing the immaculately pressed uniform of an SS Hauptsturmführer, or captain, the same rank as the men who ran *Granitwerke Mauthausen*. The Hauptsturmführer was sitting erect and alert at a table in the middle of the rail yard. One by one, every person who had offloaded from the boxcars passed the man, who turned out to be a doctor. As they went by, he would look at them for an instant, and then order them to the right, or to the left. In that instantaneous assessment, he decided if they would live a while longer, or be dead within hours.

I've known about 'selections' for as long as I've known about my father's year in the camps, but the concept still shocks me. One man, looking at you for less than a second, decided if you would live or die. You could have been a marathoner, but if you'd had a runny nose and sniffled right then, you'd die. You could have had the strength of Hercules, but if you hadn't slept well in the cattle car and looked haggard, you'd die. Nothing about your past, nothing about your life, nothing about your accomplishments and capabilities counted for anything in that moment when the SS Hauptsturmführer at the table in the middle of the rail yard gave you a quick glance and sent you to the left or the right. To me, it was terrifying.

My father was sure the man he encountered for that fateful second was the infamous Dr Joseph Mengele. Mengele wasn't the only Birkenau doctor assigned to make selections, but he was the most zealous, and by far the most well-known.

Kapos and *KZlers* guided people in the direction the SS officer had pointed, creating new lines. My father was sent to the right, as was his brother-in-law, Hannah-Leah's husband Bernát. He noticed the elderly, and nearly all the women and children, were sent to the left. Others, too, were sent left, though at that moment my father didn't know why. The rest of his family went that way: his mom, his sisters, all his nieces and nephews, and his oldest brother Lazar with his wife.

My father went to the right as he was told, heading to where a new line was forming, but then he stopped. Turning around to look back, he saw an image he never forgot, a permanent imprint on his memory. He saw his mother and his two sisters standing together, with the younger children clinging to their dresses. They had gone to the left, and they hadn't noticed him staring. They seemed to be absorbed in the process of keeping their place in their new line. Suddenly my father knew this was all wrong. A spotlight appeared to be illuminating them, making them stand out from the throngs of Jews milling around. He felt a pain in his heart. Why had they been separated? It wasn't men to one side, women to the other. It was men like *him* to one side, young, self-assured, healthy, strong men to his side, and women, kids, overweight men, much older men, to the other side.

He started raising his hand to get their attention, but just then his mother's head snapped towards him. It was for only a heartbeat, or maybe two. He shuddered as his mother's eyes locked on his. He immediately sensed from her that he would never ever see her again. In his head he heard her words again, 'in a "luxury way",' and he understood she had been sending him off, sending him into a breathtakingly dangerous world she knew he would emerge from, while she would not. She had been saying good-bye.

Then in a flash he lost her and the rest of them as other Jews crowded into his line of sight. He didn't truly know the importance of that last look just then, but it stayed with him until the day he died.

My father was directed to a reception barracks where he undressed and showered. *KZlers* shaved his head, and issued him new clothes. They were unmistakably prison clothes, with vertical black stripes and a Jewish star on the left breast. The only item of clothing he kept, that everyone was required to keep, were his shoes.

He was assigned number 71890-U, U for *Ungarn*, German for Hungary, his country of origin. The number was imprinted on a label sewn onto to the left breast of his prison uniform and stamped on his Prisoner Personnel Card. It was not tattooed on his left forearm, which was only done to prisoners who stayed to work at Auschwitz or one of its sub-camps. Uncle Villi had a green-ink number tattooed on the inside of his left forearm.

Even at this point, hair shorn, wearing prison garb and assigned a number, my father said it still felt to him like everything would turn out alright as the family was resettled in Germany, or wherever they were, or were going to be. What he kept wondering about, though, was what had happened to his mother, sisters and the children after he had turned around to see them, after that shudder he felt, after they had gone to the left? He asked a Polish *KZler* standing by a window.

'Look there,' the Polish prisoner said in Yiddish. He pointed to thick brown smoke emanating from a stack they could see out the window. 'That's where your family is.' He smiled a nearly toothless smile. 'Up in smoke.' He exploded open the fingers of his clenched fist in front of my father's face.

Dad looked at the plume of smoke, and then back to the man's opened palm and fingers. The fingers were short and stubby, like their owner. And then he looked at the gummy, smiling face. The man's smile never reached his eyes. He was deadly serious and now my father felt numb.

'I wasn't sure what the Polish *KZler* meant,' my father said to me. 'It seemed crazy. I thought maybe he was crazy. Maybe he was playing a game with me. How could they have gone up in smoke? I had never heard of gas chambers and crematoriums, so that thought never entered to my mind. But I started to think. I was thinking now, for the first time, maybe this was not a relocation camp.'

Incredibly, Birkenau's true purpose was simply not penetrating.

Still contemplating the silent, ghastly sight of the smoke spiraling up from the smokestack, my father was directed into a rickety barracks building with no furniture. Instead of bunks, the barracks floor was covered with straw, and he made himself comfortable against one wall as best as he could. His brother-in-law, Bernát, still with him, settled into the straw beside him. Known as Hershy by his friends and family, he was a friendly and unathletic businessman of thirty-four who was adored by all the Hersch cousins, and who carried on his frame a few pounds too many for his average height. Other Hungarian Jews were already in the barracks. My father immediately noticed Hershy was among the oldest men there.

A couple of times that day, 'selections' occurred in the barracks. SS troops barged in, fingered weak-looking men, and marched them out. The veterans in the barracks, having been there two or three days already, told my father and Hershy what was happening. The truth was now becoming frighteningly evident to them. Men who had somehow gotten past the first train yard 'selection' were being discovered and sent to the gas chambers. The meek were not inheriting the earth, they were being slaughtered. Reality finally began weighing on Dad's shoulders like a heavy cloak. There was going to be no resettlement in Germany, no baker's job in some new place. He felt certain his family was gone. And he knew if he was picked in a 'selection,' he'd join them. Yet, leaning against that barracks wall, a feeling of serenity descended over him.

'I felt no fear, Jeckeleh,' my father said with intense seriousness. 'I wasn't afraid of anything. I knew I would not be selected to die in Birkenau.'

'Why were you so sure?'

'Because I was strong.' He puffed out his chest. 'I was young, and I could see the others who remained in the barrack.' He pronounced it 'bah-RAHK,' exactly like U.S. President Obama's first name. 'They were all like me.'

My father was seemingly too sure of his own youthful immortality to be afraid. But I've since learned differently. I learned he couldn't grasp the enormity of what he was experiencing. Instead, he had gone completely blank. Normally highly observant, his sense of reality had completely deserted him. It was all too much for an eighteen-year-old to comprehend. He was in a state of shock.

How do I know? How can I be so sure?

Because he always maintained that he was in Birkenau for a week or two. But the official Nazi date stamps on my father's *Häftlings-Personal-Karte* show he was there only *three days*. While he and Hershy were in the Birkenau barracks, every minute must have felt like an hour, and every day must have felt like a week. My father was in the red-hot core of the greatest killing apparatus every created, and his mind could not assimilate any of it. He had shut down.

On the second day in Birkenau, my father and Hershy were moved to a barracks that had beds. No mattresses, no blankets, but wooden bunk beds. He was assigned to a bed with three others, yet another form of degradation my father and the others in Birkenau endured. And the 'selections' continued. My father calmly waited them out.

Obviously my father was never 'selected' during the few days he spent in Birkenau. But many other were, and as they were shoved out of the barracks, others prisoners, mostly Hungarian Jews, took their place. During those scary days my father not only managed to stay in the barracks with his brother-in-law, but they were joined by his good friend from Dej, Izsak Mozes, the younger of the two brothers.

On June 10, 1944, my father, his brother-in-law Hershy, his friend Izsak, and everyone else in their barracks, along with a few hundred other Hungarian Jews, were loaded in groups of fifty onto boxcars. This was not a 'selection' for the gas chambers. Ordered to sit twenty-five down one side of the boxcar and twenty-five down the other side, they were not told where they were going. The big door slammed shut with a loud metallic click, and my father was once again plunged into darkness. The trip took three nights and four days, the car door remaining locked for all but an hour during the second full day. My father said the putrid interior became sweltering in the late spring heat, and some of the men passed out. A few were soon near death.

When the train stopped that one time and the SS guards slid open the big door to allow in air, my father and his boxcar mates begged the storm trooper in charge for water.

'We were so thirsty you wouldn't believe it,' my father said. 'The SS man for our car was a German. The other SS were Ukrainian.'

'How did you know?' I asked.

'We heard them speaking, so we knew where they were from. The Ukrainian SS were the worst. All the time they were much worse than the Germans.' SS soldiers hailing from Ukraine were not unusual. The occupied countries provided the Reich with thousands of troops who volunteered for both the SS and the regular army.

My father said their German SS guard acquiesced, allowing them to move as a group to the train station's water fountain. The Ukrainian guards, meanwhile, refused to let their charges out of their cars.

'I felt so bad for them, but there was nothing we could do.' My father's sadness was reflected on his face. It was, I noted, the first time that evening he'd appeared so sad. Even describing the last image of his mother didn't alter his expression this way. It was empathy, I supposed. He knew exactly how the Jews in the other cattle cars felt, because he'd felt it himself.

On June 13, 1944, my father's train with its human cargo pulled into the Mauthausen *Bahnhof*, the town's small train station.[1]

---

1 In German, all nouns are capitalized. When I use German nouns, I will follow their custom.

The portrait of my father that I saw on the KZ Mauthausen website in 2007. It was undated, but was most likely taken in 1943, when he was seventeen or eighteen. (Author)

My father, on the right, with his older brother, Villi, in the rear storage area of their father's small soap factory in Dej. The picture is dated 1938, when my father was twelve or thirteen. (Author)

My father with his sister, Rosie, in an undated photograph inside their home. My father believes he was fifteen or sixteen, while Rosie was around nineteen. (Author)

My father, second from left, in an undated photo. He is assembled with his Hungarian Labor Service battalion. The two men in front and on the far left are Hungarian officers. Note the yellow armbands on the two battalion members to my father's left, signifying that they are Jews. Presumably my father is wearing one as well. (Author)

My father and two of his friends in 1942 or 1943, when he was around seventeen. The man on the right is Izsak Mozes, who was with my father during most of his time in the camps. The man in the middle is Yanou (it has not been possible to establish his last name). Being Jewish, he was sent to the camps as well, and did not survive the war. (Author)

My mother. The picture is dated July 30, 1951. She was 21. (Author)

My mother in 1944, when she was fourteen, with her younger sister, Renee, and their uncle, David Grossman, a medic with the 16th Regiment of the US Army's 1st Division. The photograph was taken in London. On the morning of June 6, 1944, while my father and most of his family were being locked in a cattle car to be sent to KZ Birkenau, David landed on the Normandy beaches at H-Hour. Surviving that day uninjured, he was seriously wounded at St. Lô, France, a few weeks later, and evacuated. (Author)

Ignaz Friedmann, in his World War I Austro-Hungarian Army uniform. The photograph is undated. (Mauthausen Memorial)

Barbara Friedmann, in an undated image.

My father's Prisoner Personnel Card. His prisoner number, 71890U, which stayed with him from KZ Birkenau until liberation, is in the upper right corner. The birthdate, 13.6.25 (June 13, 1925), is incorrect. He was born July 13. His mother's (*mutter*) first name is also incorrect. It is Malvina. Date stamps show he entered Auschwitz-Birkenau on June 7, 1944, and Gusen on June 13, 1944. The red stamp on the bottom left, HOLLERITH-ERFASST (registered by Hollerith) signifies that my father's card had been tabulated by the Nazi's IBM card sorting system. (Author)

KL.:		JUDE	Häftl.-Nr.:
			71.890 U

Häftlings-Personal-Karte

	Überstellt	Personen-Beschreibung:
Fam.-Name: H e r s c h	am: 13. Juni 1944 an KL.	Grösse: cm
Vorname: David	GUSEN	Gestalt:
Geb. am: 13.6.25 in: Des	am: an KL.	Gesicht:
Stand: led. Kinder: -0-		Augen:
Wohnort: Des	am: an KL.	Nase:
Strasse: Racz u. 6		Mund:
Religion: mos. Staatsang.: Ungarn	am: an KL.	Ohren:
Wohnort d. Angehörigen: Mutter:		Zähne:
Abraham geb. Malome	am: an KL.	Haare:
KL. Auschwitz		Sprache:
Eingewiesen am: 7.6.44	am: an KL.	
durch: RSHA		
in KL.: Auschwitz		Bes. Kennzeichen:
Grund:	Entlassung:	
Vorstrafen:	am: durch KL.:	Charakt.-Eigenschaften:
	mit Verfügung v.:	Sicherheit b. Einsatz:
Strafen im Lager:		
Grund: Art:	Bemerkung:	
		Körperliche Verfassung:

KL./B/XI. 43-500000

The photograph that my father's siblings mailed to him in 1946, during his recuperation in the Kohlbruck Klinik in Passau, Germany. Uncle Villi is on the left, Aunt Rosie in the middle, and Uncle Isadore on the right. (Author)

My father, center of the back row, among unidentified fellow patients – all 'survivors' – in the Kohlbruck Klinik. The image is dated 1945. As they are outside and not dressed for the cold, I think the picture was taken that summer, meaning my father had been liberated just two or three months earlier. You can see how much thinner he looks here than in the 1946 Klinik picture on the next page. His indomitable spirit pours off this page. (Author)

My father in a hospital bed in the Kohlbruck Klinik in 1946. After initially making good progress in his recovery from his illnesses, in the fall of 1945 tuberculosis led to peritonitis and jaundice which nearly killed him. Here he is seen finally on the mend. (Author)

This portrait was taken in 1945, while my father was recuperating in the Kohlbruck Klinik. The concentration camp uniform is authentic, but borrowed. He wanted to have a photograph of himself in a camp uniform. (Author)

My father on an Israeli beach in an undated picture. Similar photographs are dated between 1951 and 1953, so he would have been between twenty-six and twenty-eight years old. (Author)

This is the evening in 1965 when my parents celebrated their purchase of a small stake in a senior citizen home, the business my father had entered as a busboy when my parents came to the US in 1958. I am seven; my brother is three. In exactly twenty years my father had gone from 'Hitler's Nightmare' to the American Dream. (Author)

Chapter 21

Sanitary Camp

Angelika and I are walking along the path paralleling the camp's south wall leading to the front gate. She tells me that the field I had been eyeing from the parking lot, now on our left, was actually two fields during the war years. The part closest to the parking lot was a ball field used by the SS guards for recreation. 'They played football on it,' she says, 'your soccer.'

Football? Soccer? I am so astounded that I stop. The Nazi guards had a soccer pitch to play on? So they could stay in shape, relax, forget about their cares and have a good time in between details guarding and beating and killing men like my father? 'How nice,' I finally say, and Angelika's weak grin shows she gets my sarcasm.

She tells me the rest of the field was originally called *Russenlager*, or 'Russian Camp.'

Dad was there, I think to myself.

Continuing, Angelika says when Hitler turned on Stalin in 1941, Mauthausen's *KZlers* covered the field with new wooden barracks anticipating an influx of Russian prisoners of war (every wall, structure, barracks, and path in KZ Mauthausen was built by its prisoners). But while the Russians originally came in sufficient numbers to require their own section of the camp, by the time the *Russenlager* was completed most of them had been killed, so instead the barracks became a camp infirmary.

I tell Angelika my father spent time between late 1944 and early 1945 in the *Russenlager*, in what he always called the *Revier*, pronounced like Paul Revere.

She says she recalls me writing about that in an email, adding that *Revier* is short for *Krankenrevier*, German for infirmary, or military hospital.

'But this was not the main *Revier* at Mauthausen,' she clarifies. 'Also, when your father was there it was not called any more *Russenlager*, as you wrote, because there were no Russian prisoners there. Instead it was called *Sanitätslager*, the Sanitary Camp. There were doctors there, and very sick prisoners, but they had almost no medicines. But yes, I understand why your father called it the *Revier*.'

I study the field more closely, and Angelika steps away from me, giving me space. My father had been somewhere on that turf for three months. Though it is now barren, I easily picture row after row of German field-grey barracks filling the field when Dad was a *KZler* here. *This* is why I have come. *This* is what I want to see. Places where my father existed, places where he persevered, places where he beat the odds.

My palms are moist and I am sweating in spite of the pleasant temperature. But at least my hands are steady now. I'm somewhat overwhelmed, as if I'm nearing sensory overload. This field in front of me is where my father lay on a bed, or a cot, or a plank of wood, or I'm not frankly sure what, and tried to remain among the living. My senses are operating in overdrive, like I am taking in too much too fast. My heart is pounding in my chest.

I try for a moment to relax my breathing. After a short spell I am ready to move on.

Reaching the southwest corner of the stone wall, we turn right and pass a series of memorial sculptures, gifts from nations whose citizens were murdered here. A few steps more, another right turn, and we come to the huge wooden double-doors of the KZ Mauthausen main gate. The gate today remains exactly as it was in 1945, though without the Nazi eagle above the doors. The camp's prisoners passed through this every morning on their way to the quarry, or to whatever work *kommando* they were on, and they passed through it again on their way back to their barracks after a day of inhumanely exhausting effort, no doubt some number fewer than in the morning.

Kommando is a German word meaning 'unit' or 'command.' It usually refers to a group of soldiers, but the Nazis appended the word to the names of the various working groups in their concentration camps, perhaps to lend a military legitimacy to what they were doing. My father used *kommando* liberally in his story.

Angelika and I step inside the camp. Finally, I am here.

Immediately in front of me is a wide, straight street covered in black asphalt, with barracks buildings on my left, a row of one-story buildings on my right. During the war this main camp street was where roll call was held twice a day, and public punishments and hangings were conducted nearly as often. Angelika tells me the asphalt surface is new, put down for the many tourists who now come. During the Nazi era it was covered in a coating of crushed granite stones from the Wiener-Graben quarry, like a suburban gravel driveway. The camp had a *kommando* whose sole function was to pull heavy and unwieldy cement rollers up and down the street, smoothing the stones. Working seven days a week in the broiling sun of summer and freezing bite of winter, it was a difficult *kommando*.

Running the length of the street on my right are three connected wood-and-stone one-story buildings. They once contained KZ Mauthausen's administration offices, kitchens, showers, the camp's prison, and its small gas chamber. Many of the interiors are preserved as they were during the war, while one of the buildings is now Mauthausen Memorial's museum.

Facing the street on my left are three wooden barracks, painted pale green, as they were during the war. When KZ Mauthausen was operational there were a total of thirty-two barracks in the camp. As we walk towards them, Angelika tells me that since the barracks were made of wood, in the years since the war it was too hard to maintain them against the harsh winter weather prevalent in this area. So all of them, save these three on the main street, were razed.

Hearing that, I wonder: if wooden barracks couldn't handle the harsh winters, how did the prisoners? How did my father? How did anyone make it out of this place?

Chapter 22

Normandy, France: D-Day: 679 Miles Away

At 6:30 in the morning of June 6, 1944, the same day my father, his mother, and most of his family left the Dej ghetto and boarded a cattle car to Birkenau, American, British and Canadian soldiers landed on five wide beaches in Normandy, France, to begin the assault on Hitler's Europe. The day is now known as 'D-Day.'

Normandy was attractive to Allied military planners because it was unappealingly far from British ports. The distance meant the Nazis did not consider Normandy among the most likely Allied invasion beaches. Instead, the German High Command presumed Pas de Calais, the closest French shore to England, to be the most likely invasion target. The 155,000 Allied soldiers who parachuted and waded into Europe that morning needed that bit of surprise, as well as every scrap of luck they could garner, as General Erwin Rommel, the man Hitler assigned to defend the French coast, intended to stop any invasion at the beaches, throwing the Allied troops back into the English Channel.

The 53-year-old Rommel, known as the Desert Fox for his fighting exploits in the arid wastelands of North Africa, was one of Hitler's best generals. He worked tirelessly to craft defenses all along the French coast which would be impenetrable from the English Channel. But though there were close calls that D-Day morning, particularly in the American sector codenamed Omaha Beach, Rommel's soldiers failed to halt the invasion at the shoreline. By the end of that day, while my father and his mother sat in a dark and cramped boxcar heading north into Poland, young Allied soldiers, many of them no older than Dad, were digging foxholes in France.

Exactly one week later, my father's train pulled into the Mauthausen town *Bahnhof*. During those seven days, Allied troops and tanks fought their way west and south, so that on June 13, 1944, they were 679 miles from Enns, Austria.

General George Patton and his Third Army was not part of the Normandy invasion or these first thrusts on the Continent. The brilliant armored commander and his 350,000 soldiers were being held back for a ground-attack role which would begin in the heat of August. Third Army's troops and tanks would take the field south of Normandy, on terrain more suitable for the fast-moving armored warfare Patton loved. Once in combat, Patton and his soldiers would not disappoint.

Chapter 23

Wall Plaques

I step into the first of the identical barracks on the left side of KZ Mauthausen's main street. The building has no insulation, just wide slats of wood nailed to a wooden frame, exactly like my bunk in summer sleep-away camp in the Poconos when I was twelve. The similarity ends right there.

Each barracks building is made up of two large sleeping rooms, one on either end, with rows of wood bunk beds that could each sleep as many as six prisoners. There are only two bunk beds in the room this morning, but later, in the camp's museum, I see drawing done by prisoners of barracks interiors showing them as crowded as they once were. A central core between the two main rooms contains a large washroom and an equally large bathroom. The washroom has two round cement basins with faucets every few feet, enabling many prisoners to wash up at one time. The bathroom has a sheet-metal urinal trough running along one wall, and holes in the floor at the other, where a bank of tightly-spaced porcelain toilets used to be. Privacy was non-existent for *KZlers*, and hygiene barely so.

Angelika and I cross the main street to explore the buildings on the other side. Tourists mill about. Most are teenagers moving in clusters, and as we near them I overhear them chattering excitedly in Italian, German and French. Angelika tells me the camp is an important destination for high school students throughout Europe. I am pleased by that.

We walk slowly through Mauthausen's shower room. I tell Angelika my father was in here at least twice, once when he arrived at KZ Mauthausen, a second time when he'd returned to Mauthausen after being in KZ Gusen, and maybe a third time when he left the *Revier*, the *Sanitätslager*, to return to the main camp. The room is forty feet on a side, with bare, grey cement walls. Eight rows of pipes hang from a high ceiling, with ten evenly spaced shower heads on each row, meaning it could handle eighty prisoners at a time. There is a set of valve handles at the center of the front of the room. They are round and oddly large, looking like demented musical instruments, which, in a sense, they were.

I picture my father standing under one of the showerheads, and I wonder what he thought then. Showers for me are refreshing. Were they for him? There were no showers in the barracks, so this was a rare event. Was it renewal, a new start, a chance to literally wash off where he had been before?

I wish I could ask him, but I think to myself that he died too young. Maybe if my father had lived longer I would eventually have learned of his 1997 trip here. Perhaps, when Vivi called to tell me about the photograph on the internet, he could have been my next phone call.

I sigh.

Past the shower room we enter a hallway leading us to the camp prison (it seems *KZlers* who violated the rules were not always summarily killed), and then to the camp's small gas chamber.

Each room I pass through contains a small plaque or two explaining its purpose in English and German, black letters on a white background. I carefully read each one, but I find myself strangely disconnected from the words. I read, 'A wooden bullet trap stood in the left hand corner of the room, in front of which the SS killed prisoners with a shot to the back of the neck.' And I read, 'From this room, the poison gas was piped into the gas chamber.' They are simply worded, and I can understand each word I read. But I cannot fully comprehend the full meaning of what I am reading. I cannot picture what these plaques are describing. I can't string the words together to absorb their true intent.

It is not a trivial thing to shoot someone who is not resisting, whose hands are tied behind their back, someone who is merely standing in the corner of a room in front of a wooden bullet trap waiting to die in an instant or two. It is not a simple thing to close a heavy, airtight door, turn a dial to allow poison gas to be piped in, and know in twenty minutes every human in that white-tiled room will be dead.[1] But that is what the plaques say. And maybe those

---

1 It is generally believed it took between a few minutes and ten minutes to kill everyone in a Nazi gas chamber. The time varied, and could have been as long as twenty minutes, depending on how crowded the chamber was, the age

Nazis who fired the shots and piped in the gas felt it was trivial and easy, and maybe they slept well at night.

But for me, I absolutely cannot connect the words with the actions that took place on these spots where I stand. The words are too ordinary, too plain for me. There are no exclamation points, no screams, no echoes of jackboots on hallway floors, no screeches of fingernails scraping gas chamber ceilings trying to get out, no sounds of men dying for no reason. Maybe I am back in the sensory-overloaded state I experienced in front of the *Russenlager-Sanitätslager.* I may be so overwhelmed by what I am seeing that I cannot take in the words and shape them into the facts and pictures and horrors they represent. Maybe I am shutting down, the way one does at the instant of impact during a car crash, or when a bullet strikes.

Or when my father arrived in KZ Birkenau.

I have the unmistakable impression that I am experiencing the same feeling he felt during his first days in the camps, when he lost track of time. Psychologists would say we were 'dissociating.' We were detaching ourselves from our environments, severing ourselves from our realities to cope with the extremes we were seeing and feeling. Obviously my father's dissociating was very different than mine. He was on a real-world journey through hell. I am safe and secure, but simply can't get my mind wrapped around words I've been reading since childhood. The effect is the same.

After taking my time walking through the camp's small museum, Angelika and I head back to the main gate. I consider that I can spend all day here, and not cover everything I'd like to see. But I've seen what is important to me, I've taken away what I need to better understand my father's story. I now know enough of what is within the black granite walls of KZ Mauthausen: the single row of barracks standing in silent memory to the prisoners who existed – *lived* is not the proper word – within the camp's walls, the gas chamber, the shower room where my father had been, the prison, the bullet trap, the administration buildings, the museum.

Walking out of the main gate, we head straight, again passing the monuments to those killed here, to a chain-link fence fifty yards ahead. The fence keeps one from falling 100 feet down into the Wiener-Graben quarry. It marks the top of the quarry, the top of the sheer granite wall KZ Mauthausen's prisoners were enslaved to mine until they died. The fence wasn't here during the war.

---

and health of the prisoners in the room, the number of gas pellets used, and their proximity to the pellets.

Though my father never worked in this quarry, it is important to see, because for many people this quarry *is* KZ Mauthausen. Even though KZ Gusen had quarries too, where my father slaved and which I will shortly visit, the Wiener-Graben mine represents the pinnacle of Nazi brutality.

And now I am looking at it.

From this elevated viewpoint, the surface of the mine ten stories below looks covered in grass and appears pastoral. No doubt, from 1938 till 1945 it was anything but. To my right, 200 or so yards away at one end of the quarry, is a long flight of steps climbing most of the way to the height where I stand. The steps were infamously known by the prisoners as the Stairs of Death. From my distance the staircase doesn't look very impressive. But I know that's wrong, so I need to go down there and see it from the point of view of a *KZler* in the quarry.

Before turning to leave the fence, I raise my gaze. Looking out into the distance, the view is tranquil, one of farm fields and white fences and meadows atop rolling green countryside. How utterly cruel this was to KZ Mauthausen's prisoners, this view of an unreachable life. It was one more sublime torture, only this sort of torture didn't leave a mark on the body. In the middle distance to my left I can see Enns, its medieval belfry jutting through the afternoon haze. To a prisoner in Mauthausen, Enns might as well have been on the moon.

Chapter 24

Parachutists

A ngelika and I return to our cars and she leads the way to the Wiener-Graben mine. A few hundred steep yards downhill from the Mauthausen parking lot we turn right, and after a short drive we park in a clearing. I get out of my car and follow Angelika into an open area of clumpy grass, dirt, and rock, about the size of a local shopping mall parking lot. The area feels intensely claustrophobic. Suddenly I realize why. Just ahead, forming the back border of the field and towering high above me is a hundred-foot high wall of granite. I am standing in the middle of the Wiener-Graben quarry.

A few minutes earlier I was at the top of this wall, looking down. Now I am peering at it, squinting as I look into the sun dangling high above the wall's crest. This monster is almost 300 yards wide, and bends around to my right. Weeds and small brush growing out from the wall initially camouflaged its true size, but now as I bring it into focus, the gigantic brown and grey mass makes me shiver. It seems ice cold and foreboding in the still air. I wouldn't be surprised to find steam escaping from deep within its bowels, though I know it is inert. Dante could not have conceived anything more infernal. I am in a hell on earth.

Walking further into the quarry, I think about how thousands of lives were stolen here to produce the granite facades and roadbeds and rail track ballast of Hitler's Germany. I tell Angelika that I cannot imagine facing this sinister mass every morning for years, as some of Mauthausen's *KZlers* did. She agrees.

To my left are the Stairs of Death. Harder to spot from ground level than from above, the staircase is tucked against the far granite wall and masked among the wall's green growth. It projects steeply upward to a height of approximately ninety feet, with a slight right dogleg two-thirds of the way up.

The Mauthausen prisoners who lived and died on these stairs belonged to the camp's penal company, the *Strafkompanie*. Assignment to the penal company was a true death sentence, more certain than assignment to KZ Mauthausen in the first place. Penal company *KZlers*, who were being punished for various camp offenses, carried granite boulders weighing as much as 100 pounds on their backs, in crude and uncomfortable wooden backpacks, up the staircase's 186 steps. They made eight or nine trips in a typical day, if they lived that long. As if things weren't difficult enough, the steps were built from the mine's granite and were uneven. Step heights varied, and the length of each step – the 'run' in builder's parlance – was shorter than standard. It was a torture track. The stairs were so famous that visiting Nazi officials made a point of having their photos taken on them.

Once at the top, assuming they made it to the top, the *Strafkompanie* prisoners weren't done. They still had to walk five-eighths of a mile up a pitted and unpaved path to reach Mauthausen's main gate. The granite they brought out of the quarry was used to construct the camp, its walls, buildings (except of course for the wooden barracks), and its streets. The remainder of the granite mined at Wiener-Graben was taken from the base of the quarry by truck or rail to the Danube for loading on river barges to be transported throughout Europe.

It is incredible to me that anyone walked up and down these steps multiple times a day carrying the loads forced on them. Going up and down once, Angelika and I discover that the short 'run' makes walking down almost harder than going up. One hundred feet to the top of the quarry, the stairs plus the unpaved path, is roughly equivalent to a ten story building. Put another way, every day the prisoners in the Wiener-Graben penal company climbed and descended the equivalent of the Empire State Building, if they lived that long. I have seen, and experienced, enough to confirm the impossibility of surviving the Mauthausen *Strafkompanie*.

Long after the war, a local researcher identified sixty-two ways a KZ Mauthausen prisoner could die. The list included the basics, like being shot, hung, starved or gassed. And it contained the more esoteric, such as being forced under a freezing cold outdoor shower during the camp's brutal winters, until dead. Then there were the ways to die unique to the Wiener-Graben quarry. Some forms of murder even doubled as entertainment for the SS guards.

For instance, in one game a guard on top of the granite wall would order a prisoner to push a second prisoner off the edge of the wall, to fall to his death 100 feet below. Guards called prisoners who jumped, or were pushed, 'parachutists,' and that part of the wall was called the 'parachute wall.' If the first prisoner refused to push the second prisoner off the wall, he would be shot, the guard would make the same demand of a third prisoner, and the game began again. Nobody ever won.

Another game was a stair race. Prisoners from the *Strafkompanie*, burdened by their wooden backpacks loaded with 100-pound boulders, would race up the stairs to the top. Sometimes losers were shot, or pushed off the top, becoming parachutists. Other times the race continued until all the participants had quit of exhaustion. Then they were shot. Again, there were no winners.

One more and then I'll stop, but this one was so over-the-top nasty, I have to tell it. While climbing the stairs, the huge weight of the backpacks left the prisoners of the *Strafkompanie* precariously balanced. And they were usually packed together so tightly that if one prisoner faltered, it could cause a chain reaction of stumbling prisoners behind him. Photos still exist showing how tightly they were bunched. If a prisoner on the staircase fell backwards hard enough, those behind him might be knocked over like dominos, all the way to the bottom. So sometimes, just to watch it happen, a guard would shoot a prisoner high up on the stairs.

My father was lucky he never slaved here. He did, however, work in a quarry no less difficult to survive, Kastenhof. Angelika and I return to our cars and head there, to the Kastenhof quarry in Gusen, the Austrian village that lent its name to Mauthausen's two sub-camps where my father spent most of his time as a guest of the Nazis.

Chapter 25

Arrival in Mauthausen

Dad stood to remove his suit jacket, draping it over the back of his dining room chair. Sitting back down, he took a long drink of his club soda. I supposed the memory of that murderously hot train car on the way to KZ Mauthausen made him thirsty, and maybe even a bit warm. Or perhaps he was preparing himself for what was to come. He continued with his story.

'We arrived in Mauthausen,' he said, 'and the first thing the guards made us do was take a shower.'

As with the Dej ghetto, that simple sentence, I found out later, was not the whole story. It was completely true, but left out an important detail. One of the many things I learned when researching KZ Mauthausen was that the concentration camp did not have a train station. Its quarry, the Wiener-Graben, had a special-purpose, narrow-gauge rail line connecting it to the Kastenhof quarry, and linking the two of them with the Danube River. But the granite-walled prisoner camp itself had no train tracks leading to it.

Instead, in the afternoon of June 13, my father's cattle car from Birkenau pulled into the small train station in the river-side *town* of Mauthausen. He would turn nineteen in exactly one month, if he managed to remain alive until then. Dad and the others dropped down from the rail cars, formed up into rows, and marched in the afternoon heat to KZ Mauthausen, three miles uphill from the town's *Bahnhof*. The last part of my drive to the concentration camp, when I got out for a few minutes to stand on the roadside, took the same route my father and his fellow prisoners hiked that hot afternoon. The last half-mile is especially steep.

A three-mile uphill march in the heat of a mid-June day, after four days broiling in a boxcar, is not something easily forgotten. Yet every time my father told his story, he said exactly what he said to me on our last Passover evening together: his train arrived in Mauthausen, and then the SS guards made him take a shower. He had omitted this march purposely.

I wondered why.

My first guess was that he felt this tiny piece of his wartime experience was, to him, simply not worth mentioning. He was still in good shape – just one week earlier he'd been a well-fed teenager running a bakery – and maybe the walk really was not remarkable, his typical 'no big deal.' Of course, what was not remarkable, not a 'big deal' to my father might have been especially remarkable, a *huge* deal, to me or anyone else whose life didn't include time in a Nazi concentration camp.

Or perhaps, after spending four days overheating in the boxcar, my father's mind was fried and he didn't recall the walk. Perhaps he remembered it only as a nightmare, or maybe it didn't register at all. That seemed unlikely given the level of detail he recalled about that year. As I learned the fine particulars of my father's year in concentration camp, I discovered that though he occasionally got things wrong, he generally remembered distances and times with savant-like accuracy.

Lastly, I came up with this. Maybe the march uphill was so horrendous, his first full taste of the Nazi brutality he'd face in the coming year, that he didn't *want* to recall it, and moreover, didn't want me to know about it. That afternoon he was exhausted, hungry, dehydrated, scared, and burning up inside and out. What good would it do to talk about it? He remembered it perfectly well, but what would it add to his story of perseverance and survival to remind himself of that uphill slog? Why should he recount it? Why should he go there? And why should he share it with me? Why did I need to know about it? He was protecting me, as well, by omitting the worst this first march.

In the end, any of my guesses could have been it, though I figured out later I was on to something with that last one.

Once at the top of the hill, my father's introduction to KZ Mauthausen started with his prisoner number being logged in to the camp's rolls, followed by that shower. Sweating and thirsty after the march, he stood under one of the eighty showerheads, his face turned up to absorb all he could get. But the Nazi guards weren't going to make it that easy. Standing by those oddly-large valve handles, they cruelly switched the water temperature back and forth between ice cold and scalding hot. It was perfect for catching colds, or even pneumonia, and for generally weakening prisoners, both physically and mentally, right at the start of their internment at KZ Mauthausen. That was the idea, of course.

'I didn't care about the water,' my father said with an air of nonchalance and a wave of his hand. 'I knew they wanted it to bother me, but it didn't. It cleaned me off after the "transport".' Already he had decided he was not going to show weakness. 'Hot water, cold water, all the time they changed it. It didn't matter to me. After the shower we were sent down to a new camp a few miles away, Gusen II.'

I not only missed my father's hike up from the train station, I missed asking about this trip, too. I have no idea how my father, his friend Izsak, and his brother-in-law Hershy traveled the two-and-a-half miles to Gusen II. They may have taken one of the regularly-scheduled trucks running between the camps, or the narrow-gauge train from the Wiener Graben, though I suppose they could have easily marched it, as well. Once there, the three of them were assigned to the same barracks, where they slept six to a wooden bed, three with their feet facing one way, three facing the other. For each of them, their sole personal possession was a blanket.

Chapter 26

More than Luck

My father continued with his Seder story. 'The Nazis thought I was a baker. That's what I was doing before the "transport."' Even KZ Mauthausen's entrance log, on the line where he was signed in, gave his profession as baker, which he had very recently become.

Now with a sly grin, he added, 'Can't you imagine, Gusen II had a very little use for a baker.'

'I'm sure it didn't,' I agreed. From my many years of hearing his story, I knew what was coming next, and unable to prevent it, I too, cracked a small smile.

'So when the *kapos* asked me what else I could do, I told them I was a carpenter.' Now he revealed his killer smile, and our dining room got much brighter.

Though the father I knew had passable carpentry skills, as a teenager I don't think he had ever done more than hang a picture in his house in Dej. But he'd sensed carpenters had it easy in Gusen II, so he said he was one. When the Nazis had come looking for a baker in the Dej ghetto, he'd raised his hand even though his baking ability was almost nonexistent, and that had worked out splendidly. Why not again? So while Izsak and Hershy went to work their first day in the Kastenhof granite quarry *kommando*, my father went off with the carpenters.

'By the end of the second day they saw that I wasn't a carpenter, so they put me with Hershy and Izsak in the Kastenhof *Kommando*.'

That, of course, was why Dad was smiling. He knew from the start he would never be able to keep up with real carpenters. He'd tried, and he'd been caught. But he made his reassignment to the quarry *kommando* sound routine. He didn't fit here, so try over there.

Like so much of my father's story, his transfer from the Carpentry *Kommando* to the Kastenhof *Kommando* couldn't have been as easy as he'd made it out to be. After all, this was a concentration camp, a place where men were thrown off cliffs for sport and knocked down flights of stairs like dominos for entertainment. I think my father was incredibly lucky the *kapo* in charge of the Carpentry *Kommando* didn't kill him for the ruse.

A *kapo* was a prisoner like everyone else, but a first among equals, with privileges not granted the regular prison population.[1] Generally, *kapos* did most of the managerial work in the concentration camps, running *kommandos*, for instance. They got much better food and worked far less hard. But there was a catch: their responsibilities often included quotas – pounds of granite moved, number of prisoners killed. Failing to meet their quota could mean death. Or it could mean worse: being put back into the regular prison population, where they were likely to be killed by vengeful *KZlers*.

I wasn't surprised my father had tried to slot himself into an easier *kommando*. Nothing he tried to pull off that year surprised me. But what I never considered until my trip to Austria was what it *meant* that he was never punished. If Dad had learned a lesson by claiming to be a baker in the Dej ghetto, it's that bold action could improve his lot. If there was a lesson for him in this carpenter maneuver, it's that the downside of taking a risk might be nothing worse than ending up where he should have been all along.

How could the downside be so minimal, so inconsequential? How is it he wasn't killed for lying? This story made me seriously consider that my father's survival wasn't just a matter of luck. Certainly luck played a huge role – or maybe it was divine intervention, if you believe in that. And so did sheer bravery, or balls, or nerve, or some similar notion. It took indescribable guts to escape the way he did, two separate times. And it took at least that much guts to walk into the boiling cauldron of Gusen II and claim to be a carpenter, knowing he was not.

But it took something else altogether to avoid being *punished* for that outright lie.

I am one hundred percent certain that after his second day as a carpenter, the *kapo* in charge of that *kommando* did *not* approach my father, put a hand lightly on his shoulder, and say, 'Y'know, Dave, I

---

1 It is often spelled *capo*, though I will spell it *kapo*. As with ghetto, the source of the word is lost to history, but I turned up guesses including the Italian *capo*, meaning 'head' or 'boss,' the mafia usage of *capo*, 'captain,' and a shortening of *kameradschaft polizei*, a German word meaning 'police comradeship,' or 'police group.'

don't think you're particularly well suited for this line of work. Let's see where you might fit in better in our organization.' Not a chance.

But what *did* the *kapo* say? What did my father say in reply? In what language? What exchange did they have that resulted in Dad joining Izsak and Hershy in the quarry *kommando*, with no repercussions for his stunt?

Knowing the sort of transgressions that could get a prisoner killed in concentration camp – moving too slowly, giving a *kapo* or SS guard a wrong look, being in the wrong place at the wrong time, even just waking up that day – the number of times my father was not killed for the things he did defied logic. In searching for reasons, I considered it might be his personality, his easy manner, his open and friendly way of being, or even simply his smile. Yes, I think even his good looks might have had something to do with it.

Even in a concentration camp, where my father said men were reduced to behaving like animals in order to survive – actually, to *being* animals, he always said – human interaction, the connection of one person to another, the way people related to one another, still counted. *Maybe* my father is an example of how it counted. Maybe his winning smile, coming from his young and approachable face, softened hard-bitten *kapos* and fanatical SS guards just enough to make them go more lightly on him.

Perhaps, too, my father's remarkable ear for languages played a role. Maybe he and the carpenter *kapo* had established a rapport, a connection, simply by unexpectedly – for the *kapo* – sharing a common language. Mixing together a smile, a language bond, and a common threat of death hanging over all of them might have produced the grease smoothing my father's path, allowing him to get away with things that would have meant death for any other *KZler*.

Earlier, I'd asked Angelika if she had any thoughts about my father's knack for avoiding death in the camps. She agreed with my supposition about his sunny personality and multiple languages. She thought his ability to communicate with the SS guards in German, and his ability to connect with other *kapos* by conversing in their language, would have gone a long way.

She also suggested another reason. She proposed he might have been treated better because he didn't look Jewish. Perhaps, she said, he was given leeway because his looks didn't produce the loathing for Jews so many of the *kapos* and SS guards generally felt, which a more Semitic-looking prisoner might have produced. Though my father had wavy dark brown hair and brown eyes, his hair was cut short, while his features were unmistakably Slavic: high flat cheekbones, thin lips, small nose. Everyone knew he was Jewish, it said so right above the left breast pocket of his prison uniform. But their inherent hatred, fomented over years by being fed anti-Semitic vitriol, might have been blunted by the fact he didn't look like the caricature Jew they were hard-wired to vilify. Add the other ingredients, and perhaps, just perhaps, that made all the difference when his life was on the line.

Chapter 27

Gusen II

KZ Gusen II had opened its doors just three months before my father showed up. The camp had been constructed quickly and on the cheap. Instead of being enclosed by high stone walls topped with barbed wire, as KZ Mauthausen and KZ Gusen I were, it had only electrified barbed wire fencing around its perimeter, augmented by gangly wooden guard towers standing at intervals along the fence and scattered throughout the camp.

No one today knows why, but Gusen II became a haven for the meanest *kapos* and SS guards in the entire Mauthausen concentration camp system. *Kapos* dictated life and death over the lesser, ordinary prisoners, and in Gusen II the *kapos* used their rank murderously. My father said most of the camp's *kapos* were long-term prisoners from Poland, many who had already been in KZ Mauthausen three years or more. Like *kapos* in other camps, they walked around with long rubber whips, short leather truncheons, and wooden sticks my father called two-by-fours.[1] But unlike other *kapos*, according to my father the ones in Gusen II had been charged by their Nazi overseers to kill ten prisoners a day, every day. On one of the first days there, my father's brother-in-law Hershy helped fill that quota.

The day after his lack of carpentry skills had gotten him shifted to the Kastenhof mine *kommando*, my father was working with Izsak and Hershy, moving boulders around the quarry. One of the *kapos* spied an especially large boulder, one that couldn't possibly be picked up by any one person, probably not even by four people. The *kapo* ordered Hershy to pick up the boulder and move it. Clearly not cut

---

1 The sticks they carried for beating prisoners were considerably narrower than standard two-by-four lumber. But that's what my father called them, so that's what I will call them as well.

out for hard manual labor, in only a few days in Gusen II Hershy had already picked up the nickname, 'the banker.'

He didn't stand a chance.

The world's strongest man wouldn't have been able to budge that boulder. Sweat pouring off his fleshy face, he gave it everything he had. The *kapo* beat Hershy with his whip as he tried, failed, and tried again, and again, to move the boulder. Then, sharks drawn to blood in the water, other *kapos* joined in.

My father turned away as the thwack of two-by-fours and the crack of whips tore into his brother-in-law until he was dead. It hadn't taken long, but Dad had learned to harden himself. And that hardness never left him, though it didn't manifest itself very often. It only appeared when he talked about the camps. In every Seder telling of the story of that year, including the last one in 2001, death was merely a detail, a feature to be related, and not something to be dwelled on. He would never pause for even a moment to reflect, never stop to let his mind go back to happier times with Hershy, maybe to a family dinner or to Hershy's wedding to his sister.

Instead, as he did each time he told it, that Seder night Dad said, 'They killed him, and I continued working.'

And then he went on with the story.

Maybe that's why I never dug deeper into my father's years under the Nazis. Maybe that's why I never showed much interest, except as a rapt listener at the Seder table. My father's familiarity with death was so total, I never noticed its importance in his story. His brother-in-law, my uncle through marriage, was killed and his death was, to my father, just a line at the end of a sentence. And that line passed through me without ever stirring a single reaction. It was just a story.

I needed to think about that.

While the days in Gusen II were frightfully dangerous for my father and his fellow prisoners, the nights were no less risky. Unlike KZ Mauthausen, Gusens I and II did not have bathroom facilities inside the barracks. Instead, they were in special-purpose latrine buildings centrally located between prisoner barracks. My father called these special-purpose barracks 'latrines,' or 'washrooms,' because they also contained sinks and, in a few cases, laundry facilities. After lights-out for curfew, Nazi guards high in the towers would shoot at prisoners making their way to the latrines. Just for target practice. Every night my father would hear gunshots ringing out, and every morning there would be four or five bodies scattered around the camp, their only crime having been the need to pee.

Chapter 28

Gusen I

Nothing could be worse than Gusen II,' my father said to me, shaking his head. 'Nothing. The *kapos* were so cruel, every day you thought you would die from their hands. So three weeks after we came there, Izsak and I volunteered for a new work *kommando*. We didn't know what we were volunteering for, but it could only be better than what we had.'

They were put together with fifty-eight other volunteer Jews from Gusen II, and the sixty of them were marched across the 130-yard wide field separating the two Gusen camps. They were moving to Gusen I. They had lucked out.

'This was a regular camp.' Even at that Seder evening fifty-seven years later, I could hear the relief in his voice. 'It had stone walls and it was organized properly. We felt it when we came inside the gate. No question, Jeckeleh, the move saved my life.'

After arriving in their new camp, Dad, Izsak and the other prisoners were assigned to a barracks in the Jewish section of the camp. They were each given their own bed and blanket in wooden bunk beds.

'It wasn't the Ritz, but it was much better than before.' My father smiled again.

Even better for my father and the Jewish prisoners who'd joined him, the *kapos* overseeing them in Gusen I were a slightly gentler breed than those in Gusen II. They and their SS overseers seemed to be marginally more interested in mining granite, and slightly less interested in outright torture and murder than the *kapos* and guards in the newer camp. Rather than killing ten prisoners each day to fill a quota, *kapos* in my father's *kommando* had no quota that he knew of. Instead, he said prisoners around him in the quarry were dying at the rate of one or two per day, mostly because of malnutrition, illness and accidents.

My father quickly learned the one serious negative to his move to Gusen I. The work.

'We were in the Stone Crusher *Kommando*,' he said. 'It was very hard labor, Jeckeleh, harder than the Kastenhof *Kommando* in Gusen II. We worked so hard, and we worked without a break, except for lunch. Every day we worked like this.'

The Gusen stone crusher was famously the largest of its kind in Europe. Finished in 1941 and costing the lives of 2,000 prisoners to build, it was Gusen's Pyramids. It was actually a trio of interconnected cement structures. One, a square two-story building with a wide garage-door-like opening in front, contained narrow gauge rail tracks, cables and hoists for maneuvering heavy granite slabs, and a large hole its floor. It also contained workspace for stone artisans, men skilled at cutting and shaping granite to exacting architectural specifications.

Attached to this building was a giant cement structure that looked like a shoebox turned on its side. This building was fifty feet tall and contained fourteen storage chambers. Crushed granite was stored in the chambers, awaiting shipment. The third structure was thirty feet away and smaller than the other two. It housed the massive mechanical crusher itself, the machine that pulverized raw granite into small stones of varying sizes, all the way down to nearly powder.

Today only the attached buildings remain – the structure with the hole in its floor and the shoebox-on-its-side. The separate building containing the huge crusher itself is gone, as are the cables, conveyor belts, and their associated machinery.

'What was your job? What did your *kommando* do?'

'We took heavy stones from a central collection point and loaded them into wagons.'

My father pronounced 'wagons,' 'vah-GONS,' as in German. He was referring to what are commonly called mine wagons, mine carts, or hunds, small iron containers with rail wheels – so they could ride on tracks – regularly seen around mines. The Mauthausen Museum has one. I spent a long time studying it when I visited.

My father continued. 'Then we pushed the full wagons to the stone crusher and unloaded them.' He was breathing noticeably faster. I sensed he was back in KZ Gusen.

Reaching the stone crusher's middle building, the one with the garage-door opening, he and the others in his *kommando* emptied the mine wagons, dropping the granite down the hole in the building's floor. From there the stones rode a conveyor belt up to the crusher machine. After they were crushed into varying sizes, the stones took a conveyor belt up into the storage building.

'How far apart was the central collection point from the stone crusher? I mean, how far did you have to push the wagons?' I was so caught up in the story, I nearly pronounced 'wagons' the way he had, but I caught myself in time.

'Not far, I think 200 meters, 200 yards, something more something less.'

'Not far,' my father said, 200 yards, give or take. 'Piece of cake,' I think I heard him imply. Every day, hour after hour, he filled mine wagons with hundreds of pounds of raw granite, pushed them along steel rails to the stone crusher building two football fields away, unloaded them, then pushed them back empty, to load them again and push them to the stone crusher again. And again. And again. It may not have been far – to him. But to me it was the definition of Sisyphean torture.

What made my father's *kommando* especially difficult for him was that the labor was non-stop. They lifted heavy granite boulders into and out of mine wagons, and pushed those wagons between the central loading point and the stone crusher all day long, without breaks or downtime, except for lunch. He contrasted it to his work in the granite quarries while living in Gusen II. *KZlers* in the quarries moved heavy granite boulders to each quarry's individual collection points. Once the quarry was emptied of raw granite, *KZlers* would move away from the quarry while the rock face was dynamited, exposing and creating new raw granite. Those dynamite breaks could last for hours, and my father missed them. Time was a commodity cherished by the prisoners, and downtime was the most valuable commodity of all.

What my father didn't say, and what I never asked, was how the granite got from the three Kastenhof quarries' individual collection points, to the central collection point where he worked with the mine wagons. The answer, I learned, was the granite was brought there by Kastenhof's own penal company, its *Strafkompanie*.

Like KZ Mauthausen's *Strafkompanie*, Kastenhof's penal company prisoners were in their own unique hell which only ended when they died. Like their fellow prisoners up the hill, Kastenhof's *Strafkompanie* men carried granite boulders often weighing 100 pounds or more in wooden backpacks. With the boulders on their backs they jogged 200 to 500 yards from the three quarries to the central collection point where my father worked. They had to run in single file, close together, without a gap between them.

111

If a gap formed, SS guards or *kapos* would yank out the first prisoner in the gap and beat him to death. If a prisoner lost one of his shoes, he had to continue barefoot. If one fell out of line exhausted, he was killed. And if this wasn't enough, Kastenhof had a replica of the Wiener-Graben Stairs of Death. Supposedly, no one ever lasted longer than two weeks in the Kastenhof quarry penal *kommando*. I wonder what my father thought when he'd see the *Strafkompanie KZlers* jogging towards him with another backbreaking load of granite.

Chapter 29

A Day in the Camps

My father never spoke about the small details of each day in the camps: when he woke, when he ate (although he spoke about *what* he ate), how long he worked, how long he slept. The story he told contained the highlights, the scenes which stood out most vividly when remembering his 334 days from the Dej train station to liberation. But he never talked about his day-to-day existence.

That might be because he viewed every single day as something to be endured and survived, and not anything worth remembering individually. If he'd told me about a typical day, he would have had to recall it. And perhaps, unlike the highlights, remembering each interminable day was worse than those few moments where he did something particularly interesting, or where his life hung in the balance (which is interesting in its own precarious way).

I'm sure whenever my father replayed the 'ordinary' days in his mind, he recalled working extraordinarily hard, eating very little, going to sleep hungry, and then doing it all over again the next day. Each of those days contained no hope, no excitement, and nothing to look forward to except more pain, more hunger, less hope, and more chances to die.

But a question as big as what was my father's typical day is, *why didn't I ask about it?* Not once in all the Seders, never in all the times I'd heard the story, did I ask my father about his daily routine in the camps. It's only since Vivi's phone call that I realized I had a gaping hole in my knowledge.

While hoping the trip to Austria would help me understand *why* I never asked, before going I knew that with a little effort I could close this particular hole, or at least make it much smaller. Scouring the internet and books, I came across many descriptions of typical days told by former *KZlers* in the Mauthausen camp system, as well

113

as in other concentration camps. While there were differences, there were also many similarities, so I figured out for myself what a day in the life of *KZler* Dave Hersch was about.

His day began at 5:00 am, 4:30 am in the longer days of summer. My father and his barracks mates had thirty minutes to wash, use the bathroom, clean their bunk and barracks, and get to an all-hands roll call, the *Appell. Appell* was held on the *Appellplatz*, the roll call square, or place. In KZ Mauthausen, the *Appellplatz* was the camp's wide main street. In Gusen I it was a large open space on the eastern side of the camp. Accounts I've read speak traumatically of the *Appell*, describing sometimes hours of standing at attention, regardless of the weather, as they were counted and recounted by *kapos*, ending with every prisoner in unison clicking their heels while removing and returning their caps to their heads. My father never even mentioned it. I suppose to him it was 'no big deal.'

After *Appell*, his breakfast each day was a small piece of salami, an equally small piece of cheese, some jam, and a thin slice of bread. Then he reassembled on the street with the other *KZlers* and their *kommandos*, and marched off to work.

Around noon, my father was given a few minutes to eat lunch, usually a soup of some sort. Working the soup line properly was an art form. If he stood in line too soon, the soup would be watery. If he got in line too late, he risked running out of time to eat, or the cooks running out of soup to serve. The sweet spot of the line was the middle, where the consistency of the soup was a bit thicker, and a piece of potato or other vegetable might make it into the bowl. But since everyone knew that, it was a challenge for my father to get it right every day.

After lunch, work resumed until he had put in a day of between eight and eleven hours, depending on the time of year, the whim of the *kapos* and SS guards, and the assigned workload at the stone crusher. At the end of the day he marched back to the barracks, stood for another *Appell*, and was served dinner, the soup again, sometimes with another piece of bread. Finally he stumbled back into his barracks to sleep.

My father never talked of having a day off, a rest day, and I never asked him. I assumed he worked seven days a week because he spoke as if he did. Accounts I've come across describe a range of times off, everything from no work between Saturday noon and Monday morning, to two days off each month, to no breaks at all. I can't be certain, but I believe my father never got a day off work, with one single exception he told me about later in the Seder evening.

114

Along with sadistic SS guards, maniacal *kapos*, and an infinite number of diseases facing every prisoner in the KZ Mauthausen system, hunger was my father's ever-present companion. The minimal quantity of food coupled with the heavy labor was a recipe for mind-numbing starvation, malnutrition and eventually death. A prisoner might manage to dodge diseases or find himself beaten less than others, but fierce, all-consuming hunger was inescapable. It struck everyone, and without food it was unconquerable. The meager rations my father and the others received wouldn't have been sufficient even if the prisoners had done nothing more strenuous than lounge around all day. But for men working in rock quarries, the caloric intake was grossly insufficient.

'We were so hungry all the time,' my father said to me at the Seder. 'All I wanted was to feel full just once.' He patted his belly. 'Just one time I wanted to feel like I wasn't so hungry.'

One morning, to feel full, my father did something he said amazes him when he looks back, something I find utterly inconceivable.

A regular bartering system existed among the prisoners for one food or another. Some *KZlers* who had been in the camp longer had managed to get slightly more, or slightly different, food than others with less guile or fewer resources.

My father said, 'Many days I traded my salami, which didn't fill me up very much, for three small potatoes which another *KZler* always got.' He made the OK sign with his thumb and index finger to show me how small. 'The potatoes filled me up more than the salami, but it still wasn't enough. It was never enough.' His voice trailed off.

That morning he spotted a group of prisoners eating smoothed granite pebbles. When he asked them why, they replied that it made them feel full. Full? Really? For my father, suddenly his previously unattainable goal was within reach! He never considered the consequences of putting rocks into his intestinal tract, but he was a teenager, and anyway at his level of hunger, the goal trumped the risks. So one morning he traded his salami for a few pebbles. And sure enough, after swallowing them, he felt much fuller.

Later that afternoon, he watched one of the prisoners who had told him about the pebbles keel over and die while clutching his sides in agony. That evening, a second pebble-eater died. My father asked, and was told by their friends those two had eaten pebbles for a few days in a row. The pebbles were blocking their bowels and they were dying in terrible pain. That did it. My father's first foray into eating smooth pebbles was his last. Lucky for him, the ones he ate passed through his system the next day and that was the last time he tried that trick.

Chapter 30

Gusen Memorial

Following Angelika's car in my rental as we drive from the Wiener Graben quarry to KZ Gusen I, I'm thinking the same thoughts I had on my way to KZ Mauthausen earlier, after meeting Angelika's family. This is a nice drive. The sun warming the ground has lifted a misty haze into the air, painting the fields and farmhouses on either side of me with pastel watercolors. For a moment, it seems to me to be an idyllic and peaceful place to live. For the first time, I realize what a shame it is that this part of Austria is forever poisoned by the overbearing presence of KZ Mauthausen. I feel now perhaps such a harsh sentence is undeserved, and I decide to accept that this part of Austria is actually quite beautiful, in spite of what my father and so many others went through here.

Driving west on a road first called *Hauptstrasse* and then *Georgestrasse*, we soon arrive at the spot where KZ Gusen I had once been. We've driven just over two miles from the quarry. *Georgestrasse* runs east-west, and once formed the southern border of both Gusen I and its adjacent sister camp, Gusen II.[1] Yet nothing on the road alerts us that we've arrived. Unlike KZ Mauthausen, most, though not all, of Gusen I's granite perimeter walls had been torn down. There was no road sign announcing, for instance, 'Here was Once the Entrance to KZ Gusen I, a Concentration Camp,' or something to that effect.

Instead, I know we've arrived only because Angelika calls my cell phone to tell me. She phones just as I pass, on my right, a pair of long, narrow, one-story buildings of brown stucco with white window

---

1 *Georgestrasse* actually runs northwest-southeast, but to more clearly describe the road and its physical relationship to Gusens I and II and the Kastenhof quarry, east, west, north and south are sufficiently accurate.

frames. They had been guard barracks for Gusen's SS contingent. I recall, from seeing wartime U.S. Army Air Force reconnaissance photos, that the structures were part of a cluster of barracks buildings marking the southeast corner of Gusen I. Only these two remain.

On *Georgestrasse*, adjacent to the SS barracks, I pass two fragments of the camp's original granite wall. They have opposing rounded corners, and each had been cut down to six feet in height, making them look nothing like the imposing eleven-foot-tall barriers they were in wartime. Back then they marked the start of a sixty-yard long access road leading away from *Georgestrasse*, north to the main KZ Gusen I gate. Now they mark the start of a driveway to a private home. I make a mental note to return to these fragments.

A quarter of a mile past the SS guard barracks, we arrive at the Gusen Memorial, built to remember those who'd slaved and died here. Its location once marked the southwestern corner of KZ Gusen I, the opposite end of the SS barracks. Angelika, still on her cell phone to me, tells me not to drive into the memorial just yet. We pass it and pull over at an intersection another 130 yards ahead. We are at what would have been the eastern border of Gusen II. Again, I see no signs on the road, no indication of what was once here. As before, I know we are there only because Angelika has told me.

On May 23, 1945, a few weeks after liberating KZ Gusens I and II and KZ Mauthausen, the U.S. Army burned Gusen II to the ground because of a typhus epidemic that had raged among its prisoners. It had been constructed entirely of wood, and not a single structure remained. Every barracks, every boundary fence post, and every guard tower was turned to ash. There was nothing left.

I leave my car to talk to Angelika. Standing by her Citroen I see, where Gusen II once was, now are small, pretty homes and quiet suburban streets. It is as if the notoriously brutal concentration camp that imprisoned my father for three weeks never existed. I wonder if that's exactly what people living here want.

Angelika tells me that after the war no one had much money. The government sold small plots of this land cheaply to young families, many of whom built their homes themselves. Now that it's a community, she surmises ('this is not her opinion,' she stresses to me) perhaps the people living here don't want to be reminded of something started and run by the Nazis, of something that tainted Austria unwillingly, of something so ghastly.

Right. I'm about to say something, then think better of it and go back in my car. I decide to keep an open mind for now.

Most of Gusen I was also wiped away after the war ended, and replaced with homes. The Russians, controlling this part of Austria for a time after World War II, eventually destroyed or burned almost everything in the camp, including all the wooden barracks, and most of its stone exterior walls. The building housing the stone crusher was destroyed, and the crusher and conveyor belts were carted off to Russia. But the paired stone crusher storage chamber and conveyor loading buildings (the shoebox-on-its-side and the building with the garage door opening) were left intact, and remain there today.

Besides the paired stone crusher buildings, one thing that didn't burn – because it obviously couldn't burn – was the crematorium. It was six feet high and comprised of two ovens which could each fit a human body. As KZ Gusens I and II were slave labor camps, the crematorium had not been built to handle high volume.

In the early 1960s, the Gusen Memorial was built around the crematorium. A plain square cement building was constructed, with the ovens in its center. It is big enough for a dozen people at one time to enter and see them up close. The crematorium building was then set within a roofless enclosure made of grey cement walls ten feet high. These walls are striated, rows of thin grooves running their length, reminiscent of the cement walls of the stone crusher storage structure, the shoebox-on-its-side. The ground within the walls is covered in crushed granite pebbles, exactly like what once had covered KZ Mauthausen's main street.

Inside the memorial, the eastern wall contains ten plaques, identical except for their language. The English plaque, all capital letters and without punctuation, reads:

**WITHIN THESE WALLS
ON THE ACTUAL SITE WHERE IT WAS BUILT
UNDER THE NAZI REGIME
REMAINS THE CREMATORY OF GUSEN I AND GUSEN II
THE MOST MURDEROUS COMMANDOES OF
KZ MAUTHAUSEN**

**FROM 1940 TO 1945 MORE THAN
37,000 PATRIOTS OF ALL NATIONALITIES
WERE INCINERATED THERE
AFTER HAVING KNOWN THE MOST CRUEL
PHYSICAL AND MORAL SUFFERING**

THEY DIED
FOR THE INDEPENDENCE OF THEIR COUNTRIES
FOR LIBERTY
FOR THE SALVATION OF MAN

MAY THE MEMORY OF THEIR SACRIFICE FOREVER
REMAIN IN THE THOUGHTS OF THE LIVING

I stand in front of the plaque, reading it a few times. I like it. The words register with me, unlike earlier today when I was disassociating from the small plaques inside KZ Mauthausen's buildings. It seems I am growing accustomed to all this horribleness. But as I step away, the granite stones crunching loudly under my feet, I feel my face growing flush.

This is inadequate. This is nowhere near enough. I don't think this little crematorium building inside this open-air enclosure with well-worded plaques in multiple languages properly memorializes the 37,000 or more dead whose dried blood and sweat lay under my feet. I don't think it honors those very few others who survived – like my father – but who left everything but their souls, and maybe those, too, behind on this land.

I ask myself if I'm being too harsh, and instantly know I am not. The best way to memorialize concentration camps, to remember and honor those who were murdered in them, is to leave them untouched, like KZ Mauthausen, KZ Auschwitz and KZ Birkenau. Those camps are now full-throated warnings, teaching tools, red flags to the world, reminding everyone of what can happen when prejudices and power are left unchecked.

But what about camps that were burned to the ground, as the U.S. Army did with Gusen II? How should their victims be remembered? Looking at the memorial's grey walls, I decide all this land should have been left bare. Blank. Instead of houses and streets, it should be empty. Sacred ground. Like the World Trade Center in New York City.

Manhattan real estate is among the priciest land per square inch on the planet. Yet the ground where the Twin Towers once stood is rightfully considered hallowed, never to be built on. A well-conceived and executed memorial now occupies the land, ensuring no one ever forgets what happened. I've been there. It's powerful. It hits home.

To me, the land under Gusens I and II is no different. Officially, 37,000 people were slaughtered here, and that figure is almost certainly conservative. It was important, and admirable, that the

Gusen Memorial was funded and built. I'm grateful for its presence. Its centerpiece, the camp's crematorium, is certainly a fitting symbol of the horrors the Nazis inflicted on their victims. The word 'crematorium' instantly connects me (and probably most people) with the Holocaust and Nazi atrocities.

But I am having trouble understanding how the rest of the site could become middle-class housing. Yes, I know the Austrians didn't perpetrate the Nazi's death machine, and they were, mostly, as much victims of Hitler and his followers as Germany's many good citizens. I get it. But that doesn't mean they didn't have a responsibility to do things to keep the memory of what happened in, and to, their country alive for future generations to see and learn from. That's why memorials are built, so we don't forget, so that we teach our children and grandchildren, so that the human race improves. They have to be impressive. They have to make a statement. They even have to be a burden: they have to take something away so visitors leave with something important.

It seems to me the Austrians missed an opportunity here.

That's what I think.

Chapter 31

Latrine *Kommando*

My father had broken into a grin again.
'Why are you smiling?' I asked.

'I was just remembering something. Every day, no matter how hard I worked, no matter how *hungry* I became,' he really emphasized that word, 'my mind never stopped working. All the time I was thinking of some way I could find to make things easier for myself.' He was pointing to his temple.

A month after arriving in KZ Gusen I, after four weeks of long, exhausting hours working at the stone crusher, he thought he'd uncovered the ideal way to ease his burden.

'A gypsy *kapo* was in charge of the Latrine *Kommando*. I don't know how he became a *kapo*. The Nazis hated the gypsies almost as much as they hated Jews.' The grin stayed on my father's face as he spoke. He was back in the camp again, the gypsy in his line of sight. 'So I became his friend. He was a *kapo*, and I was just a *KZler*, so I wouldn't say we were *good* friends, but we were friends. I begged him every day to take me into his *kommando*.'

My father explained that the Latrine *Kommando*'s job was to empty the dozens of barrels collecting human waste under the latrine barracks. The men in the *kommando* carted the barrels to a dump, emptied and cleaned them, then returned them back under the barracks. He told me that, although the work was incredibly unsavory, even revolting, it wasn't the physically demanding, will-sucking, Sisyphean drudgery of loading, unloading, and pushing a never-ending stream of granite boulders in small mine wagons to the stone crusher. Working on his new friend, pleading and cajoling over the course of a week, the gypsy *kapo* eventually relented, and recruited my father for his Latrine *Kommando*.

123

'I felt like I'd won the lottery!' My father beamed, clapping his hands once in celebration.

Once again, his personality must have played a role in getting himself switched from heavy labor to his, er, dream job. As a gypsy in an environment where everyone viewed him disparagingly, the *kapo* must have felt isolated and lonely. In the eyes of the Nazis, only Jews were lower than gypsies. Even for Europeans generally, gypsies occupied the lowest rung of society. My father knew that, and had probably bonded with the *kapo* over their shared miserly status.

Dad's first day went exactly as he'd expected. He collected barrels of human waste from under each of the latrine barracks, moved them to a dump, emptied and cleaned the barrels, and returned them to the spot where he'd gotten them. He said the stench made him throw up at first, but like everything else in his new life, he found a way.

'You could get used to anything,' he said emphatically to me.

Once he'd adjusted to it, moving barrels of human waste was just what my father had hoped for: effortless compared to his old job. His initiative had worked. He'd taken a chance, and made things better for himself.

And then, in the middle of the second day, a barrel he was carrying toppled over.

'I couldn't move a muscle,' my father said. 'I just stood there looking at the mess.'

The gypsy latrine *kapo* had been nearby, saw the spill, and instantly descended on him. My father finally moved, but the *kapo* was faster. The gypsy's rubber whip tore at him while he frantically worked to clean up the mess and get it back in the barrel, bit by disgusting, slimy bit.

'Another *kapo* joined the gypsy, this one had a two-by-four, and they both beat me while I made the ground spotless.' My father was smiling again while he said this. Smiling! Then he let out a short burst of laughter, and continued. 'I managed to finish cleaning up everything, took the barrel to the dump, emptied it, and then finished my day in the *kommando*.' The *kapos* were done harassing my father.

I saw nothing funny about this. I mean, my father's life was hanging in the balance that afternoon while the *kapos* beat him as he labored to clean up the reeking mess. It wasn't an embarrassed laugh, either. It was genuine. Where was the humor in this?

In all the years of hearing the story, I'd never asked, but this evening I did. 'Dad, what was so funny?'

'Jeckeleh, I did what I had to do to survive.' After a brief moment, again he smiled.

That was it. That was his explanation, and he felt he'd said enough. Later, I learned it was even worse, even more brutal, than my father had said. Once again he'd left off an important detail that revealed his experience to be many times worse than he'd said. I never wondered how he'd 'made the ground spotless.' I assumed he'd used a broom, a squeegee, a shovel, rags, or I-don't-know-what. It was revolting obviously, but it didn't seem that physically difficult, and so I never asked about it.

But researching his story, I asked my uncle what my father had *really* done to make the ground spotless. He'd used his bare hands. He'd used his fingernails. He'd used his prison clothes. That's how he cleaned the shit off Gusen's dirt path, until it was 'spotless.'

How in the world did he clean a barrel's worth of shit off the dirt with his fingers?! How did he bring himself to do that?

And then I had the answer. Now that I knew the whole story, I knew exactly why my father was smiling and laughing that Seder evening.

He was smiling at *Death*. He was laughing at *Death*. More than that, he was taunting *Death*. He was telling *Death* he had beaten him that day, and he would beat him again. 'Don't bother showing up in the operating room this July, *Death*. You're wasting your time. You've got nothing on me.'

In the few weeks since my father had been shipped by cattle car to KZ Mauthausen, he had discovered that if he dug down deeply enough, if his will to live was profound enough, he could laugh at *Death* while it hovered over him, while it hung close to him as he scraped other people's shit off the ground with his bare hands. My father discovered that afternoon he had that *Will*, the *Will* to live. He could do what others could not, or perhaps even would not, do. He could do far more than what the average person thinks is ordinary, or do-able, or survivable.

He could do whatever it took to stay alive.

As long as I've known my father, when things got tough, I never saw him down, never saw him sink into a funk. Not once. Dealing with the pain of losing his wife, surviving a heart attack, then a second one, having two triple-bypass surgeries, learning his mitral valve was failing, nothing depressed him. And if it did, it didn't last long enough for me to notice.

During those difficult times, Dad would say to me, 'Jeckeleh, it beats the alternative.' These phrases, these expressions he had – 'not so terrible,' 'no big deal,' 'it beats the alternative' – were not only his shorthand way of making a point, they also served a valuable purpose for him: they put life's events in perspective. 'Beats the alternative' meant being alive – no matter what he had to do to remain alive and no matter how difficult that life might be – was better than being dead. Every single time. That's what he found in himself that day in the Latrine *Kommando*. Cleaning the latrine barrel spill with his hands and fingers and clothes 'beat the alternative.' It beat dying. It beat succumbing to the *kapos* and Nazis who wanted him dead. He would do whatever it took to avoid it.

That's why he smiled and laughed when he told that story.

Now I knew how my father managed to get from day to day while in the camps. When I awakened to this capacity my father had, I immediately wondered if I had the same thing in me, if I possessed that *Will*, too. Could I dig down as deeply as he had? Could I do whatever (*whatever!*) I had to do to live, to survive, to make it to the next day?

That evening, my father returned to his barracks after the other work *kommandos* had finished for the day. Stepping inside, his *Blockältester*, the barrack's block leader, screamed at him to get out, to stay away, that he stunk worse than the dirtiest barnyard imaginable. Dad stripped, scrubbed and cleaned himself and his clothes in the latrine barrack's large sink, returning soaking wet, bruised, battered, and exhausted. But clean. The next morning he asked to return to the Stone Crusher *Kommando*, and the *kapo* took him back.

Of course he did.

Chapter 32

Third Army Takes the Field, 658 Miles Away

By the end of June, 1944, the fifty-mile-wide front in Normandy the Allies had secured during D-Day's harrowing first twenty-four hours had been expanded to encompass France's entire Cotentin Peninsula. Their forward line ran east-west, with the Americans on the western side, the British and Canadians to the east. Mixed in with the latter were Polish and Free French armored divisions.

In spite of their successes, Allied gains through June were coming more slowly than originally planned by the overall ground forces commander, British General Bernard Montgomery. The Germans still held most of France, controlling the southern half of Normandy and everything east of the outskirts of the city of Caen. Montgomery simply didn't have the weight of men and materiel to shove back the powerful German formations facing him. But with more Allied troops, tanks, and artillery landing on Normandy's beaches every day, it was only a matter of time before the Wehrmacht was brought to a decisive battle and kicked out of northwestern France.

To buy himself that time, Montgomery sent his British and Canadian divisions, positioned near Caen, into a series of assaults, drawing the best of the German military to their front. This not only thinned out the German forces facing the Americans, it also kept the Germans busy, preventing them from organizing their own offensive actions.

Finally, on July 25, 1944, with enough American troops now in position and with the Wehrmacht leaning towards the British and Canadians, the U.S. Army launched Operation Cobra. Smashing through German defenses and fighting their way south, within a week the Americans reached open country and turned eastward, so they now faced the direction they really needed to go: towards Germany.

Meanwhile, Patton's Third Army was shipped across the English Channel and moved into the line, ready to play their part. The 65th Infantry was not yet among the divisions moved to France. They were still in Camp Shelby, Mississippi, training day and night to prepare for a role they would play in the late winter of 1945.

With Third Army now in position, on August 1, 1944, Patton flew to Normandy to take the reins. Immediately ordering his troops into combat, he sent divisions both east and west. Westward, they fought to extricate German forces from Brittany and secure Atlantic Ocean and English Channel ports for Allied use. Eastward, Patton drove rapidly into central France, paralleling British and Canadian forces thirty miles to his north.

It quickly became clear that if Patton's troops in the south and the British and Canadians in the north all moved fast enough, they could form a giant pincer, surrounding and cutting off the retreat of the entire German army stationed in Normandy, 100,000 men plus hundreds of tanks and artillery pieces. German commanders saw this encirclement developing, but they were under orders from Hitler to hold their ground. The area that would soon entrap the Wehrmacht is now known as the Falaise Pocket.

Patton's divisions were speedy enough, but were held up by higher command, which feared his troops would be stretched too thin to effectively seal in Nazi forces. Patton argued vociferously, but he obeyed orders and held his ground. Fighting against stiffer resistance than Patton had encountered, British and Canadian forces, along with Polish and Free French armor, were moving more slowly. Still, by August 21 the gap between the Allied armies was closed in the town of Chambois, ensnaring most of the Germans and, in spite of Hitler's order, forcing them to sneak or fight their way out individually.

By midnight the next day, the Battle of the Falaise Pocket was over. Between 10,000 and 15,000 German soldiers had been killed, and 40,000 to 50,000 became prisoners of war. The rest threaded tiny gaps in the Allied cordon, alone or in small groups, escaping to the east to fight again.

Patton's Third Army was now 658 miles from Enns, Austria.

Chapter 33

Closest Call

Only weeks since being yanked out of his safe and comfortable life in Dej, my father had nailed down how he would get by in Gusen I. He would take chances. His antenna would be up and searching for ways to improve his life, all day, every day, 'all the time,' as he said. Because every time he'd tried and failed, the consequences were nil, a reset, a return to the starting grid, back to wherever he'd been before he took that chance. And he would tap into that *Will*.

But then came the day he was nearly killed.

September 1, 1944 was the fifth anniversary of the start of World War II, five years since Germany invaded Poland without warning, or even pretense. It's also the day of my father's closest call, a day far worse, much scarier, than when he spilled the latrine barrel. He knew the date because everyone in camp – from the *KZlers* to their SS guards – was aware of yet another anniversary in a war that seemed to have no end.

'It was a Friday,' my father began. His mood had turned dark. 'The *kapo* in my *kommando* ordered me and five other *KZlers* to move a metal pipe. We used pipes to bring gas into the stone crusher, and once in a while we had to move the pipes from here to here, or from there to there, or replace them.'

That morning, the six of them hoisted a length of heavy pipe on their shoulders in unison and without much difficulty. But while the other five were roughly the same height, my father was somewhat taller, making the group slightly unwieldy, though my father hadn't noticed. Nothing seemed amiss as they began walking with the pipe. But the *kapo* monitoring them came up from behind, and without saying a word, with his two-by-four walloped Dad with a shot to the head that spun him to the ground.

WHAM!

'Jeckeleh, my God. I never before had been hit like that.' My father touched his cheek with the tips of his fingers. 'Never.'

He instantly recognized he was in deadly trouble. He used every ounce of strength he could muster to get up, but he was dizzy and hurting, and before coming fully to his feet the *kapo* struck again.

WHAM!

My father staggered again, but this time he didn't fall. He took a third hit, a blow that should have dropped him, would have dropped anyone else, but he did not, would not, *could* not, go down. He looked straight into the *kapo*'s flaming eyes, and knew with absolute certainty: to fall again was to die.

Like struggling to walk against the strongest of gales, he went back to the pipe, took his place among the other five, and resumed carrying it. Blows from the *kapo*'s two-by-four rained down on his arms, his legs, his back. But. He. Would. Not. Fall. Again. He would not succumb to *Death*, though he could hear *Death* begging him to come, he could hear *Death*'s pleas to make the pain stop, he felt it so close by. But my father could only remember his mother's promise of the next train trip in a 'luxury way.' He focused all his energy on that promise. He was not going to die, not now, not there, not today. He was going to keep his place among the *KZlers* carrying the pipe, and he was going to be on that train.

Eventually the *kapo* had enough. And somehow my father stayed with his *kommando* the rest of the day. When he came back to the barracks that night he was stiff and sore, black and blue all over, in agony everywhere.

'But I was alive.' My father's eyes were moist. Blinking to keep the flood back, he said, 'I knew right then, right then, I was going to make it. Jeckeleh, can't you believe it, I felt something inside me I didn't know was there. It came from so deep down, I can't tell you where it came from.'

My father paused for a drink of club soda and to gather himself. After a moment, he concluded by saying that, after *Appell* and his bowl of soup for dinner, he settled into his bunk in the barracks to sleep, the hard wood igniting new waves of pain in his shoulders and buttocks. But for the first time in a long time, when he closed his eyes, he was hopeful.

And a smile of sorts returned to his face.

I couldn't smile along with him. Not after this one. This time, the only time, my father clearly had omitted nothing. It was all there, and I hurt right along with him.

Chapter 34

Walking Gusen I

Though the grounds of KZ Gusen II are only a short walk from the Gusen Memorial, I know there is truly nothing to see in the space where one of the most ferocious concentration camps in all of Europe had once been. Not unless I want to walk its pretty, paved streets lined with nice homes, and become even angrier. So Angelika and I leave the memorial and drive back in our cars to the twin SS guard barracks on *Georgestrasse*, where we park. Now walking north along a narrow lane by the barracks, we are quickly in the middle of what was once KZ Gusen I.

As with Gusen II, I see around me only small, well-kept single family homes. There are streets and sidewalks. Compact and mid-sized cars, and SUVs and small pick-ups, are parked against the curbs. Men and women push baby carriages and walk their dogs and go about their business. One smiles at Angelika and me, and we smile back, but most ignore us. In place of the concentration camp my father existed in, was tortured in, and nearly died in, Gusen I is now a collection of cute homes and tree-lined streets with names like Garden, Park, Cedar and Flower. I am aghast. My face becomes flush all over again.

The eastern border of the community, where we are walking, is defined by a tightly bunched row of trees and brush. Peering behind the growth, I spy a partially camouflaged segment of the camp's original outer wall, this one is its full eleven-foot height and fairly long, fifty yards or so. As with the two cut-down fragments of wall along *Georgestrasse*, which serve as an entranceway, this piece is made of the same medieval-looking granite as KZ Mauthausen's sinister walls.

Why hadn't this been torn down? It serves no obvious purpose. It doesn't mark a boundary, or divide anything, or support anything, or keep anything in or out. It doesn't memorialize anything. It's just here, overgrown with brush and hard to spot. The hair on the back of my neck is standing up. As much trouble as I have with the idea that people now live here, I have even more trouble understanding why they accept this wall in their midst.

I reckon if the government was going to take the time and trouble to replace KZ Gusen I with this delightful little community, it would not have taken much more effort to remove *all* the concentration camp's original granite walls. It seems incredibly peculiar to me that the people who live here see this every time they walk their dog, every time they drive by in their car, and are not bothered by its presence. It is like someone leaving an electric chair along a sidewalk and the neighbors taking it in their stride as they go about their day. It is completely incomprehensible, to me at least.

Angelika and I walk further north, towards the back of the development, where we pass a couple of commercial buildings housing small local businesses. Standing defiantly just beyond these buildings is another part of Gusen's perimeter wall, this a segment of the north wall. Made of dark granite blocks like the others, this one is twenty five feet high and doubles as a retaining wall, holding back earth. The ground slopes upward here, and Gusen I had been dug into the slope.

Looking past the wall, I notice a cliff of brownish-grey rock mixed with green brush, and speckled with trees. I estimate it to be 300 yards away from me, or perhaps a bit further. It captures my attention and I stare at it for a long while, not thinking of anything as I do.

Angelika breaks the silence. 'That is Kastenhof you are looking at,' she says.

It takes a few seconds until I register the significance of what I've just heard. That wall is the granite mine where my father worked, where he slaved while a prisoner in Gusens I and II. It is higher than the Wiener-Graben quarry wall, and maybe more imposing, if that's possible.

Then Angelika adds, 'And that building there,' pointing to my left, at a windowless, greyish-white structure set back from the slope, closer to me and partly hidden by trees, 'is the part of the stone crusher that is still existing.'

I shift my gaze to take in that building. I recognize it as the shoebox-on-its-side part of the three-building stone crusher complex, the one containing the storage chambers. It seems unremarkable and nondescript from this angle and distance. I notice stacks of light-colored rock and modern machinery scattered about.

'It's not still a working quarry, is it?' I ask, though I see enough to know the answer.

'Not exactly,' Angelika says softly, and explains what's here.

I'm shocked. I assumed that, like the Wiener-Graben quarry, Gusen's Kastenhof quarry would be shuttered, or even turned into a memorial. I am quite wrong. Although no longer an operating rock quarry, it is a fully-functioning, commercial granite distributor and mill. The Poschacher family owned Kastenhof, or parts of it, since the 1800s. They reacquired it after the war, and now they run it again the way they had before the Nazis showed up. As if nothing ever happened here.

I have to go there. 'Can we get inside?' I already know what I will do if Angelika replies in the negative. I don't see any sign of activity, and being Saturday, I figure the quarry is empty of workers.

'I think maybe yes,' she says, and the laugh lines around her eyes give away that it might not be too kosher. 'Let's take my car.'

Chapter 35

Stone Crusher

Leaving my rental car by the SS barracks, Angelika drives us west on *Georgestrasse* and turns right just past the Gusen Memorial. A quarter of a mile up, we make another right, into a two-house dead-end street, and park. This is post-war Gusen's northern border.

Marking the end of the street and blocking our way is a decorative brick wall about four feet high. A white wrought-iron gate in the middle of the wall allows access. Beyond the brick wall and the gate is a narrow field of uncut grass running the length of the Gusen development. Past the grass is the Kastenhof – now Poschacher – quarry. Through trees and brush, at the far end of the field I can make out the shoebox-on-it-side building. I need to get past the brick wall and its gate.

'They keep it locked,' Angelika says. 'I tried to enter into here before today.'

I've come this far, I'm not going to let a dainty four-foot decorative brick wall stop me. I place one hand firmly on the top of the iron gate, another on the top of the wall.

'It is private property,' Angelika reminds me, though I'm thinking her bland tone reflects her indifference to my upcoming transgression.

I start heaving myself up. The iron gate swings open under my weight, nearly throwing me on my face.

'I guess someone left it open, so it is permissible for us to enter,' Angelika now opines, deadpan. This was meant to be.

Stepping over the field's wild grass, we soon come to the stone crusher storage structure. I feel a hand pressing down hard on my chest, making it difficult to breathe. The ground around me, around this building, is *precisely* where my father worked while a prisoner here.

Stopping on the south side of the shoebox-shaped building, it seems bigger and more threatening than its thirty-foot height. The first floor is open and vacant except for a series of evenly-spaced support columns, so train hopper cars could roll directly underneath the storage chambers. From the second floor up, it is a windowless, eighty-foot wide, solid face of cement. The cement is striated, like the Gusen Memorial walls, and its color is a progression – nearly black on top, melting to an aging greyish-white lower down.

I suggest to Angelika that the black on top must have been caused by fire, and she agrees. When my father was a prisoner here, a wooden structure two stories tall sat atop the cement shoebox, bringing it to its full fifty-foot height. The wooden assembly contained machinery for sorting crushed granite coming up from the mechanical crusher via conveyor belt, and then dropping the granite down into any of the fourteen storage chambers. Today the black scarring at the wall's top is all that remains.

Seven rusted metal funnels jut out of the building's striated facade, about fifteen feet off the ground, lining up with the seven pairs of storage chamber rows inside the shoebox. Railroad tracks ran not only under, but also alongside, the shoebox, so hopper cars could be loaded both by coming under storage chambers, and also from these funnels on the building's side. During the war this must have been an incredibly busy place. All the train tracks had been taken up long ago, either by Stalin, or by townspeople who'd put the steel to better use.

We walk around the corner, to the eastern side of the paired buildings, and the pressure on my chest intensifies. I am now in front of the garage-door-like opening that faces the quarry. I am completely lost in my head. This opening was the destination for the small mine wagons filled with raw granite boulders my father loaded, pushed, and unloaded. Every single day my father was in KZ Gusen I, he slaved from morning till night between the central collection point where the *Strafkompanie* left off their loads of granite boulders, and this exact spot where I am now standing. I am stepping on the same ground my father walked on in the wooden shoes he was given after his own shoes came apart. The ground is uneven, strewn with rocks, pebbles and bits of grass. I involuntarily search for shoe prints. I find none. During my father's time here it must have been all dirt, trampled smooth by the prisoners' constant traffic. I wonder if he is watching me.

Scattered everywhere are piles of polished grey granite blocks twinkling in the bright sun. Some blocks are short and narrow, others longer and wider. Some are in neat piles on the ground, a few are on wooden pallets piled high, ready to be loaded on trucks, and still more lay around haphazardly. Halfway to the Kastenhof quarry wall, I see a jumble of granite blocks of all shapes and sizes twenty feet high. It is the discard pile, made up of incorrectly cut stones and excess granite. Intuitively I figure it must be close to what had been the central collection point where my father loaded his *kommando*'s mine wagons.

Angelika waits by the stone crusher buildings as I walk over to the pile and make my way to the top to get a better view of the quarry. It is stable, each fragment of granite so heavy that my weight isn't shifting it. Balancing on a jagged piece at the top of the pile and looking north, The Unterbruch Kastenhof quarry 100 yards away rises high above me. The young trees dotting its face makes it seem somehow less monstrous, though I know that is illusory.

I rotate slowly, hands out to keep my balance on the uneven granite beneath me. Now facing south, the Kastenhof wall is at my back, while Angelika and the empty, paired stone crusher buildings are ahead of me and to my right. Directly in front of me is a row of new one-story structures, part of the modern Poschacher operation. Behind them is Gusen I. Or used to be.

I let my imagination roam.

My father woke up every day somewhere inside there, in the concentration camp that had once been behind these new buildings, in a barracks that is no longer there, on a wooden bed with only a blanket to call his own. He ate what little they gave him for breakfast, some days trading salami for potatoes (and once for smooth granite pebbles), lined up for *Appell*, and then clicked his heels and marched with his *kommando* to here, to me, to near where I now stand, to work a miserable, endless day. Somewhere around me he paused once during the day for a lunch of thin soup. Maybe he sat with his precious soup near the mine wagons, or maybe he sat in the shade of the stone crusher buildings, or maybe the *kapo* didn't let him sit at all. And then he finished his work day, left this place with his *kommando* again, to go back to the other side of the granite wall for another *Appell*, a bit more soup, and another empty night.

I stand on the pile, taking in all I can see and hear and feel. The sun shines intensely, giving color and clarity and life to every black and white photo I ever studied of this quarry and the prisoners in it. A light breeze flicks at my shirt. At this instant I am looking through my father's eyes. I feel him with me. I can almost hear him breathing. It is 1997 again, but this time he has invited me along.

My father's story *never* conveyed how monstrously isolating, how insanely solitary this feels. He never projected to me how extraterrestrial this landscape is. I focus on the shell of the stone crusher building, the one with the garage door opening facing me, the one that once had a hole in the floor and hoists on the ceiling. The distance between me and that structure was my father's entire world for those months he was here. He must have felt so unreachable, it must have seemed like he was in outer space, like he was on another planet in a different solar system. Certainly no one on planet Earth would have permitted Stone Crusher *Kommandos* and *Strafkompanies* and ghettos in forests and Gusens and Birkenaus. It occurs to me he must have felt completely abandoned here.

And then the sensation becomes familiar. I've experienced it before. My father must have felt as abandoned as I felt after my mother died, as abandoned as I feared I might be again when he had his first heart attack. I know it's not the same thing. He was physically abandoned in a place that was trying to kill him. I only felt abandoned in my mind, and in places no more dangerous than my bedroom or kitchen. Still, standing here I now understand, a little, how he must have felt.

I can't help but wonder: how did he wake up and face the massive granite wall behind me, and those mine wagons, day after day? How did any of them, any of the very few who'd survived? And then go on to raise a family, tell jokes and stories, read good books, and enjoy good meals?

How can I ever equal this? How can I ever do anything in my life that shows I have the same *Will* to live as he had, the same desire to enjoy life in spite of pain and loss and hardship that my father exhibited? How can I prove I have what it takes to be the son he deserves to have?

I don't know. I have no idea how.

I stand on the granite discard pile and long to hear him call me 'Jeckeleh' one more time. I long for it now, as much as I've ever longed for anything in my life.

138

Chapter 36

Out of Gas, 384 Miles Away

After decimating the Wehrmacht in northwestern France, Patton's forces mounted their tanks and went back on the offensive. Driving eastward at a surprisingly rapid clip for such a large armored force, by August 31 Third Army troopers were in Verdun. During World War I, Verdun was the site of a battle between France and Germany that cost nearly one million casualties. This time, a single combat command with 5,000 men from Patton's 7th Armored Division captured Verdun without stopping, keeping the Wehrmacht on the run.

Two weeks later, Third Army reached, and liberated, a line of French towns near the German border, from Metz in the north, to Luneville, fifty miles to the south. Not all the towns behind the line were free of Nazi troops, but Patton had a much bigger problem. His forces were running low on fuel. Allied logistics commanders had not yet solved the problem of efficiently getting gasoline from Britain to the European continent, and then to combat units at the fast-moving front lines.

Worse for Patton, Field Marshal Montgomery (he'd been promoted on September 1, 1944), now commander of British forces in the ETO, the European Theater of Operations, was allowed to grab all the gas he might need in order to execute a major assault code-named Operation Market-Garden. Montgomery sold Market-Garden to the Supreme Allied Commander, future President of the United States Dwight D. Eisenhower, as a war-shortening thrust. The Field Marshall intended to circumvent formidable German border defenses facing Patton and other American generals, by doing an end-run around their north.

Montgomery's plan was to drive British tanks along a narrow sixty-mile-long highway through the Netherlands. The highway crossed numerous rivers, and so was dotted with bridges. The bridges would first be seized by American and British paratroopers, who would defend their positions until ground forces reached them by that single, narrow road. The last bridge, the one furthest out, was in the Dutch town of Arnhem, twenty miles from the German border. From there, Allied forces would pour into the heart of Germany and power ahead until the Nazis capitulated.

Patton was now triply-furious. First he'd lost whatever fuel he might have gotten to Montgomery, whose fighting skills he did not respect. Second, he believed his Third Army had the Germans backpedaling so fast, he could end the war in weeks if he would just be given the gasoline to keep moving. He didn't think the German army's border fortifications facing Third Army were as impenetrable as Montgomery was saying. Finally, he gravely doubted Montgomery's single-highway plan was militarily viable. But Montgomery had convinced Eisenhower that he should be given a fair shot at his northerly route into Germany, and so Eisenhower, the overall ETO commander, ordered Patton to make do with what meager fuel supplies he had.

Market-Garden was launched on the afternoon of September 17, 1944, against what Montgomery believed would be weak German resistance. He was very wrong. Wehrmacht troops and tanks stationed in towns near the narrow highway route, soon dubbed 'Hell's Highway' by those who battled on it, were in greater number, and of far higher caliber, than the British commander expected. Eight days later Operation Market-Garden was declared a failure when British tanks were stopped by the Nazis just short of Arnhem – a bridge too far.

That same day, September 25, 1944, Patton's gas situation became so acute he was forced to halt his troops. They had plenty to do, capturing Nazi-held towns near their lines, cleaning up resistance behind them, and preparing their equipment and themselves for winter combat. But for now, their rapid progress through France had ceased thirty miles short of the German border. They had covered 274 miles in twenty-five days, and were 384 miles from Enns.

Chapter 37

Yom Kippur 1944

September 27, 1944, a Wednesday, was the Jewish holiday of Yom Kippur, the Day of Atonement, the holiest day in the Jewish calendar. The prisoners at Gusen had no calendars, of course, but like the anniversary of the start of the war, there were enough *KZlers* keeping track that they knew when the important Jewish holidays fell.

Most mornings, between 800 and 900 men lined up in my father's *Appell*. Yom Kippur, 1944, was a regular workday in Gusen I, no different from the other days. The men were arrayed with their *kommandos*, including my father, who was fully healed from nearly being beaten to death four weeks earlier.

My father was now sitting bolt upright in his dining room chair. 'That morning,' he said, 'the *kapos* counted one worker more than they needed.' He was holding up his index finger. 'Just one more, just one extra *KZler*. They picked me to stay behind in the barracks.' His smile was back. The odds had been 800 or 900 to one. 'It was a *good* selection,' he concluded. It may have been his single day off work.

My father squared his shoulders, stepped out of the *Appell*, and walked to his barracks alone, without looking back at Izsak Mozes and his other friends in his *kommando*.

Once in the barracks, he never said if he fasted that day, as many Jews do on Yom Kippur. I assume he didn't, because the Jewish religion, even at its most orthodox, does not require one to risk one's life to carry out commandments, and missing a day of meager rations seems, to me, to be flirting with death. It was the same principle guiding my grandmother when she ordered her son to buy pork before their 'transport' to KZ Birkenau.

'I spent the morning in the barrack with Rabbi Rabinovitz,' Dad said, pronouncing the name as a Yiddish-speaking European would, rah-bin-OH-vitch. 'We *davened* together.' *Davened* is Yiddish for 'prayed.'

My father explained that Rabbi Rabinovitz knew many of the Yom Kippur prayers by heart, so together they prayed to God, as they would have done in their home towns, in their respective synagogues. My father never said who Rabbi Rabinovitz was, where he came from, what language he spoke, whether they had met before while in KZ Gusen, or why, like him, the rabbi hadn't been assigned to a work *kommando* that day.

Like so many aspects of my father's year in the camps, I never asked for more detail. So now every Yom Kippur I think about those questions. As the answers are impossible to come by, I have, instead, come up with a few myself. I've decided that Rabbi Rabinovitz was sent to KZ Gusen just to spend Yom Kippur with my father. He arrived that morning, and when the sun set on that holy day, he left the way he had arrived, returning to wherever he had come from.

Who had sent him to Gusen? My grandmother, of course.

Jews believe that during the ten days between the Jewish New Year and Yom Kippur, God contemplates our fate for the coming year, weighing whether to inscribe us in the 'book of life,' or in the 'book of death.' At sundown at the end of Yom Kippur, He ('He' for expediency's sake, as I am not assuming God is male) makes a final determination, live or die, and writes down His decision in the appropriate book. In Yom Kippur services now, sitting in my temple's pew and saying prayers I will never know by heart, I often picture my father and Rabbi Rabinovitz side by side in the drafty concentration camp barracks praying from memory, Rabbi Rabinovitz's mostly, thanking God for helping them survive to that point and asking that they be written in the 'book of life' for the coming year. It must have seemed to them like such an impossible request. As I pray to God to give me a good year, *another* good year (because they're *all* good years, because they all 'beat the alternative'), I think about how my father's prayers were clearly answered.

Whether Rabbi Rabinovitz's prayers were answered, I could not tell you.

'It wasn't just on Yom Kippur, Jeckeleh,' my father said, continuing the theme. 'I prayed to God every day in the camps. Every day.'

He said he didn't know all the prayers by heart, but he knew a few of the most important ones, and those he recited. It took him five minutes, and he did it while rushing to get ready for *Appell*. He was checking in, saying thanks for being able to wake up to a new day, and asking God to watch over him during another day in hell.

He concluded. 'And I always said *kaddish* for my father.' *Kaddish* is the prayer for the dead that is said daily by the orthodox for the first eleven months after losing a parent, and then once a year on the anniversary of that parent's death. My father was saying it for his father, who'd died suspecting the worst was coming. My father never mentioned saying *kaddish* for his mother, and I never asked why. I'd never even thought to ask. Now I can only assume an answer. I assume he wasn't certain she was dead, so he erred on the positive side.

My father's eyes welled up for a second time that evening. Maybe he was thinking of his parents right then. I know he never doubted that his survival was not happenstance, was not just luck, was not just the force of his upbeat personality and monumental willpower. In his view, he'd had help. His mother's 'luxury way' premonition was proof. My father had held on to the possibility of that train trip and he held on to God making it a reality. And when he survived, he committed himself to saying those same few prayers, to saying 'thank you,' every day for the rest of his life.

I feel the same way as my father, though my faith has never been tested as his has. I believe God saved my father's life, and I believe He watches over my family and me, as well. I have no scientifically rigorous proof that He's done anything especially good for me, or that He's kept me from anything especially bad. But I have never asked for proof. My father's presence is proof enough. I accept that my life is going the way He means for it to go. So like my father, I take five minutes out of every morning to pray. It's an important part of my wake-up ritual. Shave, shower, dress, pray.

Having known many concentration camp survivors, I've learned they each had very diverse and personal views of God. Some, like my father, believed that if not for God, they would have lost their lives. Others, like my father's older brother, Uncle Villi, were on the opposite side. Uncle Villi believed there couldn't possibly be a God, because what benevolent god would have him suffer the loss of his beautiful wife Dora and young son Tibor? What god would allow six million Jews to be slaughtered, or, for that matter, more than fifty million human beings to die in a war? Instead, he attributed his survival purely to luck. Other survivors I've known have had views all along the spectrum between those of my father and my uncle.

In spite of my own strong belief, I can't argue with my uncle Villi's viewpoint. To accept that there is a God, knowing what we know about the lives taken and the lives ruined in World War II, or in any war, you must believe that understanding God's ways is a frivolous and unnecessary exercise. You must take the stance that 'God has a reason.'

I hear those four words, 'God has a reason,' all the time. Shortly after Sam, my oldest child, was born, he was diagnosed with cerebral palsy. Today he's a bright, handsome and engaging college student running straight-A's studying Classics. He uses a power wheelchair to get around. My ex-wife Karen and I raised him as ordinarily, as normally, as we could. He attended regular schools. We took him and his twin sisters everywhere we went. We took them on ski vacations (Sam skied in outstanding disabled ski programs, with dedicated and wonderful paid and volunteer staff), we sat on beaches, we toured the country's National Parks, and we visited relatives.

It was when we'd be out in the world with Sam that I would hear that phrase, 'God has a reason.' Well-meaning people would see us, and if they had a chance to catch my ear, they might say that to me. It often came out of the blue, perhaps while we were about to board an elevator, or in line at Disney World, or waiting for the next ski lift. They might ask me how old he is, or what his name is, or where we're from, and then they'd just blurt out those four words.

I have to say, believing 'God has a reason' didn't make it easier for me to raise him, and I guarantee you it doesn't make Sam any happier to be disabled. My ex-wife and I did, and still do, the best we can, but we never once thought to ourselves, 'This is wonderful, God has a reason!'

I think it is permissible for me to believe strongly in God, and yet be unhappy with His choice of Sam and my family facing disability. The two aren't mutually exclusive. My father firmly believed God enabled his survival, but it doesn't mean he was happy he'd spent a year in the camps and lost so much of his family.

Everyone has burdens of one sort or another. Some are more overt, you can see the person and understand, to some degree, what they're confronting. Others are less so, perhaps deep inside their bodies, or just deep inside their heads. No matter how tough I might have thought it was to raise Sam, he has had it much harder than I – he's the one who doesn't walk. What do I deal with? In comparison to him, I think nothing.

Knowing this makes keeping my head on straight relatively easy. This isn't to imply I'm any more normal than the next person, because I'm certainly not, but whatever extra load my son's disability puts on my life is something I happily carry.

Fifty million human beings died in a war that earned the instigators absolutely nothing. And Sam can't walk.

I'm certain God has a reason, probably more than one. I don't know what they are, but I have no doubt the reasons somehow, in some way, make sense (though those reasons may forever remain a mystery). For a true believer, that's sufficient. It was for my father. It is for me.

Chapter 38

Jourhaus

Angelika drives me back to the SS barracks so I can retrieve my car. Before getting in and driving away, I remind myself that I need to see one last thing.

I am parked next to the two granite wall fragments bracketing the original Gusen I access road from *Georgestrasse*. At the end of the access road is a building that, during the war, served double-duty. It was both the camp's main gate, as well at its administration building. It was designed with a cut-out in the center wide enough and high enough to fit a large truck. It was sealed by a set of heavy wooden double-doors. It was known as the *Jourhaus*, and most concentration camps had one.

In the camps a *Jourhaus* had a multitude of purposes including administration building, guard tower, command center, prisoner induction center, prison, and sometimes all of the above. It isn't normally also a gatehouse, though it was in Gusen I. The Gusen I *Jourhaus* still stands at the end of the access road leading north from *Georgestrasse,* by the trimmed-down wall fragments. But it's no longer an access road. It's a driveway. And it's no longer an administration building. It's a home. A family now lives in it. I guess they are relatively well off, as this is by far the largest home in Gusen.

Before leaving, I just *have* to see this. Angelika accompanies me, though she doesn't appear enthusiastic about it.

We start at the back of the house. The small lawn is manicured, with a swing set and a small storage shed off to one side. The yard is cordoned off from the rest of the Gusen housing development by a high white stucco wall and hedges. The house, too, is of white stucco, same as it was during the war.

Granite stones in the shape of an arch define the KZ Gusen I camp gate cutting through the center of the house. These stones were always there – they're clearly visible in photos of the *Jourhaus* from the war – but today instead of heavy wooden doors filling the arch, the owners installed plate glass. On the second floor, bay windows face the interior of the Gusen housing development. Period photos show the bay windows also were always there, enabling anyone standing by them to monitor the entire camp's goings-on. I guess now it's a bedroom window. I bet they have a great view of the Kastenhof quarry face and the stone crusher buildings when they wake up every morning. How cheery.

But wait, there's more.

We come around to the front of the building. Standing in the center of the access-road-now-driveway leading from *Georgestrasse*, I see the owner had filled in this side of the old granite arch with plate glass, as well. The home's front door is centered in the middle of the glass. The south-facing glass probably let in lots of light. How architecturally perfect.

I have seen enough. I stride up the driveway to the front door. Angelika keeps a step behind me, her body language making it clear she wants nothing to do with this, but I don't ask her, and she doesn't volunteer. I knock. A pretty blonde woman about my age answers the door. She is wearing jeans and a t-shirt, she was not expecting company. She looks from me to Angelika and back to me.

Angelika is silent. I ask the woman if she speaks English. She does, a little. She appears uncertain.

I'm stuck. I was expecting a monster, an ogre, a storm trooper I could slam to the ground with one *zets* to the face. Instead I am confronted by a woman who looks like she could be in my circle of friends.

'Have you lived here long?' I finally ask.

She hesitates for a moment. 'Yes, for twenty years. Who are you and why do you ask me this?'

I explain to her that my father was a Jew who worked in the Gusen concentration camp, in the mines. She responds by inviting me in to look around. I pass, it feels like I'm intruding. She continues, telling me that when she and her husband bought the house the plate glass was not there. They had done much work to it over the years, she says, and are raising a daughter.

I want to ask her if she and her husband hear footsteps, if they hear the ghosts of the thousands of lives lost here screaming in the night. But I don't. Instead, I tell her she has done a nice job with the remodel and wish her a nice day.

She offers for me to return any time. As I turn to leave, she has one more thing to add. She tells me that prisoners were never kept in the house.

Oh. Wait. So that makes it OK to live here? Until that comment, I was feeling guilty for thinking so poorly of her. She and her husband are strivers, making their way in the world. But then she says to me that it's OK that they live there, since no prisoners were ever kept there. First, I know that's not true. A pastor beloved by KZ Gusen's prisoners was tortured to death in the basement. And second, it was merely the gatehouse and administration building to one of the two worst concentration camps in the world. But she believed no prisoners were kept here, so that made it acceptable?

I give away none of this to the woman of the house, whose name I didn't ask and don't want to know. I walk back along the driveway, every molecule in my being vibrating with a need to get away from there. And so Angelika and I get in our cars and leave.

We have more important things to do. We are going to find the exact places where my father escaped.

Chapter 39

Suicide

Through the fall of 1944, my father continued working in his *kommando*, loading, unloading and pushing those small mine wagons with raw granite to and from the Kastenhof stone crusher. Every day was an effort to wake, to eat, to manhandle the wagons, to survive. From Yom Kippur 1944 until early November of that year my father's days blended together.

Until one day they didn't.

'Jeckeleh, I couldn't go on not one more day,' my father said. He had rolled up his white shirtsleeves in a manner he'd been doing his whole life, as if he was getting down to work. Copying him, I had rolled up mine, as well.

He continued, his voice quieter than before. 'I had seen enough, and I had suffered enough. I was so hungry all the time, I was just so tired, and I decided I wanted to die.'

Even knowing my father's story from prior Passover Seders as I do, it shocked me every time I heard those words coming from him. He was the last guy I would peg as suicidal. He was perpetually happy and upbeat, his glass always half-full. I saw what he'd faced in *my* lifetime, and each time he'd met those challenges head-on. He was not a man to seek a way out. But it was a mark of the severity of the never-ending demonic forces defining his life in the camps that suicide was on his mind. Still, this was surprising, out of character, and a drastic switch from his hopeful tones of just a few minutes earlier.

'What about your mother's train ride in a "luxury way"?' I asked.

My father shook his head. 'I know, but I just couldn't. I couldn't go to that stone crusher not one more time. The things I told you tonight, the stories I told you and your brother over the years, it's maybe only ten percent, or twenty percent of how bad it really was.'

And there I had it, my father admitting he was holding back, not telling me everything. It wasn't even a hint – he *said* it. He said it was worse than he was describing.

I now know I blew it right then. I completely missed the import of that comment. In spite of my father's admission that things were worse than he'd ever said, I never asked him to tell me more, to tell me about what made it so much worse. I never suggested to him that I wanted to understand better what he'd been through.

Instead, all I said was, 'It was that bad?'

It was a weak question, which garnered an equally weak reply. 'Yes, Jeckeleh. Yes it was.' I could have done much better.

It was in the first week of November 1944, my father does not know the exact date. When he woke that chilly morning, he began scheming how he would die. He'd watched many others do it, he said. It didn't seem that difficult, especially compared to the effort necessary to live. The two methods of suicide most common in KZ Gusen I were either grabbing the high voltage wires bringing electricity to each barracks and running along the top of the granite camp walls, or jumping from the top of the Kastenhof granite wall, more than 100 feet up.

To my father, each method had its downside. The electrified wires were not easily reachable. Whether atop a barracks or on the granite perimeter wall, the wires could only be reached by climbing. My father said many *KZlers* did it, and the guards and *kapos* didn't mind because it was one more prisoner whose return was not desired, who now would not be returning. But Dad doubted he had the strength to make it either to a barracks roof or to the top of the wall. And if he tried and failed, the SS guards would beat him to death, which was the result he wanted, but in a slow and unquestionably uncomfortable way, and he didn't want to face that.

His problem with the other common suicide method, jumping from the top of the Kastenhof cliff to the bottom of the quarry, was also not solvable.

'I was afraid that if I jumped, I would just break a leg,' he said to me, a smile back again on his face. 'And then the *kapos* would beat me.' Surely the *kapos* or SS would not only beat him, they'd kill him. But again it would be in a way he'd prefer to avoid.

When I was nineteen years old I wondered about what time the on-campus pub closed, and whether between now and then I could convince the blonde freshman from Illinois to come back to my dorm room with me. My father, at the same age, wondered about whether jumping from ten stories up would kill him, or just leave him broken.

The fact that he wondered at all about whether he'd live after jumping was notable. 'Dad, how could you think you'd survive falling from 100 feet up? No one could fall that far and live.'

My father just shrugged. Sitting in his dining room on this Seder evening at seventy-five years of age, it was clear he believed it still. He wasn't going to articulate his belief in his immortality. The shrug did it for him.

It says a lot about my father, that he wasn't sure a fall from such a height would kill him. Most people would be certain jumping from that high, or even from half that height, would leave them dead. I researched people who'd fallen or jumped from 100 feet, give or take, and learned to my surprise there were survivors. There weren't many, but those that lived were almost always in great health *and* had landed on soft ground, or on the roof of a car, or on something else that had cushioned the shock of landing.

My father had none of those advantages. His health was far from good. He probably weighed 100 pounds at that point, down from his starting weight of 160 pounds. He had been eating poorly, he had been beaten multiple times, and he was depressed. And the base of the quarry was, by definition, rock-hard ground. It was clear that if he jumped, he would die.

Yet here he was at the Seder table, still believing he might not have died if he'd jumped.

Besides his *Will*, his luck (or God), and his personality, I am convinced a big part of my father's concentration camp survival tool kit included his unwavering confidence in his immortality. It's not that he thought he would *never* die, it's just that he thought he would not die in KZ Gusen I. Surviving the pipe beating had left him with a feeling of control over his own destiny. *Kapos* weren't killing him, hunger wasn't killing him, luck wasn't deserting him. The only thing that *could* kill him, was him.

So although, in his opinion, there was no sure-fire way to die in Gusen I, that morning he decided he had to try *something*.

In that morning's *Appell*, shivering in place with his *kommando*, my father turned to the man next to him, a 27-year-old Hungarian who'd arrived in KZ Gusen I a few weeks earlier. My father had befriended him, as they spoke the same language and so connected over more than just their shared circumstances. He doesn't remember his friend's name and doesn't believe he survived the war.

Dad said to me, 'We were in the *Appell*, and I turned to my friend and I said to him that I'm going to kill myself today. I thought maybe he'd have an idea how I should do it. He leaned close to me so I could hear him, and he grabbed my arm and he whispered in my ear. He said to me, "No you're not."'

My father paused for a moment, so I asked, 'Is that all he said?'

'No, I was just remembering him for a second. He said to me this. He said, "I spent four years in a Labor Service Battalion on the Russian front. I'm here because I got typhus and spent a month in the hospital. I was so sick I didn't even know my own name for a time. But I survived. They thought I was finished as a worker so they sent me here to die." That's what he said. He was holding on to my arm so tightly I thought he would break it. He was such a strong boy. Then my friend said "They can go to hell." Of course he meant the SS. He said to me, I'm not allowed to take my own life. They can take it from me, the *kapos*, or the SS can, but I can't. He said it's in the *torah*, I'm not allowed.' The *torah* is the first five books of the bible.

'What did you say back to him?'

'What could I say? I didn't say anything. He was right.' The smile again. *Death* missed yet another chance.

That was it. The feeling had been erased. Suicide was off the table. The friend's sharp retort had snapped my father out of his suicidal mood. In that instant my father had decided his friend was right. He didn't know when his end would come, or how it would come, but he wasn't going to help it along. Maybe the biblical reference helped, but, listening to my father, I think it might have been peer pressure, the competition of it. If his friend, who'd been sent to Mauthausen specifically to die, could hack it, he would too.

And his Mother's prediction came back to the forefront of his mind. He returned to survival mode.

Chapter 40

Bahnhof Section

The days went on. One morning my father realized that in the four months since marching across the field from KZ Gusen II to Gusen I, the only constants in the barracks were him and his friend Izsak Mozes. They were the only survivors of the original sixty-man *kommando* that had come over from II. As the *kommando* had grown, new prisoners had come, they had died, they had been replaced, the replacements had died, and they, too had been replaced. My father figured more than a thousand Jews had passed through his barracks.

Every barracks had a *Blockältester*, a block elder, or leader. The *Blockältester* lorded over the barracks, though he was just as likely to be killed by his Nazi overseers for a mistake as a *KZler* from his barracks. The *Blockältester* in my father's barracks, whose name Dad didn't recall, was a German sent to KZ Gusen I because of a criminal past whose details my father didn't know. The German, too, had noticed my father was still alive when almost all the others were dead. One evening in early November, not long after his brush with suicide, my father sensed that the *Blockältester* had had enough of him.

'I didn't know why he felt like this,' he said to me, 'but I had a bad feeling he didn't want me around anymore.'

'He never told you why?' I asked.

'No. I couldn't ask him, he was the *Blockältester*. Maybe it was because I was a walking skeleton, I was nothing, just skin and bones. Maybe he didn't like the way I looked.'

'Didn't everyone look like that?'

'Yes, but I was so skinny. I was skinnier than everyone else in the barracks.'

It struck me as an odd answer, but it's what my father always said when I'd ask him about what happened that night in the

155

camps. To his credit, he never lacked for vanity, no matter where he was.

That night, when his *kommando* had returned from another grueling day on the mine wagons at the quarry, the *Blockältester* pulled my father aside and accused him of soiling his bed. I found that claim fascinating, because until then I hadn't realized that lack of cleanliness by a *KZler* was a punishable offense. Apparently it was.

'I did nothing wrong,' my father said to me. 'My bed was as clean that morning as it was every morning.'

No matter. His punishment was twenty-five lashes on his bare backside with a rubber whip. The *Blockältester* ordered my father to pull down his pants and bend over a waist-high whipping stand purpose-built for just such occasions. My father said he took the first ten strokes of the whip, biting his lip each time, but holding himself together. Barely, but holding.

'I was counting,' my father said. 'At eleven, I lost it. Never once did I let myself go since my first day in Birkenau. Not even when the *kapo* beat me when I was moving the pipe for the gas.' His face had become drawn. 'I threw myself down on the barrack floor, screaming like I don't remember when I screamed like that. I remember he hit me four more times, and then thank God he stopped.'

'What were you thinking when he was hitting you?'

'Thinking? I wasn't thinking, Jeckeleh. I wasn't thinking of anything.'

'You didn't think you should have really tried to kill yourself a few weeks before?'

My father shook his head.

Though he said nothing was going through his mind, I can't imagine that was true. Had he shut down? Short-circuited? Was it just all too much? Was every fiber in his emaciated body screaming for the end to come? Or was he thinking about how he could have missed *all of this,* every minute of his time in the camps since early June, by hiding in the attic of the Christian family in Dej and letting his mother get on that 'transport' to Birkenau without him?

I had never asked him that before. It seemed inappropriate, but tonight it felt right. I asked him that Seder evening if he'd regretted boarding that cattle car.

'Of course not,' he said, and then added a *look*, a direct, intense look right into my eyes. My father didn't have a *look*, like some people have in response to certain questions. But for this question he came up with one that was unmistakable. This *look* said he never went there, he never allowed himself that question. It was out of bounds for him, for me, for anyone.

No doubt this was an extension of my father's faith in God, that 'God has a reason.' My father had made a choice, to go with his mother, and in the end, it had worked out: he lived, he got married and had kids and was still having a good and happy life in the U.S. If he had remained in Dej, hiding in the attic, he might have ended up on the same exact post-war path, only without the traumatic experience of the camps. Or maybe not. To my father, it didn't matter.

But to make it absolutely clear to me, my father said, 'Jeckeleh, I went. And thank God, here we are at another Seder together.' Adding a smile, my father had just given a very small demonstration of his *Will*, just for me.

The next day the *Blockältester* changed tactics. He still wanted my father out of the barracks, but he had something of a heart. It may have been microscopic, but it was definitely there. Consider that the night before he had stopped at fifteen lashes, when he could have gone to twenty-five and almost certainly murdered my father.

Dad never displayed any animosity towards him when he told his story. He didn't mention him with an edge in his voice or spittle on his lips. I didn't detect warmth either, but I never had any doubt the *Blockältester* was not my father's enemy. The relationship between my father and him seemed to me to have been very complex. Certainly master and subject. Father figure to my teenage dad? Maybe. Friend? Almost certainly not, but I could never rule it out entirely. And definitely not murderer. Not his potential killer. I felt that counted for something. I've wondered often who he was, and if he'd survived the war.

'The *Blockältester* ordered me to go to the *Revier* and to tell to them that I have diarrhea, and to ask them to admit me. I told the *Blockältester* that I don't have diarrhea. He told me to fake it, and make sure that I don't come back.'

Did the ex-con smile when he said it? Or even smirk? How I wish I knew the answer.

The Gusen infirmary, the *Revier* as my father always called it, was not what most people think of when they hear the word. It had beds and it had doctors, as any infirmary should. But the doctors were prisoners with few medicines, no anesthesia, only a few dirty bandages, in short, almost no tools of their trade. Most of the time the doctors could do nothing for those admitted, except watch them die.

I was amazed KZ Gusen I even had an infirmary. It was a concentration camp, whose reputation for depraved human existence knows no modern parallel, so what was the point of an infirmary? Why would the Nazis want to heal the same prisoners they were trying to kill? Was there a shortage of slave labor? If so, then why the murderous conditions in the first place?

Asking Angelika and others connected with Mauthausen Memorial, I came up something of an answer. The labor concentration camps often required highly skilled workers. While it took no skill to haul granite around a quarry in mine wagons, it took great skill to cut raw granite into the exact shapes used for building facades. It was the same for Messerschmitt AG, the German military aircraft manufacturer. The company built plants near KZ Mauthausen and KZ Gusen to produce plane parts, and relied on concentration camp prisoners with highly specific technical knowledge to staff the plants.

These skilled *KZlers* had tangible military and monetary value to the Nazis. The SS could starve them to within an inch of their lives, but if they got sick, they needed to be healed, because replacing them could cause manufacturing delays. Hence, the *Revier* in KZ Gusen, and even a building called 'the hospital' within the granite walls of KZ Mauthausen.

Continuing the story, my father said, 'So after *Appell* that morning, I went to the *Revier* and told the doctor I had diarrhea. He asked me how many times a day do I go. I said six times. He laughed at me.' Hahaha, my father demonstrated in a surprisingly deep voice. 'He told to me that I don't have diarrhea, I should stop wasting his time.'

I had to admit to myself that my father could have answered this better.

Slinking away, he knew he'd have to face the *Blockältester* again. Sure enough, when he reported his failed attempt at gaining admittance to the infirmary, the *Blockältester* threw punches and kicks for a few minutes, all the while yelling, 'Idiot! Six times isn't diarrhea. Twenty is. Say twenty next time!'

My father got the message. After spending the rest of the day with his *kommando*, the next day he went back to the *Revier*, reporting to a new doctor that he had diarrhea.

'Thanks God it wasn't the same doctor,' my father said to me. 'This one also asked me how many times a day do I go, and I said twenty five.' Dad chuckled. Then he turned somber. 'The doctor said to me very seriously that yes, I have diarrhea, and he assigned me to a bed in Barrack 31, the *Bahnhof* ward of the infirmary barracks.'

The infirmary was divided into two sections. The first was for those who were sick or injured and likely to recover. It didn't have a nickname. The second, Barrack 31, was for prisoners who were near death and were not expected to survive. Gusen I's *KZlers* had nicknamed this section the *Bahnhof*, German for train station, because it was presumed everyone in there would soon be leaving on their final journey.

Being ordered into the *Revier's Bahnhof* section revealed my father's true physical condition in those days. Though he didn't have diarrhea, the doctor, an experienced professional, believed he was close to death. That was the only reason a *KZler* went into the *Bahnhof* ward. The doctor clearly did not know his patient.

Once in the infirmary, my father was allowed no food, a crude but effective way of treating his diarrhea. If nothing went in, nothing could come out. And it was an equally effective way of hastening his death. The *Revier Blockältester* who took Dad to his assigned bed warned him if he was caught eating, he would be killed, which seemed ironic to me. Or maybe just absurd.

Food rations in the Gusen I *Revier* were less than the food given working *KZlers* in the barracks. They got a slice of bread with margarine for breakfast, small portions of watery soup for lunch and dinner. *Bahnhof* prisoners were fed even less. In the *Bahnhof*, starvation was a means of murder. But, as with everything else in the concentration camp, there were ways to game the system that would improve one's chances of living.

My father's willingness to barter food for pebbles so he could feel full demonstrates the lengths he, and others, were willing to go to satiate their indescribable hunger. But the lengths my father went to in the infirmary were on another level entirely. The methods he related to me had to do with the dead. This was survival at its most base level. Like my father said: people became animals.

The slice of bread distributed to each prisoner in the infirmary every morning only went to patients who were alive. Obviously. Dead patients had no use for food. But my father had a use for the dead patients. Starting on his first morning in the *Bahnhof*, as soon as he woke he checked the patients in the beds on either side.

'If one had died overnight, I would talk to him as if he was still alive,' he explained. 'I would grab his hand, touch his shoulder or stroke his face, anything to make the *kapo* handing out the food believe he was still alive and talking with me. I would tell the *kapo* to just put it on his bed. And the *kapo* would leave him his food.'

It worked every time.

The other technique required no less a descent into pure animal. To make it seem to their brains and stomachs as if they had more food than they were actually getting, *Bahnhof* patients often ate half of their bread slice in the morning, leaving the remainder for later in the day. But to be sure they could safely keep that half a slice until later, they would put it on their chest, or under the small of their back, or under their bed sheet. Everyone was naked in the infirmary, so no one had pants or shirts with pockets. Excess food was safe only if it was under a sheet or literally on your body.

If a patient died during the day, the food they had stored would of course go uneaten. When my father saw someone expire, he would immediately check under the sheet and around the person to see if the dead man had hidden food for a later that was never going to come. And so my father managed to eat even though they'd stopped his food ration.

Still alive a few days after being admitted to the *Bahnhof* infirmary barracks, the doctors wised up and moved my father to the ward for patients who were expected to live.

'They must have been realized that I wasn't leaving the station,' my father said, and his grin bloomed into a full-blown smile.' He was not leaving their *Bahnhof* on any trip not including travel in a 'luxury way.'

Chapter 41

Soup

The SS came through the *Revier* every few days making selections, culling it of patients who were taking too long to heal, or too long to die. They would be shot, hung, beaten, left outside in the cold to die, forced into ice-cold outdoor showers, or killed by another of the sixty-two ways at the disposal of the KZ Gusen SS guards. Incredibly, and by now perhaps not surprisingly, my father was never selected, and remained in the *Revier* for nearly the rest of November 1944. He was allowed to eat after being moved out of the *Bahnhof*, but the slice of bread in the morning and soup later in the day was nowhere near enough, and so he lay in bed, eating what they gave him and using the dead for help, saving his strength but still melting away.

Near the end of November, the Nazis ordered every patient in the KZ Gusen I infirmary capable of walking to prepare to hike up to KZ Mauthausen, two-and-a-half miles up hill. The *Revier* was being closed.

'When I heard the SS walking through the *Revier* giving this order, I thought this was the end.' My father's voice was still strong, his story coming out exactly the way I remembered it from so many times before. I knew what was about to happen, and I knew it wasn't the end. But at that moment in 1944, my father truly thought it might be.

He assumed two things that day. First, that those who couldn't walk, those who were to remain behind, would be killed, and second, that those who went up to KZ Mauthausen would be sent to its small gas chamber, also to be killed. KZ Gusen I didn't have a gas chamber, so the move made perfect sense to him. He had battled so hard and overcome so much, but that day he resigned himself to what was coming.

Late that afternoon, shoulders drooped and hope gone, my father assembled outside the Gusen I *Revier* with 250 other patients. It was snowing, with already two inches on the ground and more coming down. The air temperature was dropping rapidly as night approached. Dad's breath came out as vapor. He was wearing prison pajamas and his Nazi-issued wooden shoes, insufficient for a cool summer evening, let alone this. He shivered uncontrollably, the cold passing through him like he was made of paper, which, in a way, he was by this point. He knew he would never make it all the way uphill to Mauthausen. Looking around at the others, he bet none of them would survive even a mile.

They began walking. Dad looked up at the path they were on. In the fading light and his dimming brain he doubted he'd reach the scraggly bushes 200 yards ahead. But he put one foot in front of the other, and kept thoughts of his mother's 'luxury way' in his future. Then, almost as soon as he'd started, the SS guards halted the column and huddled to converse among themselves.

'We had to stand there in the cold and the snow. I blew breaths on my chest, fffff, fffff.' Showing me how, he billowed his dress shirt with his hand, and making a big overbite, blew air down onto his chest. His tie was in the way, but I got the point. 'It made me feel a little warmer.'

A minute or two later, the SS men turned the column around. They didn't say why. They might have been cold, too. Or it could be they didn't feel like marching two-and-a-half miles uphill in the snow. They decided, instead, to put the prisoners in a small passenger wagon attached to the narrow-gauge train line linking the Kastenhof and Wiener-Graben quarries. So everyone tramped back in the direction they had come, to the narrow-gauge train terminus just outside Gusen I's walls.

'The train wagon could fit one hundred *KZlers*,' my father said. 'There was not enough room for me, so I figured I would have an extra night that I could live before I reached to the gas chamber in Mauthausen.'

My father and the remaining 150 prisoners were ordered into one of the camp's latrine barracks. The barracks had terrazzo floors, trough urinals and porcelain toilets at one end, sinks at the other, and enough room in between to fit a few hundred men at one time. They were unheated, but at least they offered protection from the snow and wind.

It was dinner time, and now the strangest thing happened. The SS men accompanying them ordered soup served to my father and the other infirmary *KZlers* in the latrine. That's not the strange part, soup was standard evening fare. The strange part was they were not served the usual ration. Instead, they were served all the soup they could consume. It was 'bottomless bowl' night in the KZ Gusen I latrine barracks.

'You wouldn't believe it,' my father said. 'I thought I was dreaming. But it was real. They were really serving us all the soup we wanted. I knew that it was the worst thing. It was very dangerous.'

'Why? Isn't that what you always wished for? One more chance to fill your stomach?'

'Jeckeleh, you can't go so many months or so many years not eating proper food and then suddenly fill yourself up with so much soup. It would kill you.'

'How do you know?'

'How do I know? I know.' A sharp nod emphasized he knew. 'Some of the other *KZlers* knew, too.'

My father didn't give me a reason for knowing it – it may have been instinct – but he was right. Human beings cannot go months, or in many cases years, being slowly starved into oblivion, and then consume unlimited quantities of food. The sudden flood of vital nutrients can send their bodies into shock, over-stimulating and shutting down their organs and stopping their hearts. My father had a couple of bowls and stopped. He felt full enough, and he said that was a marvelous feeling. He remembers nothing more. He had fallen deeply asleep on the icy tiled floor, and stayed that way until morning. While slowly sipping his soup, and before nodding off, he had watched others gulp down four or five helpings.

The next morning, more than a hundred of the prisoners in the latrine barracks with him were dead. Two-thirds of the men who had gotten what they had probably dreamt of for years – all the soup they wanted – who then fell asleep on the cold, hard latrine floor had died. My father guessed some had died of exposure, the barracks was that frigid. But most, he thinks, died from whatever one dies from after eating too much.

'It was really sad, Jeckeleh,' he said. 'I had friends there. Not such good friends, but I became friends with some of them. We talked all the time, we used to say "just let me have a full stomach one more time, and I can die happy." And then they did!' My father chuckled again.

I know now the chuckle was my father's unique was of accepting just how gruesome it was that one hundred prisoners were killed by being allowed to eat all they wanted. It was also his way of accepting that he'd dodged yet another bullet. No matter how he knew not to eat too much, the willpower it must have taken him to be offered more and to *refuse* it, is staggering to contemplate. It was that *Will* again.

Concentration camp historians see my father's soup story not as Nazi largesse gone bad. They see it as murder, no different than the gas chambers, perhaps a sixty-third way to kill *KZlers*. The Nazis knew most of the *Revier* prisoners that night would not have the self-control to limit their food intake, and they knew too much food would kill them. They didn't *let* it happen, they *made* it happen.

After waking, true to their word the SS guards put my father and the fifty living infirmary patients on the narrow-gauge train on its morning run up to KZ Mauthausen's Wiener-Graben quarry. Once there, unlike my father's worst fears, they were not sent to the gas chamber. Instead, after hiking up the Stairs of Death to get from the quarry to the main camp, they were sent first to Mauthausen's showers, the same showers that ran hot and cold water in my father's introduction to the camp on June 13, 1944. This time the water was merely cold. Then they were moved to what my father inaccurately called – and I will continue to call – the KZ Mauthausen *Revier*, the sprawling collection of barracks in the field below the concentration camp's south wall first known as *Russenlager*, and now known as *Sanitätslager*, the grass field I stood over years later, Angelika by my side.

Chapter 42

Westwall, 359 Miles Away

Patton wasn't happy idling while other Allied generals in the European Theater of Operation drove their men forward, but between Eisenhower's orders and the lack of gasoline, he had no choice. Ill-suited to a defensive role, the General did the next best thing. He ordered his troops to 'patrol aggressively,' a tactic enabling them to slowly take new territory adjacent to their forward positions.

The speed of Third Army's advance across France meant pockets of German troops had been left behind. So while some of Patton's soldiers inched Third Army's lines forward, others spent October and November 1944 clearing their rear of Nazis. In several bypassed towns, German resistance was especially tenacious. The fortress town of Metz, for instance, now well inside Patton's lines, was not completely secured until November 22, after weeks of very difficult combat that cost the lives of many of Patton's finest troops.

Also in November, the gasoline situation began improving sufficiently to enable Patton to focus his attention on the German border, thirty miles to his east. More important than the border itself was the Saar River, five miles inside Germany. Patton was zeroing in on the Saar for two reasons. First, it was a significant natural barrier near the French-German border that his soldiers would have to cross. Second, the river was only a few miles west of *Westwall*, Germany's main line of defensive fortresses, pillboxes, and anti-tank obstacles facing France, Luxembourg, Belgium, and the Netherlands. Once past the Saar River, *Westwall* would have to be pierced.

Though it looks like an English word, *Westwall* is German, meaning 'western defensive wall.' It stretched for 390 miles, starting south of Patton's positions, and running north all the way to the Netherlands. Allied planners believed penetrating *Westwall* would be the toughest part of their advance into Germany. Getting past it was expected to be so difficult, it had compelled Montgomery to conceive of – and Eisenhower to approve of – the ill-fated Market-Garden assault that, if successful, would have taken Allied soldiers around the northern end of *Westwall*.

Typically, Patton saw the battlefield picture differently. Displaying the confidence in his troops that gave Third Army such *esprit-de-corps*, he saw no reason his soldiers couldn't punch their way through the section of *Westwall* right in front of them. He'd said as much when Field Marshal Montgomery was arguing for Market-Garden. To put his divisions in position for that major thrust, Patton's troops spent the late fall of 1944 fighting their way over the German border, and establishing small bridgeheads across the Saar River near the town of Saarlouise.

By the middle of December 1944, Patton's forces were gassed up, armed, fitted, rested, and in position to assault *Westwall*. They were 359 miles from Enns, Austria. On December 19, they would launch an attack propelling them deep into the heart of Germany, and within striking distance of Enns.

Hitler, however, had other plans.

Chapter 43

Back in KZ Mauthausen

My father spent three months, most of the winter of 1944–45, in the KZ Mauthausen *Revier*. I don't know what diagnosis kept him there so long. I know that besides being severely underweight, he suffered from boils that had appeared mostly on his arms. They were common among prisoners, were painful and debilitating, and needed to be treated. In a fully-equipped infirmary, that would have meant lancing them with a sterile knife, ice or some other numbing agent to minimize the pain, and bandages to prevent infection. The KZ Mauthausen *Revier* had none of those things.

'They had to cut them down,' my father explained to me at the Seder, 'and I said it's OK, you do what you have to.' Dad bore, without anesthetic or antibiotic, whatever the doctors did to treat his boils. It could not have been fun. Eventually, he said, they went away.

'And once they healed, they let you stay in the *Revier*?'

'Yes. The boils took a few weeks till they were better, then I had dysentery. And I had a bed. They didn't need the bed so nobody complained.'

I've often wondered about the winter my father spent in the *Revier*. It seemed to me a long time to be allowed to stay there. The boils and dysentery needed a month or so, but then I would have expected him to have been ordered back to KZ Gusen I or KZ Mauthausen and put into a work *kommando*. Or else taken out through a selection and killed. Yet he remained in an infirmary bed, not working, not being selected, just existing.

Maybe my father had worse things than boils and dysentery and he didn't remember. Or maybe he remembered but he didn't want to tell me. Now that I know how much he'd held back in his story, this possibility was very real. At the end of the war he was diagnosed with typhus, pneumonia, and tuberculosis. Maybe he was fighting all three by then, and the doctors allowed him to stay. Maybe he was so close to death that it was pointless to send him out to the work *kommandos*, though in that case, he should have been selected and killed. Maybe no one kept track of him. Maybe, like he suggested, no one cared that he was occupying a bed. Maybe, because of his youth, some doctor was looking out for him, protecting him.

Another reason I've come across is that, as KZ Mauthausen's prisoners were mostly non-Jews, there was resistance among the *kapos* and *KZlers* to 'polluting' the camp's prison population with Jews. It's a reminder that European anti-Semitism was not exclusively a Nazi trait in those years. By this theory, the camp's Nazi overseers were content leaving the Jews in the *Revier*. They weren't using up much food, they weren't taking up space in the camp, so they were left alone. But then, if it was so easy to kill six million Jews, why keep a few around in the KZ Mauthausen *Sanitätslager*?

Whatever the reason, spending the harsh Austrian winter in the infirmary is certainly the only reason my father was still alive.

My father never told any stories of that winter in the KZ Mauthausen *Revier*, not at our 2001 Seder, nor before. Well, he once told me one story. It was about the lines to use the *Revier's* bathrooms in the morning: short lines to urinate in troughs, and long lines to defecate. When my father had dysentery, some mornings he couldn't wait to go. So he would use the urinal latrine for both needs, by turning around. The story goes on, but this is one anecdote I'm not going to pass along in any further detail.

In early March 1945, SS troopers came into the *Revier*, telling the patients that anyone who wanted to go to the main KZ Mauthausen camp, inside the granite walls, would be permitted to go.

'I didn't believe them,' my father said. 'Since when did those SS offer the *KZlers* anything? They did selections all the time, they murdered us like they would cut their fingernails, and now we were being offered something without giving to them back anything in return?'

Yet my father said the SS soldiers insisted this wasn't a trick. 'They promised us they weren't going to gas us.'

My father volunteered because his streak was still intact. And besides, maybe this was a repeat of the Gusen I *Revier* clean-out? It turned out to be exactly that. Those who volunteered – my father didn't say how many were with him – were given new prison clothes and lined up outside the infirmary's barracks. Then together they marched up the granite stairs to KZ Mauthausen. Everyone was assigned a barracks and a bed, but not a work *kommando*.

The streak continued.

Chapter 44

The Bulge: 300 Miles Away

On the cloudy, freezing cold morning of December 16, 1944, Adolf Hitler hurled nearly half a million troops against Allied forward positions in Belgium and Luxembourg. It was the bulk of his armed forces in the west. It was the biggest gamble he'd taken in the war, an all-or-nothing shot, and it had to succeed. If this attack failed, he'd have exhausted his reserves of soldiers and tanks, depleted his army's ammunition stocks, and made losing the war inevitable.

The powerful Nazi assault drove into American forces at a weak point of their defenses. Taken completely by surprise, the Americans reeled. Within a week, Hitler's army had driven fifty miles westward into the heart of Allied positions. On a map, it looked like a bulge digging into the Allied lines, hence the German assault and Allied counterattack is now called, 'The Battle of the Bulge.'

The Nazi attack was a surprise to everyone except General Patton. A few days before it began, Patton's intelligence men detected unusual military activity across the border far north of their positions. Correctly concerned, the General warned his fellow British and American army commanders in those sectors an assault might be imminent, and made contingency plans to race to the rescue, if the need should arise. His warnings were ignored, but his intelligence was accurate, and the need did arise. So when Patton got the call for help on December 16, he was ready.

In what is lauded as one of the most exceptional feats in Patton's unparalleled career, in a 48-hour span he reoriented two infantry divisions and an armored division – more than 40,000 men and hundreds of tanks – from facing Germany to the east, to facing Belgium to the north. Then he sent them charging 100 miles north to slam into the left side of Germany's assault formations on December 18. Patton's troopers soon penetrated German lines and, one week later, broke the siege that famously entrapped American soldiers and paratroopers in Bastogne, Belgium. Patton's brilliant and difficult maneuver was a major reason, though not the only reason, Hitler's gamble failed, and by January 28, 1945, the Wehrmacht was back inside Germany, beaten and now mortally weakened.

Six days before the Battle of the Bulge ended, the 65th Infantry Division landed by troopship in Le Havre, France, having finally completed their state-side training. Seven weeks later, on March 9, 1945, the division was established on the front lines in Saarlouis, Germany, alongside the Saar River. They were ready to join Patton's next major advance.

That advance began the next day, the 65th Infantry jumping off from their positions around the Saar and joining other Third Army divisions already engaged in a thrust against *Westwall*. Ten days later, the German fortifications were breached, and Patton's war machine moved rapidly through wide-open countryside, precisely like the countryside I drove through after landing in Munich. By March 29, the 65th Infantry Division was in Oppenheim, Germany, where its troopers crossed the Rhine River.

They were 300 miles from Enns.

Chapter 45

Recharge

Leaving the *Jourhaus*, I suddenly feel drained. I am emotionally spent. The trip has caught up with me. It is barely late afternoon, but I'd only slept a couple of hours on the flight the night before. Anticipating this, Angelika had not planned for anything else today and now I'm relieved she's had the foresight to stop here.

I need to catch my breath. I've been to where my father had worked as a *KZler*, where he'd been beaten, where he'd dug down into reserves of strength and resilience that were deeper than I had ever realized, deeper than I could imagine, maybe deeper than I possessed.

And I still have tomorrow ahead of me.

I need to recharge, because I have not yet done what I consider more important than visiting the concentration camps. I want to find the *exact* spots where my father escaped both times, and I want to go to the Friedmanns' house, walk its grounds, and learn its secrets about my father. I want to be ready for this, because it will be the most personal part of this journey.

Until now Angelika and I had been to places where my father had been alongside many thousands of others: philosophers, writers, politicians, gays, criminals, gypsies, communists, soldiers, the completely innocent, the totally guilty, Jews and non-Jews. My father had been in that mix, in with these people, and his story was also their story.

But that's not true of what is about to come. The story of escape, recapture and escape again is my father's story alone. What happened to him, what he pulled off, he did completely on his own, because of the force of *his* Will, because of the power of *his* desire to be free, because of *his* drive to live. Because for him, 'living beat the alternative.' I want to be ready to fully absorb what I will see next.

Angelika and I agree she will pick me up at my hotel at 11am tomorrow, after she and her family attend church, and we will use only her car. Then I point my rental towards the Hotel Romer. A few minutes later I pull into its short driveway with the sun sliding down past the hills behind me. It looks exactly as I expected: small, neat, modern. I check in and as I enter my room, I can hardly keep my eyes open. I steal a nap.

Waking a short time later, I ask the young woman behind the front desk where I might get dinner. She directs me to the Enns town square, a five minute drive. Besides food, I know from my father's story that the square houses the local police station, which played an important role in his first escape.

Night has fully engulfed Enns as I park in a space near the ancient belfry. The square is well lit by floodlights and the glow of shop windows and restaurants in its perimeter. It's larger than I'd expected for such a small town. Looking around, I don't spot a police station. Walking around the centrally-situated belfry's perimeter, I gain a clear view of every structure lining the square, but I see no sign saying POLICE, or anything close. Maybe it is, or used to be, one of the buildings with no sign at all. A bit disappointed, I resolve to wait till tomorrow, when Angelika and I will be here together.

Though I don't find the police station, I do spot an Italian restaurant that looks inviting. With the diners inside chatting loudly, I opt for quiet and take a table outdoors under a heat lamp. I sit down to eat and to write my thoughts on my laptop while they are fresh.

Tapping out the details of the afternoon, I find myself returning to a question that's been hanging over me all day. I deeply wonder if I could have survived what my father had survived, if I have what he had, if I have that *Will*. It was a question I never overtly asked myself before, though I now feel I've been asking it my entire life without being aware of it. Maybe ever since those schoolyard fights, I have been driving myself as if *subconsciously* that question is present within me.

I wanted to be an Air Force fighter pilot since my very earliest memories. That dream ended in sixth grade when my left eye became nearsighted. Lasix hadn't been invented yet, so my imperfect eyesight disqualified me from military flying. Instead, I decided after graduating high school I'd join the Army, but my father asked me not to. He said that after the losses he'd lived through in his lifetime, he wouldn't be able to handle losing one of his sons, as well. I assume he'd have given me the same line about the Air Force if my eyesight hadn't deteriorated. His argument was impossible to refute, so I went to Columbia University. As an engineering student I carried a large class load and pulled all-nighters, but nothing in college came remotely close to my father's experience in the war.

After graduating, while building a career and raising a family, I found time for a few pursuits, all of which I still do. My obsession with airplanes led me to obtaining a pilot's license and flying aerobatics planes. I earned a second-degree black belt in Goju Ryu, a strict Okinawan form of karate, and have taught it. I cycle long distances. I play ice hockey regularly. I ski, preferring steep runs on cold, snowy days. I play tennis at a competitive club level. I've run five marathons and a few halfs, though arthritis in my knees has forced me to stop going so far.

During my first marathon I tore my left calf muscle twenty-two miles in, with four miles to go. Limping and in pain, as other runners passed me I started thinking that, if my emaciated father could survive a death march in wooden shoes and in the condition he was in, I should be able to run a measly few miles in my new Asics sneakers, with carbohydrate blocs in my pockets but a small muscle tear in my calf. So I resumed running, channeling my father every painful step, all the way to the finish line. Like many first-time marathoners, I cried when I finished. But this cry came from deep in my soul. I had felt my dad running with me, stride for stride that rainy morning. I missed him terribly that day.

Until now, if you asked me why I do the things I do, I would have told you it's because I love doing them. And that's true. Each of them brings me real joy. But there's something more going on, something the torn calf in the marathon hints at. I finally see it while eating dinner and reviewing my afternoon in Austria.

These things I do are, for me, a continuous series of tests: a test to fly each flight better than the last, a test to master a difficult new martial arts technique, a test to see how far and fast I can cycle, to get to the puck before the other skater, to ski a tougher run, to stay in the tennis match even though I know my opponent is better, to run on a torn muscle. I probably subconsciously think these tests somehow relate to my father's survival. Maybe my inner self thinks that if I can do these things, if I can pass these tests, I will be able to lay claim to having some of my father's *Will*, some of his extraordinary toughness and drive to live, some of the incredible survival instincts he displayed that year. It would be nice to believe I have some of that.

Why do I want to be like him? Why do I need to prove I have the same *Will* and drive? Well, I'm his son. I'd like to know I can achieve what he achieved, survive what he survived, be as tough, as capable, as resourceful as he was. It's pretty basic, and maybe even hard-wired in humans. Or at least in me. Children want to be seen as *adults* in their parent's eyes, adults of equal stature. If they can attain that, if they can be recognized by their mothers and fathers as equals, then they're ready to assume their respective adult roles, to carry on where their parents left off. The best way to be seen as an equal is to match their parents' accomplishments. Maybe even surpass them.

I just want to know I can do what my father did.

But after today, after seeing firsthand some of what my father's year in KZ Mauthausen and KZ Gusen was really all about, I know such thoughts are sheer lunacy. These things I enjoy doing, these tests of mine, however physically demanding, don't answer that question. It's not even close. Even if I climb Mt. Everest or run the 135 mile Death Valley Ultramarathon, I won't come close. They may prove I have determination, or a desire and willingness to push myself extraordinarily hard, but that's it. Do I have the same *Will* as my father? I don't know. Could I have survived what he survived? I have no idea. And unless I'm faced with precisely the same tests my father faced down and defeated, replete with murderous SS troopers and maniacal *kapos*, I will never know.

What about my children? Do Sam, Rachel and Lauren think they need to master the same pursuits I enjoy so much in order to feel like worthy adults, in order to feel accepted in my eyes? Have I inadvertently given them high hurdles of their own to surmount? I hope not.

Does my son feel less a man when he considers all the things I do? Not only do I hope not, I hope it's the opposite. My son triumphs every day over no less adversity than his *saba* beat, adversity that may be different in many ways, but is identical in so many others. My father knew that about Sam. He never said as much, but I could tell by how they behaved with each other. They were kindred spirits. They had a common bond.

Do my daughters feel less worthy of my love because they aren't tennis pros, or pilots, or martial arts instructors? Once again, I hope not. They know their genetic make-up, they know where they came from. Plus I've shown them all the love and support I can, without condition and without judgment. At least, I think I have.

One thing I *do* know, one thing that has become crystal clear since my conversation with my cousin Vivi, is that my father avoided talking about the worst of his experiences in his story. This was hammered home to me the moment I saw Kastenhof's monstrous granite wall. My father kept his story far away from the grittiest details. Instead, he smiled and chuckled and spoke glibly about the things he went through. He never said how brutally miserable it must have been pushing fully-loaded mine wagons back and forth over the same ground, day after day, in every kind of weather. He made light of chatting up dead men so he could grab their unneeded morning bread rations. He joked when telling of eating pebbles that would enable him to feel full, though they could have killed him. He laughed about cleaning a barrel's worth of shit off the ground with his hands.

As I type my impressions of the afternoon, I still am not sure why he danced around the details, why he kept his story light and on the surface. Nor, for that matter, am I sure why I never asked more probing questions, never drew out of him more detail. I am beginning to assemble reasons for both, but I need to keep pondering this.

I suddenly remember something special about my father.

There is, I realize, one thing I might be able to emulate about him, a test, of sorts, I might be able to pass every day. At his funeral, besides all his friends that I'd expected to come, there was a group of mourners I didn't know. They were people who lived near my father's home in Long Beach. Every day, weather permitting, he walked the two miles of the Long Beach boardwalk. On the walks he would encounter people outside their homes, or on the boardwalk, and he'd stop to chat. Over the years he'd gotten to know many of these people quite well, and a dozen of them came to the chapel that day.

After the funeral service, they told my brother and me they'd come because our father was the nicest guy they had ever met. They had looked forward to his conversations, and now missed him greatly. Here was a man who'd survived the worst that humans could dish out, and his response was to be cheerful and engaging every single day. He made people feel they were worth knowing, and their stories worth hearing.

This, I figured, I could do. Or try to do. I generally think of myself as nice, but if I'm being truly honest, I'm not always. My fuse is shorter than it needs to be (why do I need a fuse at all, I wonder), and I don't always treat people with the respect they deserve. As I finish my dinner, I decide that by always being nice, by always being considerate and respectful, I can, perhaps, come close to equaling that particular accomplishment of my father.

I'm going to try.

PART III
ENNS

Chapter 46

Inbound 'Transports'

Throughout March 1945 my father watched, from his new vantage point as a prisoner in KZ Mauthausen, as thousands of Jews poured into the camp. Some were emaciated, like himself, while others appeared much fitter. Many wore standard concentration camp uniforms, but some, mostly those in better physical condition, wore civilian clothes. These new prisoners were arriving by 'transports,' that German/English word my father used often when referring to any movement of prisoners from one place to another. For these newly-arrived Jews, 'transports' meant marches, walking until either they arrived at Mauthausen, or they died: death marches.

These Jews had been death-marched to KZ Mauthausen from as far as a hundred miles away. The withered marchers in prison garb were coming from other concentration camps near the front lines, while the stronger men in civilian clothes were coming from Hungarian Labor Service battalions that were in the path of the approaching Russian army in Hungary and Czechoslovakia. Izsak Mozes' brother, Chaim, who had helped my father on his first death march, was in this latter group.

At this late stage of the war, the Allied armies were converging on Austria and the geographic heart of Nazi Germany. The Russians were closing in from the north and east, while the Americans and British were approaching from the west. The Nazis knew by now they had no chance to prevail, and equally no chance to negotiate a peace. They became desperate to keep the Jews under their control away from the Allied armies, or, failing that, to murder every one of them. No Jews could remain alive to testify to the Final Solution. The witnesses had to be kept from telling Germany's conquerors what they knew.

Force-marching Jews around the Third Reich was not a new concept in 1945. Death marches had been used throughout the war to move Jews from camp to camp, but they became prevalent as the Russians drove through Poland in late 1944 and early 1945 and captured Auschwitz, Treblinka, and other concentration camps, and uncovered the unspeakable atrocities that had taken place there. The populations of hundreds of European towns witnessed long lines of gaunt, starved Jews trudging through their streets bound for camps – as Vivi said to me that morning in 2007 – thirty, forty, even a hundred miles away. Their roadsides were littered with the bodies of those who didn't go the distance, who succumbed or were murdered along the way.

There is some slight controversy about whether the Nazis really intended to kill large numbers of Jews on these death marches. *Slight* because it is irrefutable that Jews who couldn't keep up with the marches were killed. It is equally irrefutable that many Jews on these marches were slaughtered outright, regardless of their ability to keep pace. But written orders from high-ranking SS officers were found after the war specifically requiring the marches to be conducted in an 'orderly' manner, and the Jews on these marches to be treated 'as decently as possible.' The quoted words, taken directly from the orders, were never elaborated upon. It's not known if these orders were given to all the SS officers and troopers organizing and guarding the marches, to only some of them, or if the orders were only written as a ploy and never distributed, written to protect their authors from prosecution after the war, enabling them to show concrete proof of their humane side.

To me, the narrow truth about these orders isn't important. Instead, what I care about is what actually happened. Not a shred of humanity was shown to the Jews on these marches by their Nazi guards. The accompanying soldiers routinely made it their mission to kill as many of the Jews under their charge as they could. Prisoners died every yard of every trek. If they couldn't keep up, they were killed. If they went to the side of the road, they were killed. If they fell, they would either be trampled on by fellow marchers and killed, or killed by SS guards. There are stories of able-bodied marchers being herded off the routes and killed in nearby fields. My father and other death march survivors had no doubt: the singular aim of these marches was murder. The orders found after the war are not relevant to me, and they definitely weren't relevant to my father and his fellow Jews as they marched and died.

KZ Mauthausen's south wall today. The gate to the right of the center of the picture is not the main gate. This entrance leads to an enclosed garage area for cars and trucks. In the foreground is a swimming pool, built by prisoners for use by the guards. (Author)

Looking through KZ Mauthausen's main gate to the *Appellplatz* (assembly area) as it appears today. The three surviving barracks are on the left. Camp administration buildings are on the right. (Author)

The Bungar Forest, which served as the ghetto for the Jews of Dej, as it looks today. The wooden planking is part of the memorial created in memory of those who were there. (Author)

The KZ Mauthausen shower room, in a recent photo. The overhead piping holds eighty showerheads. (Author)

The fields below KZ Mauthausen's south wall. The nearest one, marked out in granite, was a playing field used by Nazi personnel when not on duty. To its right is the *Russenlager* (Russian Camp), later called the *Sanitätslager* (Sanitary Camp). It was filled with barracks during the war. (Author)

The Wiener Graben granite quarry, from the top of the Stairs of Death. The tourists in the base of the quarry are standing on grass, which was not there during the war. KZ Mauthausen's main camp is above the granite rock face on the left. (Author)

Looking west into KZ Gusen I, showing the eastern camp wall, the *Appellplatz*, and a few barracks. The *Jourhaus* is at far left. The original image is undated.

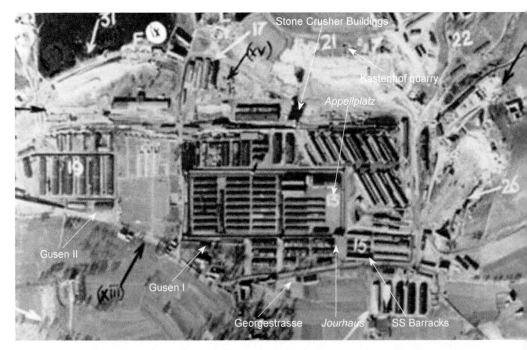

An Allied aerial reconnaissance photograph of KZ Gusen I and Gusen II, taken in 1945. The two SS barracks (to the right of the white '15') still exist today.

The stone crusher complex in the Kastenhof quarry. This undated image was taken soon after the war ended, before the complex was partially destroyed.

All that remains today of the stone crusher complex: the storage chambers ('shoebox on its side') and the destination for the mine wagons. (Author)

The front of the *Jourhaus* as it looked during the war. (Bundesarchiv, Bild 192-171/
CC-BY-SA 3.0)

The front of the *Jourhaus* as it looked the day I knocked on the front door. (Author)

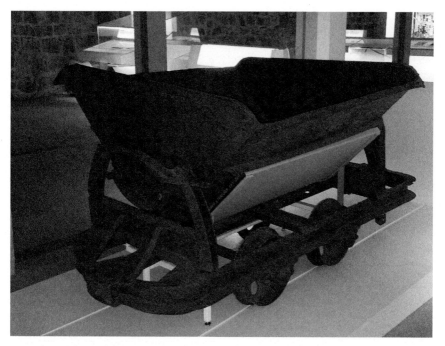

A mine wagon of the sort my father loaded and unloaded while working in KZ Gusen's Kastenhof granite quarry. This was photographed in Mauthausen's museum. (Author)

Looking north at the face of KZ Gusen's Kastenhof granite quarry, in a recent photo. The stone crusher complex is two hundred yards to the left of the photographer. (Author)

The intersection where my father escaped the first time, as it appears today. The view looks north, up *Weiner Strasse,* from the intersection's south side – what a refugee would have seen while waiting for the 'death march' marchers to pass (they would have passed from right to left). The refugee route was up this street towards the blue building. (Author)

The same intersection, looking west. Refugees were coming from the left, heading to the right. This is the view my father would have had as he stepped into the intersection. (Author)

The corner building of the Enns town square that housed the Gendarmerie outpost in April 1945. The curved door frame (under the backwards blue *Volksbank* flag) is where, according to Dietmar Heck, the symbol of the *Orpo* was positioned during the war. (Author)

The Friedmann home seen from *Kristein Strasse*. (Author)

The exact spot where my father escaped the second time, as it looked when I discovered it. During the war, the cement wall to the right was a barbed wire barrier. The path my father ran down is barely discernable directly ahead. (Author)

The "attic in their barn," as my father called one of his hiding places, the afternoon I saw it. No doubt it looked very different in the spring of 1945, when my father spent one week hiding here. (Author)

The barn my father would have encountered if he had turned *left* at the Y-intersection after leaving the Friedmann house. (Author)

The exact location of my father's second escape, as it appeared when I visited. This is the view looking north across *Doktor Renner Strasse*, formerly the B1 Motorway. The pile of dirt between the bridge railing and the cement wall was from recent nearby road construction. During the war, instead of the cement wall a barbed wire fence ran from where this wall ends to the right. The yellow structure behind the brush and trees is on the far side of the *Kristeinerbach* stream. (Author)

The 4×4 track my father had taken on Saturday night, April 21, 1945, when he got lost. This view looks back along the track, in the direction he had come from after turning right at the Y-intersection. Farm fields are to the right. The trees directly ahead, bracketing the track, cantilever overhead. The trees to the left mark the near bank of the *Kristeinerbach* stream. The grass between the trees ahead and the trees to the left is the triangle-shaped grass field. (Author)

This photo was taken ten feet to the right of the photograph above, at the edge of farm fields. The track is visible, pointing back towards the Y-intersection. The tall trees to the left border the *Kristeinerbach* stream. Most of the triangle-shaped grass field is blocked from view. One can easily imagine this view at night, with the trees bordering the track blending in with the trees along the stream, creating the illusion of a single long wall of vegetation. (Author)

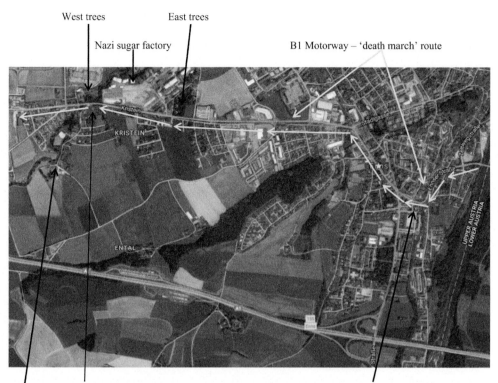

West trees   East trees

Nazi sugar factory   B1 Motorway – 'death march' route

Kristein Strasse–B1 intersection
(second escape)

Ennser Strasse–Steyrer Strasse
intersection (first escape)

Y intersection, just south of the Friedmann home

A Google Earth view of Enns, Austria, showing the B1 'death march' route, and the trees before (east) and after (west) the sugar factory. The photo also shows the Y intersection, the Friedmann home, and the two locations where my father escaped. (Courtesy of Google Earth)

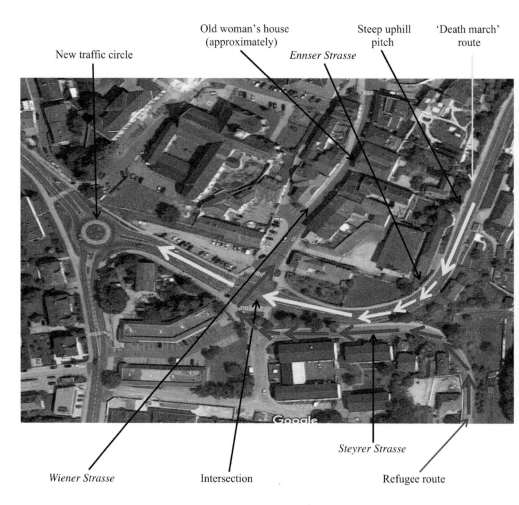

New traffic circle

Old woman's house
(approximately)

Ennser Strasse

Steep uphill
pitch

'Death march'
route

Wiener Strasse

Intersection

Steyrer Strasse

Refugee route

A Google Earth close-up of the *Ennser Strasse–Steyrer Strasse* intersection, the location
of my father's first escape. (Courtesy of Google Earth)

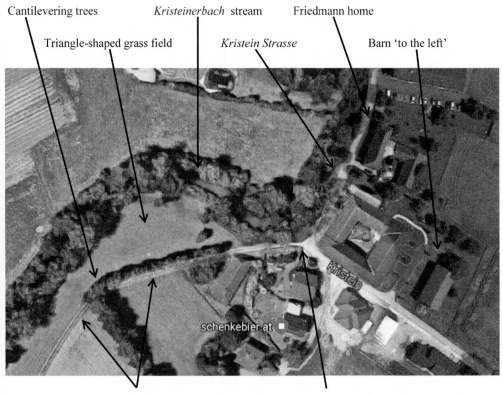

Cantilevering trees   *Kristeinerbach* stream   Friedmann home

Triangle-shaped grass field   *Kristein Strasse*   Barn 'to the left'

4x4 track   Y-intersection

A Google Earth close-up of the Friedmann home and the area where my father got lost. (Courtesy of Google Earth)

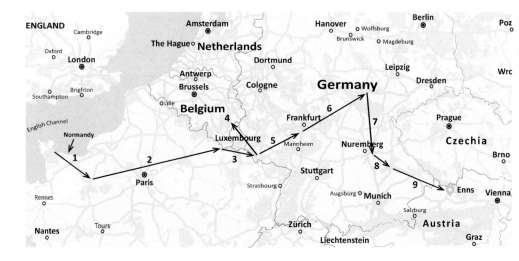

General George S. Patton's Third Army route through Europe, beginning August 1, 1944. It is clear Patton was pointed directly at Berlin until he was ordered to divert in mid-April 1945, to race to the Enns River.

Number Key

1. August 1 – August 21, 1944: Third Army lands in Europe and fights its way to Chambois, France, closing the Falaise Pocket. The army is 658 miles from Enns, Austria.

2. August 31, 1944: Third Army passes Verdun, France, 420 miles from Enns.

3. September 25, 1944: Low on gas, Third Army has bypassed Metz and halts 384 miles from Enns.

4. December 16, 1944: Patton diverts infantry and armored divisions to Belgium in response to Hitler's attack now known as the Battle of the Bulge. Meanwhile other Third Army troops advance across the Saar River to Saarlouise, Germany, 359 miles from Enns.

5. March 9 – March 29, 1945: The 65th Infantry Division joins Third Army in Saarlouise, goes into action the next day, and reaches Oppenheim, Germany, 300 miles from Enns on March 29.

6. April 16, 1945: The 261st Regiment of the 65th Infantry Division reaches Arnstadt, Germany, 241 miles from Enns.

7. April 21, 1945: The 261st Regiment attains Neumarkt, Germany, 156 miles from Enns.

8. April 28, 1945: The 261st has crossed the Danube River and captures Bad Abbach, Germany. It is now 121 miles from Enns.

9. May 5, 1945: The 261st captures Linz, Austria. It is 11 miles from the Friedmann home.

Some in the upper levels of the Nazi hierarchy were toying with a back-up plan, in case they failed to kill every Jew. The plan was to use the Jews as ransom. These Nazis hoped that if enough Jews survived the death marches, their lives could be traded for the Nazis' safe passage to whichever country might take them in. There is, obviously, outlandish irony there. Nazis doctrine was absolute, that Jews were worthless. But in this macabre calculus, the Jews were only worthless unless they could be traded for Nazis. Then they were invaluable. This back-up plan never became a reality.

In March 1945, the Nazis made KZ Mauthausen the central gathering point for Jews in concentration camps or labor battalions near North-central Austria. Mauthausen Memorial's historians believe the influx totaled at least 15,000 Jews, a staggering number considering that the concentration camp was always filled to capacity. And the total may have been many more. Typical German record-keeping accuracy was superseded by the urgent need to move Jews away from the front lines, and so how many marched to KZ Mauthausen, and from where, are now not known for sure. What my father did know for sure is, the additional Jews in the camp made it unbearably overcrowded.

To alleviate the congestion, wooden barracks were built on KZ Mauthausen's eastern side, separated from the main camp by a granite wall. It was called Camp Three, and was inhabited mostly by Jews. Its presence gives credence to the theory that my father was allowed to spend the winter in the *Revier* because no one wanted Jewish *KZlers* within the walls of the main camp – Camp Three hadn't been built yet.

When that still wasn't enough, a tent camp, the *Zeltlager*, was hastily constructed on KZ Mauthausen's northern side. Packed with prisoners and without proper sanitation facilities, conditions there were much worse than in the main camp or Camp Three. My father's name appears in a logbook in 1945 indicating he was assigned to the *Zeltlager*. The logs were sometimes wrong, and Angelika is certain my father had never been in this camp. She believes conditions there were so abysmal that my father would have spoken about it at some point. He could not have avoided it, she believes.

I think it's the opposite. I think my father absolutely avoided talking about it. I think he was precisely where the logs said he was – in the filth of the Tent Camp. And he never once spoke about it. It's yet another example of my father omitting parts of his story, editing them so that I would not know what he endured, what he survived.

In early April 1945, with KZ Mauthausen's resources stretched far beyond its limit and the Allies closing in, the Nazis initiated an operation to empty the camp of its Jews. Over a period of weeks, in groups of 500 to 1,000 Jews each day, they would be marched south and west, deep into the Austrian interior. Preferably, most would die along the way.

For my father, that was an opportunity, though he didn't know it at the time.

Chapter 47

First Escape

My father had finished another glass of club soda. Now his expression became almost whimsical and his mood lightened noticeably. We both knew what was coming.

'It was sometime in the first week of April, 1945,' he began. 'I was selected along with maybe a thousand other *KZlers* to be on a "transport." They told us we were going to Gunskirchen.'[1]

KZ Gunskirchen, near the Austrian town of the same name, was thirty-four miles southwest of Mauthausen. It eventually held more than 20,000 Jews during the last few weeks of the war, death-marched there from KZ Mauthausen and other camps near Russian and American army front lines. The camp was a true nightmare. Wildly overcrowded, it had no running water, very little food, and not nearly enough shelter for so many people. Besides the thousands who died marching to the camp, 3,000 more died of starvation and disease while waiting within its barbed wire for the Americans, who liberated it on May 5, 1945. A thousand more, too far gone to be helped, died *after* the Americans took control.

My father, to me. 'I met my friend Mozes Izsak again, in Mauthausen.[2] I left him behind in the barracks in Gusen I when the *Blockältester* sent me to the *Revier*, but the SS brought him up to the main camp, I don't know when, and he was selected for this "transport," too. Also his brother, Chaim was with us.' My father's face brightened at the mention of Chaim.

---

1 Either because of poor record-keeping, or because records were destroyed, the date of this march is not known.

2 Even forty-seven years after learning English from my mother, my father often reversed the full names of his friends, a Hungarian-language custom (also a custom in other parts of Europe and much of Asia).

Chaim had arrived a few days earlier on a death march with his Hungarian Labor Service battalion, and was by far in the best physical shape of the three of them. My father was the weakest.

'You wouldn't believe it,' my father went on, 'When we left the camp, just when we passed the gate, they gave every *KZler* a roll of bread and margarine. A whole roll and margarine!' He clapped his hands for a second time that evening. 'I was so happy.'

The schizophrenic Nazi behavior, of wanting to kill the Jews but providing them food for the march, might have been the result of those orders by senior SS officers requiring Jews on the marches to be treated 'as decently as possible.' Or maybe not. While Dad was devouring his supersized ration of bread and margarine, he wasn't expending an ounce of energy wondering why they'd given it to him.

Eating as they marched, my father and the others descended the hill towards the Danube. Three miles later, they crossed the river and the road became mostly flat.

'When we started, I felt good. Not *so so* good, but good enough. The roll and margarine helped. But then I had trouble. I couldn't walk so well. Chaim took my elbow,' my father grabbed one of his elbows with the other hand, 'and he helped me along like this. Then when that wasn't enough he put his arm under my arm and we walked this way. But it wasn't any good. I couldn't go any further.' My father's whole body sagged in his armchair.

He implored Chaim to tend to his brother instead. He slipped out of the stronger man's grasp.

Dragging himself weakly, he made it to the side of the road. To go to the side of the road meant death. It was a firm rule of the 'transports.' He sat down on a boulder, took off his wooden shoes, and waited to die. An SS trooper guarding the march spotted him sitting, and walked towards him, his pistol ready. The Nazi seemed to study my father as he approached.

'We looked right at each other. I looked right at his eyes. Then he looked at my shoes on the ground, then back to me, and I don't know what happened. He kept walking! He walked right past me! Jeckeleh, he didn't say not one word to me!'

The storm trooper had holstered his pistol and was walking on. My father was absolutely incredulous. It was supposed to be over for him. He was supposed to be dead. There were never exceptions to the ironclad rule of the march: if you sat down on the side of the road, you were declaring your intention to die. Yet once again, a rule seemingly didn't apply to my father. Once again, something went his way.

The shock of *not* being dead gave him a jolt that sprang him back onto his feet.

'For a few minutes, I felt strong again,' he said, clenching both his fists.

With his renewed energy, he pushed himself to move again. Not much further along, at the outskirts of the town of Enns, the route hit a short, steep incline, a couple of hundred yards from bottom to top. My father crested it, and that was the last of his new-found power. He'd given everything he'd had left to give. Only inertia kept his feet moving one ahead of the other. A few more yards, and he reached a major intersection. From his left, from the south, thousands of soldiers and refugees were flowing north, away from the town of Steyr and towards Enns. The Mauthausen *KZlers* were heading west, cutting across the intersection and in front of the desperate refugees.

SS guards accompanying the marchers had their hands full keeping the refugees from charging into the intersection while the *KZlers* were crossing. Boiling like lava in a volcano ready to blow, the mass of civilians and soldiers agitated while the Jews filed slowly past them. Finally, the SS halted the marchers immediately behind my father. He was the last one into the junction.

Inching across the long crossroads, step after ponderous step, he was simply too small and inconsequential for the refugees. Their scramble away from the fighting could not wait another second. They went, plunging into the intersection before my father could get through. In a second, he was drowning in a streaming lava flow of Austrian townspeople and German soldiers. Nearly panicked at first, with adrenalin flooding him his clarity suddenly became total. He could see his fellow marchers, and knew if he kept going, he would eventually reach them.

Or, if he turned quickly, he would be swept up and carried along with the refugees.

'I thought about it for just one second. Then I turned, and no one noticed.' My father's eyes shone brightly. 'I took a few steps and I was worried that I was wearing my prison clothes, but right in front of me was a raincoat on the ground. I picked it up and put it on.' Reaching down with his hand, he did it again, for me. 'It fit me exactly.'

You knew it would.

The Nazi troopers monitoring the march never saw my father's snap maneuver. He heard someone call his name, a fellow *KZler*, judging by the accent. He ignored it. He was not about to turn around. He didn't dare do anything but walk straight ahead.

185

My father's heart was booming in his chest. With his KZ Mauthausen prison uniform invisible beneath the raincoat, he blended in. Even his hair didn't give him away. The Nazis shaved a line down the middle of every Mauthausen prisoner's head, a reverse mohawk. But my father's head hadn't been shaved in weeks, and his hair had grown in enough so that the line in the center was no longer noticeable. He looked like any other refugee fleeing the fighting.

He was moving on some burst of energy that thirty seconds earlier hadn't existed, and now he could feel that energy waning quickly. He didn't have much stamina left. He took stock. The intersection was big and busy and had no houses facing it. Fields and structures on either side offered no doors to knock on. But he could see ahead that the street narrowed. Its walls bore the doors and windows of small homes behind them. He scooted to the side of the street and approached one of the doors.

'I wasn't sure what should I do. I was so tired and so hungry, I couldn't go much further, but it was very dangerous to knock.'

He had no idea who might be on the other side of the door. The person might be a lifelong Nazi and shoot him dead, or hold him until the SS came to kill him. Or the person might be sympathetic.

He knocked.

'An elderly woman with white hair opened the door. I spoke to her in German. I told her I was hungry and asked her if she would please give me something to eat. She looked at my raincoat and then she stepped back from the door, so I walked in.'

Letting him into her tidy home, she didn't ask him where he'd come from, and my father said he couldn't tell if she knew – or suspected – that he was from KZ Mauthausen. Businesslike, or perhaps just formal, she directed him to sit down. He didn't say where, whether he sat in the kitchen or the living room or somewhere else. She brought him a plate of cheese and noodles, then left him alone as he ate slowly, enjoying every bite.

'When I finished, I felt truly full for the first time in a very long time.' His face glowed. 'First there was the bread and the margarine, and now this little meal. I wasn't so full so I should be sick, but I was full enough. She told me I could wait in her little back yard. So I went back there and lied down on the grass. After a few minutes, maybe it was ten minutes, she came into the back yard. I could see she was nervous, and she said to me that I have to leave.'

Hearing the edge in her voice, my father assumed she suddenly comprehended the risk she'd taken by letting him in to her house. Maybe she'd spotted the Jewish star on his prison shirt peeking out from under the raincoat. Or perhaps his striped pants were enough to convince her she'd made a mistake. It could even be she feared a neighbor, or a refugee on the street, had seen her letting him in. She could be shot for it.

'I decided to wait just five more minutes. The grass felt so good. I hadn't had a chance to lie down on grass since the ghetto.'

It was five minutes too many. Two young SS troopers were patrolling on the street. They belonged to an SS company quartered in Enns. Flagging them down, the old woman brought them into her back yard. My father had no idea what she'd said to them.

The SS soldiers sprinted towards my father, rifles ready. He stood to face them. He was trapped. The worst possible outcome was playing out. Things were out of his control. He knew his future, if he had any, was up to these two unimpressive-looking kids with SS lightning bolts on their tunic collars and loaded weapons in their hands. But as he watched them approach, he was at peace.

'What were they going to do, kill me? I should have been dead a long time ago.'

Chapter 48

Eggs and Butter

The SS troopers were very young, my father guessed seventeen or eighteen, and they spoke Hungarian. Like the Ukrainian SS train guards on his train to KZ Mauthausen, these SS soldiers were among the thousands from occupied countries who volunteered to serve in elite German units.

My father continued with his story. 'One of them asked me, in bad German, "Who are you?" They had their big rifles pointed at my chest. I stood up as tall as I could make myself and looked at them right in their faces and I said to them in Yiddish, "I am a Jew from Mauthausen."' Dad was again sitting tall in his chair.[1]

Momentarily flustered by his brazenness, the Nazis took a step back to discuss what to do. Speaking his native language, my father understood everything as they debated if they should kill him in the old woman's back yard, kill him in the street, or take him to the Enns gendarmerie headquarters, essentially the local police station. They acted as if they didn't realize their captive understood them. Maybe they hadn't seen the 'U' for *Ungarn* on his prison shirt under the raincoat. Or maybe they didn't know what it meant.

Eventually they decided, for no reason my father could discern, to take him to the gendarmerie station in the town square. They pushed him out of the woman's yard, through her small house, and into the street, where they turned towards the square. Walking in front of the SS men, my father had time to contemplate what had just happened, and his earlier resignation was quickly replaced by frustration at what he judged to be his own stupidity.

---

1 Yiddish is very close to German, especially so in simple conversation. But my father was also daring them.

'Oy Jeckeleh, all I thought was, why didn't I leave when the old woman told me to go? Why did I knock on her door even? I was free! I should have kept moving. I would have found food along the way. Maybe a refugee would have helped me. All I thought was how stupid, what a stupid mistake I made.' My father was shaking his head as if he was once again marching up the street, Nazi rifles pointed at his back.

After what he estimated was half a mile, my father and his SS captors arrived at the gendarmerie outpost in the town square.

In many European countries, gendarmeries are nation-wide paramilitary organizations. The closest American version is a state police, or a sheriff serving rural areas. The Austrian Gendarmerie was the country's national police force before the Nazi occupation. After Germany annexed Austria in 1938, the Gendarmerie was rolled into the *Ordnungspolizei*, or *Orpo*, the German national police during the Nazi reign. Under the *Orpo*, members of the Austrian Gendarmerie retained their jobs and responsibilities, as well as their ranks as gendarmes. My father was about to meet one of them.

Dad and his escorts marched into the gendarmerie station. The lone gendarme inside, resplendent in his green *Ordnungspolizei* uniform, stood to attention behind his desk. The Nazis saluted and announced their prisoner. Returning the salute, the gendarme looked them over with great interest. My father immediately sensed this was not going to play out the way the young storm troopers had expected.

At the Seder table, he told me what happened next. 'The gendarme said to these boys, "I'll handle the prisoner," and he said it with authority, like they had better to listen to him. So one of the SS said, "Are you going to kill him?" and the policeman said, "Don't you worry. You leave him with me," and he ordered the SS boys to leave.'

Hesitating for an instant, they eventually heil-Hitlered, smartly about-faced, and left. If my father was surprised by the solitary gendarme's power over the SS men, he never said.

My father again. 'The gendarme was still standing by his desk, but he said to me slowly in German, "I won't hurt you," and I told him *"danke,"* thank you, and then I said *"ich spreche ein bisschen Deutsch,"* I speak a little German.' My father's smile was in full bloom. 'Then he asked me how I came to his gendarmerie headquarters.'

Speaking German, my father told the gendarme the story of his escape and capture. The sense of peace he'd felt when the SS men had seized him in the old woman's home had returned. Not only that, he felt surprisingly safe.

It had never occurred to me before, not that Seder evening nor any other time, but I now wonder whether my father also told the gendarme that his father had been a cavalry soldier in World War I fighting for Austria, more accurately for the old Austro-Hungarian Empire, for the gendarme's country. I can't understand why I'd never made the connection. Probably it was all part of my father's drive to keep the story light and easy, and my parallel desire to avoid asking questions. But now that the question has popped up for me, I'm intensely curious. Knowing my father, I bet he did. It might explain what happened next.

'You wouldn't believe it,' my father said to me. 'The gendarme put me in one of the jail cells. He told me that he was going to leave me in there, in the jail, for the night, and tomorrow he would get me back to Mauthausen. I tell you, Jeckeleh, I didn't understand what he was doing. He knew I was a Jew and that I escaped from Mauthausen, but he was going to let me sleep there, and then take me back to there tomorrow? And the SS in the camp would take me back just like nothing? Like I went for a walk in the woods? Can't you imagine?'

Leaving my father in the cell, the gendarme said he'd return soon, and shut the old wooden door. Dad lay down on the small cot against the wall as the lock clicked shut. He didn't know what would happen to him, but the gendarme seemed like a good man, compassionate and honest, and for now he felt secure enough to shut his eyes and drift off.

His rest was soon interrupted by the scraping of a key in the cell door's lock.

My father said, 'The gendarme walked in with a plate of scrambled eggs! I still remember the steam coming off them, like in my mother's kitchen. I hadn't seen scrambled eggs in a year.'

The gendarme left my father to enjoy his feast. After eating, he felt sleepy and lay down again. When he woke, the cell was quiet, its lone window dark. It was the middle of the night. He turned over and quickly fell back asleep.

The next morning the Austrian gendarme came into my father's cell with some breakfast rolls and butter – real butter, a delicacy in war-ravaged Europe. Then he retrieved the same two young Hungarian SS troopers who had brought my father to the jail the day before. Making sure my father heard him clearly, the gendarme ordered the SS men to return Dad to KZ Mauthausen. My father listened, but his shoulders slumped. These kids weren't going to march him back up the hill seven miles to KZ Mauthausen. They would kill him the second they had the chance, and report that he'd tried to run away again. He was sure of it. Besides, my father doubted he had the strength to walk a mile, let alone all the way to the concentration camp, in spite of the food he'd eaten in the past twenty-four hours.

'This one tied my hands behind my back,' my father said, 'and he put a stick in my back to poke me, so that I should walk fast. Sometimes the other one, he hit me with a whip he had, on my ankle. Still, it was not so terrible, and we made it back to Mauthausen.'

Seven exhausting miles on his feet, over the Danube and up the hill, but my father said it was 'not so terrible.' I had to take him at his word.

Just outside the camp main gate, the SS men untied my father's hands and left him standing there, while they marched off back down the hill. The huge main double doors swung open, and my father walked through alone. He looked up at the Nazi guards in the towers. They returned his gaze impassively. Not surprisingly, or perhaps very surprisingly, they didn't greet him. In fact, no one greeted him. No one sent him to the showers, or to the camp prison, or to the gas chamber. Maybe the gendarme had called ahead, or maybe the young SS men had said something that had given my father safe passage.

My father returned to the barracks and bunk he had been using before going on the death march the day before. He had been gone less than twenty-four hours. He said his friends in the camp were stunned by his return. He told a few of them the story, but not everyone believed him. So he stopped telling the other *KZlers* where he'd been.

Chapter 49

Intersection

Angelika pulls up in front of the Hotel Romer right at 11am. Sliding into the front seat of her red Citroen, it feels like it will be another sunny day, though perhaps warmer than yesterday. Our initial task today is to find the intersection where my father escaped the first time. To narrow our search, Angelika and I have four pieces of information to work with from my father's story, four requirements the intersection needs to meet.

First, since my father passed the intersection on both his escape attempts, it must be on the regular death march route to KZ Gunskirchen. Second, it must be near where the marchers first encountered the town of Enns. Third, both roads at the intersection are, or at least were then, major thoroughfares. And fourth, the town square and its gendarmerie outpost should be, by my father's estimate, around half a mile away.

Buckling my seat belt, Angelika tells me she had decided something important. I click in and give her my complete attention.

'I am sure that I know the intersection where your father escaped,' she states definitively. 'It is simple. Only one intersection on the march to Gunskirchen fits with your father's story.'

So much for driving around Enns scouting intersections.

She reaches into the back seat and grabs a photocopy of a map dating from the early 1900s. 'I received this on Wednesday from the mayor's office,' she explains, holding up the page.

'The mayor knows my father's story?'

'Yes,' Angelika says earnestly. 'Your father's story is very important for Enns.'

In all the time that I've been in touch with Mauthausen Memorial I have strongly sensed this. Now Angelika is confirming it. I am curious why that is, but decide to leave it for later. Hearing what Angelika knows is more important.

Pointing at the map, she tells me that once across the Danube River, the death march route to KZ Gunskirchen passes a single major crossroad just as it reaches Enns. That crossroad is in the southeast corner of the town. 'This intersection is not the same now as it was in 1945,' she says, 'but it is almost the same.'

Moving her finger north-south along a thin white line representing a road, she says, '*Steyrer Strasse* comes from the south, from the city of Steyre. That's this road. It was a very important road for refugees running from the fighting.'

Now her finger moves east-west. 'And this road is *Ennser Strasse*. This is the road your father was on.'

Peering closely at the map, I can see the junction was clearly a major intersection back then. That's one requirement. And it's located just as the marchers reached the Enns outskirts. That's two requirements.

Using the map's legend, I measure it to be a quarter of a mile from the town square. Not half a mile, as my father said, but close enough for an estimate. Three requirements.

I often wondered about my father's ability to accurately gauge time and distances in his weakened condition. Now that I am here, I discover he often estimated distances further, and time periods longer, than they actually were. This should not surprise me. Time would understandably move slower, and distances seem much greater, for someone in such poor physical shape. Still, given his physical state, his memory and powers of observation were remarkable.

Angelika adds the fourth requirement. 'It is also the same intersection your father passed by when he marched again to Gunskirchen later in April.' This is crucial, because on his second death march my father passed the intersection where he escaped the first time, hoping to pull it off again.

She puts her car in gear. 'We have to pay attention to the time,' she says as we drive. 'I have a special guest we are going to meet at one o'clock.'

'Who is it?'

'You will see. He will be very interesting for you.' Her poker face gives nothing away. Though excited, I hold my tongue.

We slide into a parking spot in the lot of a local grocery store at the intersection, and get out. Just as Angelika said, the crossroads today looks nothing like on the old map. This part of Austria has grown rapidly since the end of the war, and *Steyrer Strasse* has been supplanted by a new four-lane road that can handle much more traffic. The new road is a short walk west of the old one. The original *Steyrer Strasse* remains, but is hardly used any more. It no longer serves any important purpose. It's so quiet that we are standing in middle of the road as I get my bearings.

I walk around the south side of the old intersection, intensely sensing Angelika has called this correctly. It *feels* right. I stop at a spot where I can imagine the junction as it was in 1945. From here I can see both *Ennser Strasse*, the road from the east, still busy today with cars and trucks, and *Steyrer Strasse*, the road from the south, from Steyr, now empty. I envision my father and the other death marchers on *Ennser Strasse* slowly walking from my right, passing in front of me going to my left. I imagine battle-worn soldiers and frightened civilians standing in *Steyrer Strasse* three yards from where I stand, waiting impatiently as the death marchers cross in front of them. The refugees and soldiers, a jumble of children and adults, horses, carts and trucks, were on the run from war and capture. They would have no patience for a group of haggard, skinny Jewish prisoners crossing their path, slowing them down. They would have even less patience for a single prisoner straggling across their escape route to safety.

Something suddenly occurs to me. Every time my father told the story of this escape, and especially picturing him at the Seder table in 2001, whenever he spoke of the refugees coming into the intersection he would look to his left. And then he would swing his head and his shoulders to his right when describing how he'd turned and escaped by becoming part of the flow of humanity. Standing here, I see how that fits exactly. The refugees and soldiers would have come from my father's left, and to join them he'd have turned to his right. A fifth requirement I hadn't even thought of before.

After *Steyrer Strasse* passes the intersection – that is, on the north side of the crossroads – its name changes to *Wiener Strasse*. I now focus my attention on it, on the street my father walked after turning to go with the stream of refugees. Looking in the direction my father faced, seeing what he saw, I notice the first fifty yards of the *Strasse* is wide enough to fit five cars abreast. No houses line the street, just a church on my left, and the backsides of a few two story-buildings on both sides. The old map from the mayor's office shows the church, but the rest of the intersection in the early 1900s was empty field. There are no photos or maps showing the intersection during the 1940s, but either way – if it was field, or it was the backs of buildings – my father would have seen no doors to knock on.

Angelika and I cross *Ennser Strasse* and are now walking north on *Wiener Strasse*, just as my father did. I catch myself hunting for a discarded raincoat on the road. The church looks to be made of granite, while the other buildings along the street are cement and stucco, and painted muted greens, blues, tans and yellows, with bright white trim and red tiled roofs. It all looks quaint and very Austrian in the bright midday sun.

After fifty yards, the street narrows to a width of only two cars. We pass a few store fronts, and then come to a row of closely spaced two-story buildings on our right, the east side of the curving street. Doors every few yards are entrances to homes, or apartments. One of the doors is open. Angelika and I peer in. The interior is very small, with basic living room furniture and a postage-stamp-sized grass yard beyond sliding glass doors in the back.

The backyard is key. My father had gone into the old woman's back yard. If we hadn't seen a yard, I might have wondered if Angelika made a mistake about the intersection. But there it is. It doesn't mean *this* is the house whose door my father knocked on, but it is probably one of these. Another piece of the puzzle fits.

I call out, but no one answers. This isn't New York City. People leave their doors open even if they've stepped out. We wait a few minutes, but no one comes along to claim the house.

I see no point in either stepping into the house, or hanging around, and say as much to Angelika. The old woman's house never interested me. This isn't like the Freidmanns' home, which we know with certainty and where my father spent three weeks. Here I have no idea which house my father entered wearing a raincoat over his prison garb.

As for the old woman, she wouldn't be alive today, and I'm positive she didn't tell anyone about her few minutes of goodness before changing her mind. Not even a relative. 'Yes, I took in a Jew from one of the death marches, gave him some food, and then called the SS on him.'

Nope, she told no one.

Not for the first time today I feel anger welling up. The old woman nearly got my father killed. The least she could have done was given him a chance to gather himself up and leave. Angelika is intently watching my face. I decide to explain.

'She didn't have to call the SS on him,' I say, maybe a bit too sharply.

'Perhaps that is so,' Angelika replies, 'but it was the middle of a war. She did a good thing when she let him in and gave him to eat, no?'

'Yes, she did, but ...'

Angelika has more to say. 'The bible teaches us to help in time of need, and the old woman did that, no? And she did give your father a warning that he had to leave. Maybe she has children or grandchildren and a husband and she cannot take such a big chance.'

'So give my father another warning. Give him an opportunity to get up and go.'

'We can't know what fear was in her mind,' Angelika replies.

'Then why let him into her house at all? Why did she bother?'

'Perhaps it is because she felt sorry for your father. She saw him standing in her door and could not send him away.'

I ponder her words for a moment. Eventually, I say it. 'You're right, Angelika.'

She's not finished with me. 'Believe me, I know how you feel. But I am also a mother and I know perhaps how the old woman felt after she gave food to your father.'

I can't be angry at everyone I meet. It's not their fault my father was in a concentration camp. Sometimes I feel that way on this trip. The blonde woman in the *Jourhaus*, for example. She and her husband are just living their lives as best they can. They saw a nice fixer-upper with room for children and a yard. OK, it has a dastardly history, but why is it so wrong that they chose to live there? I wouldn't, most people probably wouldn't, but why can't they? And what did this old woman do? She took in my father and fed him. She had a change of heart, but she gave him the chance to move on. It wasn't much of a chance, but still, my father didn't take it, and so she protected herself.

I think, somewhat begrudgingly, that none of this is black-and-white.

I step away from the doorway. I decide it is a waste to become agitated over the old woman. In the end, it worked out well for my father. He got good food and a night's sleep on a real bed in the town jail.

More importantly, we've found the intersection where he escaped the first time. I now more clearly appreciate the difficulty of this escape: cutting out of a march guarded by bloodthirsty SS troopers and walking like a foreign spy down a narrow Austrian street crowded with Nazi troops and panicked refugees fleeing the battle front. My father went from the comfort of comrades on all sides of him, to the unknown of a fugitive on the run in enemy territory. No matter how weak he was, he had been relatively safe if he'd stayed with that 'transport.' He'd belonged somewhere.

I recall my father's exact words from that Seder evening in 2001. 'I thought about it for just one second. Then I turned, and no one noticed.' To me, making that right turn was bigger than lying about being a baker or a carpenter, bigger than talking his way into the Latrine *Kommando*. If the SS guarding the march had seen him do it, they'd have chased after him and killed him. If a refugee had noticed and called out, same result. If he hadn't found a raincoat on the ground, again perhaps, same outcome. Standing on this street, by what might have been the old woman's home, I appreciate the outrageous boldness of my father's actions more than ever.

And I wonder mightily if I would have been that bold, if I would have made that turn.

Angelika and I resume walking up *Wiener Strasse*. The street leads directly into the Enns town square. But starting right here it slopes uphill, which makes sense – the town's founders put the square on the town's highest point, to better see enemies approaching. And it is another reason why my father felt the walk with the SS youth covered half a mile, rather than the less-than-quarter-mile it is from this point. Uphill always feels further.

A few steps up the street, Angelika stops us. 'I see the time,' she says. 'The car is better.'

I agree, and five minutes later we are parked in a spot in the Enns town square.

Chapter 50

Gendarmerie

I am back in the square where I ate dinner the night before, though given the intensity of this trip so far, it feels as if it were weeks before. Where last night I saw buildings only in shades of grey, daylight reveals their facades are pink, grey, blue, tan and white. It is a classically picturesque slice of Austria, exactly like *Wiener Strasse*. The outdoor restaurant tables are occupied by animated lunch diners and gossiping coffee drinkers, and the shops are vibrant with regular comings and goings.

We walk towards a pink and white four-story building in the middle of the eastern side of the square. A sign declares it is the *Museum Lauriacum*.

'This is the town museum,' Angelika says. I recall that Lauriacum is the Roman name for Enns. Two men are standing in front, one about my age, one older. We walk over to them and Angelika makes the introductions.

'This is Dr. Reinhardt Harreither,' she says, and I shake hands with the one my age. 'He is the director of the town museum and knows your father's story very well.'

I'm six feet tall, he's a few inches taller, wearing black-framed glasses and a brown blazer. I say it is an honor to meet him, and he replies, in fluent, accented English that it is an honor for *him* to meet *me*. I'm not sure why that would be, but I nod and turn to greet the second man.

'And this,' Angelika continues as I reach my hand out to the older gentleman, 'is Dietmar Heck. He was very young during the war, but he knew Ignaz and Barbara Friedmann, and worked for Ignaz after the war.'

Dietmar grabs my hand and shakes it. I am dumbstruck. It is hard to believe that I just touched the hand of a man who knew the people who saved my father's life. As the Friedmanns are dead, this is as close as I can come to touching them directly.[1] I glance at Angelika and her coy smile tells me she knows she did well. For a moment, I say nothing. To me, Dietmar looks to be in his fifties, but doing the math I know he must be at least seventy. He is well over six foot, trim and fit, with small features, weathered skin, a full head of white hair, and a welcoming air to him.

'It's a real pleasure to meet you, *Herr* Heck.' It's all I can finally think to say.

He smiles back at me.

'He speaks no English,' Angelika notes, 'so I will help you.'

I have a thousand questions for him, but Angelika slows me down. 'Dr. Harreither has only a few minutes, but he wanted to meet you and answer your questions about the gendarmerie station. We can speak with Dietmar later. He will spend the afternoon with us.'

'Okay,' I say. Turning to Dr. Harreither, I ask the most important question I have on the subject. 'Do you know where the police station was in this square?' Right to the point, like the New Yorker I am. My father always said *Gendarmerie*, but I fell back on the basic English word.

Dr. Harreither knows what I mean. 'Yes, of course,' he replies, 'But why do you want to know?'

I forgot. Like the historians at Mauthausen Memorial, the museum director knows nothing of my father's first escape. Peter Kammerstätter only gave Barbara Friedmann's account of finding my father after the second one. I take a moment to tell a short version of the story. Angelika translates for Dietmar, who is listening raptly, his head tilted towards her. I find myself staring at him while I speak.

'I see,' Dr. Harreither says when I finish the story, in the way scientists say when they've been given the background they need. 'The Gendarmerie was right over here.'

He points to the building two doors north of where we're standing. We walk there, forty yards at most, to the northeast corner of the square. Three stories tall, the building houses a café on the ground floor and offices above. A glass door to the right of the café opens to stairs leading to second and third floor offices. A series of doorbells runs along one frame of the door.

---

1 On a subsequent trip to Austria I met the Friedmanns' only living grandson, an experience which, of course, brought me much closer to the Friedmanns.

'This was the gendarmerie station,' Dr. Harreither announces. 'The police have moved some years ago out of the square, to a new building of their own.'

I'm not sure what I was expecting, but this building doesn't look very police-like. I don't see leftover marks on the facade or over the doorway from signs that once said *POLIZEI* or *GENDARMERIE*, or that signified Austrian police of any sort, nothing to confirm for me that my father spent the night behind these doors.

'Are you sure this was it?' I ask.

Dietmar, hearing Angelika's translation, weighs in.

'Jack!' he announces as he lopes past me to the glass door leading to the upstairs offices. Standing by the door, he raises his hands high over his head, fingers together, palms facing each other, like a referee calling a touchdown. With his long arms, his hands reach above the top of the doorframe and he is pantomiming holding something between them.

'Gendarmerie!' he says animatedly, looking at me over his shoulder. 'Gendarmerie!' he repeats.

I get what he is trying to describe. The official plaque of the *Orpo*, the *Ordnungspolizei*, the German national police, was right above this doorway during the war. That's what Dietmar is holding over his head. He'd seen it as a young boy. This is the building alright.

Studying the structure that had once housed the Gendarmerie station, I wonder about the gendarme who had been so good to my father. Was he tall or short, young or old, in shape or did he like his beers with the boys? Did he have a mustache or a beard? Was he married? Did he have kids? And most importantly, did he realize the impact he was about to have on the young Jew standing between the two SS soldiers? The gendarme saved my father's life, but he could have as easily taken it, or caused it to be taken. Instead, he fed my father, housed him, and looked after him.

I tried finding the gendarme's name, but had no luck. The Austrian Gendarmerie was reestablished immediately after the war, and was absorbed into the Austrian Federal Police in 2005. I reached out to the A.F.P. and my contact there uncovered logs showing the names of gendarmes on duty in Enns until March 1945. Then their records stopped. The trail, regrettably, was cold.[1]

---

1 Even if the logs continued, it's highly unlikely the gendarme who saved my father's life would still be alive. The officers in those last days of the war would have been older, probably over fifty, as all the younger men were fighting at the fronts. He would be well over 100 now, and so was certainly no longer

'But your father could not have spent a night in the jail in this building,' Dr. Harreither says, interrupting my musings. 'There were no jail cells here.'

For a second, I wonder if he is casting doubt on my father's story. If there were no jail cells, then where did the gendarme put my father that night?

Dr. Harreither goes on. 'The cells were in the building that is now my museum. Come, I will show you.' I am relieved. Pieces of my father's story continue falling into place.

Walking back to the museum, I ask the group a question that has been bugging me for a long time. 'Why did the SS men obey the gendarme when he told them to leave my father with him? I mean, he's basically just a cop, and they're Nazi storm troopers, right?'

Angelika fields it. 'The Gendarmerie and the SS were directly in connection,' she says.

'Really?' I'd never heard that before. 'I thought the Gendarmerie was part of the *Orpo*.'

'It was,' she replies. 'The SS and the *Orpo* were separate organizations, but Heinrich Himmler was in command of both of them. Sometimes they worked together even.'

Dr. Harreither now chimes in, explaining that the *Orpo* contained all of Nazi Germany's police organizations. The infamous Gestapo was part of the *Orpo*, as were traffic cops, maritime police, even the railway police. National and local police forces and gendarmeries in occupied countries that had been absorbed by the *Orpo*, like the Austrian Gendarmerie, did not have to pledge allegiance to Hitler. But their members all wore *Orpo*'s green military-style service uniforms. And because a gendarmerie is a paramilitary organization whose members have some basic military training, gendarmes were accorded the respect of rank by the SS. A gendarme sergeant, for instance, outranked an SS private.

That explains why the young Hungarian SS soldiers obeyed the gendarme, and also why he had the clout to retrieve the same two Nazis the next day to safely escort my father back to KZ Mauthausen. He obviously outranked them. Without a doubt my father knew this, because he never exhibited any surprise in the gendarme's ability to order around the young SS men. It also explains why my father was permitted to walk back into KZ Mauthausen without repercussions for his escape. The gendarme had fixed things.

---

alive. But if I could have traced children or grandchildren, I would have loved to have met them and thanked them.

'Wow,' I mumble.

The *Museum Lauriacum* is housed in a thirteenth-century building originally constructed as the seat of the local courthouse. We walk through the doors fronting the town square, past the museum gift shop, and into a cobblestoned courtyard.

'There were three jail cells inside there,' Dr. Harreither says, pointing to the opposite side of the open space. A series of oversized windows, each protected by wrought-iron security bars, runs along the courtyard wall at the first floor level. Dr. Harreither leads us there.

Through a door near the windows, we enter a narrow, well-lit hallway. Three wooden doors with heavy-duty black iron locks and hinges are evenly spaced on the courtyard side of the hallway. Each door has a square, yellowed piece of paper pasted near the top, with neat script lettering: *Zelle 1, Zelle 2, Zelle 3*. Cells 1, 2 and 3. *Zelle 2*'s door is open, and I step inside.

The room is about six feet wide by eight feet long, with an arched ceiling nine feet at its highest. The walls are white. The room's single window dominates the opposite wall facing the courtyard. The room could have easily withstood a bombing, or an attack by vengeful knights. It is used for storage now, with two long metal racks filled with brown file boxes, but a narrow bed would have fit against one of the walls.

My father would have felt secure in here, away from the wooden walls and Spartan bunk beds of his barracks in KZ Mauthausen. And after his plate of scrambled eggs, he would have felt secure *and* full. It must have been an astounding feeling for him, especially after surviving the escape and the SS men's decision to not kill him. My father might even have felt invincible.

Which does not surprise me one bit.

Chapter 51

The 261st Regiment of the
65th Infantry Division;
241 Miles Away

Patton's Third Army was comprised of four corps. Each corps contained three or more divisions, and each division was made up of three or four regiments. The regiments of the 65th Infantry Division, the division I cared most about, were the 259th, 260th and 261st.

The 261st Regiment was of particular interest to me: its 5,000 soldiers are credited with capturing Enns. And one of its young men found my father. My father never knew his name.

During the first days of April 1945, the 261st was temporarily removed from the 65th and attached to the 6th Armored Division, so that their combined arms could more efficiently knife through German territory. During the two weeks they operated together, the 261st was often called on to lead the division's tanks into small German towns, seizing bridges and neutralizing anti-tank opposition so the armor could safely roll through.[1]

The 261st Regiment fought one of its biggest battles on April 7, 1945, holding off a massive Wehrmacht attack in the central German town of Struth. The battle raged for two days, but in the end the regiment, along with the rest of the 65th Infantry Division, prevailed. After that engagement, the regiment was allowed a breather, and

---

1 Though it may sound backwards – infantry troops making it safe for tanks, those forty-ton armored behemoths with big guns – it's true. Without going into infantry, tank, and combined armed tactics, German tanks could be stopped by a single American soldier with a bazooka, while a German soldier armed with a comparable *panzerschreck* (or its single-shot close relative, the *panzerfaust*) could destroy Allied armor. Infantry soldiers were needed to protect their tanks from these deadly menaces.

put into reserve, which took them off the battle front. But they weren't resting. No chance to sleep late or feel they were out of harm's way. Instead, they were tasked with mopping up German resistance behind the division's forward lines. Though dangerous, it was somewhat easier duty than being at the tip of Patton's spear.

On April 16, 1945, the 261st Regiment reached Arnstadt, Germany. It was the last day the unit would be in reserve. Starting the next day, it would return to the front lines, soldiering alongside the two other 65th Infantry Division regiments on a powerful drive southeast, aiming straight for northern Austria. On that day, the regiment was 241 miles away from Enns.

April 16 is also the day my father had a pistol placed in the back of his neck and was faced with a choice. His choice was to march, or die.

Chapter 52

The Great Escape

'When I came back to Mauthausen,' my father said, picking up where he'd left off, 'I went back to my bunk and stayed there.'

'Did they put you in a work *kommando*,' I ask, 'or did you still have nothing to do?'

Shaking his head, my father said, 'No, I still had no *kommando*. Believe you me, it was much better this way. They didn't feed us the normal ration of the working *kommandos*, but we got still a little food every day.'

'So what did you do all day long?'

This momentarily stumped my father. He probably hadn't thought about it in a long time. This was a perfect opportunity to ask about his typical day – yet I didn't. And these days were no longer typical for him anyway. The Allies were too close, the Nazis and *kapos* too nervous, the fabric of the camp too tenuous.

After an instant he cocked an eyebrow. 'Do? What we did? We talked. We talked with the new Jews who came in from the labor battalions, like Mozes Chaim. They heard a little what was going on with the war. They told us where the Russians were. We weren't so sure about the Americans, but we knew the Russians were coming much closer.'

That the Russians were closing in on KZ Mauthausen was certainly good news, but it didn't help them survive from one day to the next. Most still had to contend with their work *kommandos*, while they all continued dealing with *Appells*, hunger, *kapos*, SS guards, and their own ill health.

On Monday, April 16, 1945, my father was assigned to a new 'transport' out of the camp. Unlike the first one ten days or so earlier, this 'transport' appeared in Nazi records. It was again bound for KZ Gunskirchen. It was to be another death march.

As with the first one, my father joined with what he guessed was roughly a thousand other prisoners, a size the SS could effectively guard along the route.

'As we walked past the gate, they gave us bread and margarine again, like the last time. I didn't go very far, a few yards maybe, and I sat down. A few *KZlers* joined me. We were fifteen all together.' My father's tone was very matter-of-fact, like they'd been hiking and had decided to take a breather.

'The guards just let you sit down? They didn't stop you?'

'No Jeckeleh. We were still within the fences, the borders of the camp. Yes, we were outside the walls, but there were many other wires we had to cross. We weren't free.'

'So, you just hung out there?'

'Yes. We just stood there. I ate my bread.' My father didn't mean they literally *stood*. He used the word often, to mean waiting somewhere.

It wasn't a mutiny, though I interpreted it as an act of defiance, if only a little one. My father said they *stood* there most of the day. Incredibly, the SS guards left them alone, until around 4pm, when a trio of SS troopers approached the group and gave them three choices.

'The SS said to us that we could go back to the camp, number one.' My father was counting on his fingers. 'Number two, we could get on the road with them, with these SS, and march to Gunskirchen. Or if you don't want to go further, and you don't want to go back to the camp, we have to shoot you. They made it a choice for each one of us.'

My father said this as if he was on a game show and had been given a choice of three doors to select – just pick one. It amazed me how calmly he ticked off these live-or-die options. I wasn't sure what to ask, but I had to ask something.

'That's it? Just choose one of them?'

'Jeckeleh, I wish it wasn't like this, so simple. You should never know. Every day we saw death. Every day a *KZler* would drop on the ground right in front of me. Or they wouldn't get up from their beds in the morning. Or I would see an SS or a *kapo* beat someone to death. Or shoot him. Life meant nothing in the camps.'

'You should never know.' It was another of my father's phrases, usually used before he'd describe something extremely unpleasant. I was so accustomed to hearing it over the years that I missed its vital importance right then. To my ear it sounded like filler, my father's equivalent of 'like,' and 'um.' So I ignored it as he explained, in his way, that his year in the camps had inoculated

208

him against feeling the emotion behind the death he saw every day. I'd seen this hardness earlier in the evening, in his description of his brother-in-law Hershy's murder. It was easier for him to be this way.

Only years later, after visiting Austria and walking the grounds where he'd survived, did I recognize how vitally, crucially important 'you should never know' was to my father's post-war life. But not yet. Not that Seder evening.

After the options were presented by the SS guards, twelve of the Jews, including my father, stood up, ready to march. None asked to return to Mauthausen. Instead, the other three picked the last choice, and one of the SS men shot them dead where they sat.

'Puf, puf, puf' my father said, rhyming it with 'hoof,' mimicking the report of the Nazi's pistol while his right hand took the shape of a pistol. 'We left them there.'

Easy. Simple. For my father. For them.

The main body of marchers was miles ahead, so my father and the others moved as their own small group, their own mini-death-march. A short way down the road, still within KZ Mauthausen's outer perimeter wire, they came upon eight more Jewish *KZlers*, also sitting along the side of the route.

'The three SS with us said to them the same thing that they said to us. You can go back, you can go further, or we shoot you here. Two more said to the SS to kill them, and they did. The others joined with us to march. So we were a group of eighteen prisoners and three SS and we walked.'

Almost three hours after they'd started, around 7pm, they neared the *Steyrer-Ennser* intersection where my father had pulled off his first escape. Daylight was slipping towards dusk, made darker by thick, roiling clouds now overhead, threatening rain. They trudged up the steep incline just before the junction.

'I remembered it exactly from the first march. My mind was always working. No matter how tired or how hungry I was, my mind was always ready. I felt not so terrible, and I was hoping maybe something would be like the time before.'

Now my father's disappointment filled his face at his dining room table. His voice lowered. 'But it was quiet this time. It was not so busy to give me a chance to escape, like the last time.'

The intersection wasn't filled with the tumult and confusion of that day a week or so earlier, and even the dimmed light of the cloudy early evening gave no advantage. The crossroads were empty as my father shuffled through it, disappointment a shot to his solar plexus. His mood turned as gloomy as the gathering darkness. His feet weighed a thousand pounds each. Now the degree to which he'd blown it the last time consumed him.

He said to me, 'I saw that a week before had been my one chance. I felt that God had given me that one time, and now I felt that I would never have another one.'

The last of his energy was oozing through his pores and leaking out onto the cold road. He was growing weaker by the step. The group marched on. My father watched absently as two of the eighteen drifted to the side of the road. As with the prior march he had been on, the rule was simple: if you went to the side of the road, you would be shot. Those two were.

My father said, 'We were walking slowly, some more slowly, some less slowly, so we weren't so close to each other. I was near the front.'

Another mile, and it began drizzling, shoving my father's mood further into the dumps. His strength, bolstered by the bread and margarine he'd gotten at the Mauthausen gate, and supported by the fact that he'd escaped once and so the impossible was in fact possible, dropped to zero. He kept moving, but he had nothing left. Ten and a half months, and he finally, completely, totally had given everything he had to give.

'Jeckeleh, I couldn't take not one more step. I remember it so clearly, like it was yesterday. I was right next to a woods, some trees. I went to the side of the road.'

My father knew what this meant. The prior death march, when he went to the side of the road and the SS guard passed him by, had been a fluke. This time he would die, and he welcomed it. This was the point where every synapse in his brain, every atom in his conscious being said, 'Enough already, Dave. Let's get out of here.' He weighed eighty pounds, eighty less than when he left the Dej ghetto. He had lost half his body weight. He was a walking, talking stick figure. He was a starved and beaten animal, and he'd gone far beyond his threshold. He could tolerate nothing more.

He sat down in the dirt of the roadside by the small copse of trees. He waited, hands on the rough ground supporting him, feet out in front. As it was the time before, his mind was empty and calm. He heard the boot-steps of one of the three SS men coming up from behind. Glancing around, my father recognized his executioner as a storm trooper in his mid-thirties, older than the other two guards on their march, and coincidentally Hungarian.

Dad tipped his head down and focused on the ground in front of him. His breathing quickened. Hopefully this would be quick and painless. The boots stopped very close to his back. He heard the sound of metal on leather, of a pistol sliding out of its holster. He knew that sound, he'd heard it countless times, in Birkenau, in Gusen II, in Gusen I, and in Mauthausen. This would be the last time.

The pistol barrel pushed at the base of his neck.

WHOA, it was freezing cold!

The unexpected sting of the cold weapon launched my father to his feet like a rocket, before the SS man had a chance to say, 'Get up or I have to shoot you,' if he would have said it at all.

Standing meant my father was still a marcher. Standing meant he was safe in the unwritten rules of the death marches. The SS man moved past him, holstering the pistol and muttering to himself in Hungarian about, 'that dirty Jew,' while taking long quick strides to catch up to a few marchers who had gotten ahead.

My father was now fully upright and facing in the direction of march, but teetering like a drunk. He looked over his left shoulder. The two other SS men were only a few yards away, but walking backwards, monitoring their slower charges. In a flash, my father realized no one was watching him. He looked to his right, to the copse of trees, and, incredibly, spotted a narrow dirt path starting right at his feet and leading into the trees.

The path led who-knows-where. But the path was *possible* freedom. The road was *certain* death.

Without another thought, my father took off, bolting down the path like a scared rabbit, legs churning, eight, nine, ten steps, then he threw himself into bushes lining the path. Panting uncontrollably, he spun around on his belly. He could barely see the road through the growth, but he briefly caught sight of the two SS men, still stepping backwards. They were acting like they'd seen nothing unusual. They moved out of sight. A few seconds later he heard three pistol shots.

'Puf, puf, puf.' Again my father duplicated the reports of the guard's pistol. He assumed three more marchers were now dead.

Nobody came after my father. I think the SS soldiers guarding the marchers never saw him run. They didn't call after him. They didn't yell for him to *halt!* They didn't shoot at him. If they had seen him, I believe they would have tried to stop him. The SS guards on this march were *Storm troopers*, the Nazi military elite, the best of the best. They would never have tolerated a worn, nearly-dead Jew escaping from them. No question in my mind. Exactly like last time, Dad had gotten away with it.

211

So far.

My father lay motionless in the bushes where he'd landed, the cold rain splattering on his back. Coupled with the chill in the air and the cold of the ground, he started shivering. But he dared not move. He decided he would stay there until either he died, or he came up with a plan. Once in a while someone would walk by on the road, a car would motor past, a horse would saunter along pulling a cart. But the path stayed empty. And he stayed right there.

Dusk turned to night, and the drizzle let up. He remained quiet and still, shivering silently.

'I think it was maybe midnight, I must have been fallen asleep for a few hours. So I got up. I got up slowly, I didn't know if there were guards on the road. It was very dark.'

Austria was under a wartime blackout, but the crescent-moon's feeble light slipping through thinning cloud cover enabled my father to see just enough. He stepped gingerly onto the path and padded towards the main road. Now on the shoulder, standing on the spot where he'd nearly died, he looked left and right, straining to pick up signs of danger. It was as quiet and dark as an empty church. To his right, close by, were three bodies clustered together: the three marchers killed by the shots he'd heard after he ran down the path. One of the three appeared to be an older man. He wore civilian clothes, including a warm-looking jacket, and he had been carrying a blanket. My father surmised that he had recently arrived from a Hungarian Labor Service battalion, like his friend Chaim Mozes.

My father judged the old man to be around his size. He dragged the body towards the brush, and with some effort stripped the dead man and donned his clothes.

'They felt funny on me, but at least there was no blood on them. And now I looked like anyone from the town.'

Once again, that coldness. Once again, the dead were helping my father, giving him a chance at life after it had abandoned them. Once again, he proved he would do anything to survive. Once again, I wondered if I would have been that resourceful, if that's even the word for this.

He went over to bushes just off the path but near the road, covered himself with the dead man's blanket and tried to sleep. The cool night air bit lightly at his skin, though the coat and blanket helped, and soon he nodded off.

My father woke with the first light of the next day peaking over the horizon. Birds whistled and tweeted their welcomes to the living. Lying there contemplating his next move, he heard voices.

Concentrating, they belonged to a man and a woman speaking German. They sounded older, and used the familiar tones of a couple who had been around each other a long time. Their voices were getting louder, they were approaching. Assuming the awkwardly splayed position of a dead man who'd died where he'd dropped, my father bared his teeth in the way he'd seen the dead look, and waited.

The voices were now very close. Suddenly they appeared. My father glanced at them quickly, and snapped his eyes closed. They drew up to him. Trying to hide his breathing, he felt them standing right over him.

After an interminable few seconds, one said to the other, 'He doesn't look dead.'

My father stayed motionless, focusing intently on making his chest move as little as possible. He could not risk being found out. They debated his health for another moment, and finally moved along.

My father waited until he could no longer hear the couple. He opened his eyes, and seeing no one nearby, stood up. He decided to walk. It seemed a better idea than sitting by the side of a main road. Another 'transport' could come by. German troops might march past.

'Weren't you afraid you would be caught again?' I asked.

'Not this time. This time I felt much smarter. I spoke German. I was going to say that I am a refugee. You couldn't see from me that I was from Mauthausen. I was wearing regular clothes. My hair grew out even more than before.' My father ran the palm of his hand from his forehead back, where his reverse-mohawk had once been.

Though he believed he could pass, he left off the minor fact that he looked harrowingly emaciated, just skin and bones. But that's just another indication of his self-confidence. He assumed he would explain away anything he was asked. He felt exhausted, and of course hungry, but ready for whatever came next. Stepping onto the path, he decided to see where it led.

Soon after starting out, just as he rounded a blind bend, the couple appeared again. They were walking directly towards him, only a few yards ahead. My father willed himself to keep walking like he belonged there, though his fight-or-flight instinct was screaming at him to turn and run in the opposite direction. But the opposite direction led to the main road, and besides, he knew he didn't have the strength to run. So he kept moving forward at a deliberate pace.

They asked him to stop.

My father complied. Facing them, his nerves vibrating, he met their gazes.

'Was that you lying in the grass back there, pretending to be dead?' the man said, in German. His voice was soft, his tone kind.

'Yes,' my father admitted, matching their German and wondering where this was leading.

'We didn't think you were dead,' the woman said with a measure of satisfaction. 'Where are you from?'

My father said the first thing that came to him. 'I am from Czechoslovakia. I am an escaped prisoner from Mauthausen.' He stood to attention, drawing back his shoulders.

'You're Czech?' the woman exclaimed, suddenly brightening. 'We have so much family in Czechoslovakia!' They were both beaming. The Czechoslovakian border was only forty miles north of Enns. 'I'm Barbara Friedmann,' she said, 'and this is my husband, Ignaz.'

Ignaz Friedmann was fifty-three years old. His wife, Barbara, née Kropfreiter, was forty-one. Each was born within a few miles of where they were standing. They had gotten married in 1933, and their only child, Ignaz Jr., had been born the next year. Ignaz Sr. was a master brick mason with a good local reputation. He was responsible, along with his employees, for many of the houses and small office structures around Enns and its nearby villages. He was of average height and build, with powerful shoulders and hands, and handsome. Like my grandfather, he fought for Austro-Hungary in World War I. He was a man you'd want in your corner.

Barbara was strong-minded, smart, and a good match for Ignaz. Some even said she was more than a match. She enjoyed a good cigar, kept the books for his business, and helped him negotiate his business deals. She also had a bit of trouble keeping her weight in check. While I've been told their relationship was not warm, it was always supportive.

'I'm Dave,' my father said, illuminating them with his thousand-watt smile, and praying they didn't ask him for details. He could name a Czech city or two, but his knowledge of the country was tapped out right there.

'Are you hungry?' Barbara asked.

In the understatement of the year, my father admitted he was.

'Go back to the trees where we first saw you this morning,' Barbara said. 'Hide there and I will soon bring you some food.' Where they were standing offered no shelter from someone walking along the path. But the copse of trees by the main road, where my father had first escaped, was interspersed with bushes that could hide him. 'Tonight my husband will come back with our horse and cart and take you to our home.'

214

My father's mind raced. This made no sense to him. The Friedmanns were taking an enormous risk. Though they thought he was a fellow Czech, he was still an escapee from a concentration camp. If they were found out, they would be sent to a concentration camp themselves, or even killed. But my father sensed they really cared about what happened to him. He didn't know why they felt that way, but it was unmistakable. He had been around death and meanness and human animals for so long, he forgot people like this existed. His gut told him they were good, and they would do as they said.

'I trusted them,' my father said. 'Besides, what should I do, keep walking down the path and take the chance that I would find a better offer? A better offer than a ride to someone's house? Jeckeleh, I decided this was as good of a deal as I was going to get that morning.'

Accepting their offer, Dad let them walk on ahead of him, towards the main road. He followed at a distance until he reached the copse of trees. He found a sheltered spot off to the side where he could see both the main road and the path and, hopefully, not be seen by anyone. He settled in to wait.

An hour later, Barbara returned alone, with coffee, bread and butter.

'I was so relieved when I saw her. I was sitting there all the time wondering if I did the right thing. She could have brought a gendarme back with her, or even SS. But she was by herself. I came out from my hiding place to take the food and plan how Mr. Friedmann would come back later at night. Then I waited till he came.'

At the Seder, my father casually tossed off that day's wait as if he was waiting for a flight to announce boarding, or a TV show to begin, almost as if he'd had a couple of magazines with him. But like so much of his year in Austria, it couldn't possibly have been so easy. He had to hide in a spot where he could see the road, while not being visible himself. During this late stage of the war the road was often filled with Wehrmacht and SS troops, trucks, and tanks. Another death march could have come by. And families lived across the road and down the side streets. Something as ordinary as a kid bicycling by, or someone walking their dog on the path, could have led to his discovery. His life had been at risk every minute of daylight, and the wait must have been exhausting and petrifying. Yet he never said anything about it.

And I'd never asked. But now I wonder how he didn't go out of his mind all those hours. It was beyond my comprehension how he remained still and quiet. Maybe he just believed so absolutely in himself, his luck, his God, and his mother, that he knew he would be safe until Ignaz came.

If he came.

Chapter 53

57 Kristein

My father had taken a short bathroom break. He sat back down at the Seder table, excited to continue. 'As she promised,' she being Barbara, 'a few hours after it was dark Ignaz came back, alone, with a cart and horse. He helped me to climb up, and I lied down on the wood, on the cart. He took an empty metal pig trough and turned it over me to cover me.'

Ignaz guided his horse back to the road. As they bumped along, my father was hyper-alert for something to go wrong. The last time he'd met a local Austrian, he'd been invited into her home until she'd turned on him and had nearly gotten him killed. Maybe the Friedmanns had changed their minds during the long day, and now Ignaz was taking him to an SS barracks to collect a reward. My father scrunched himself into his hiding place, listening for clues.

After only a few minutes, they stopped. 'We're here,' Ignaz said, his voice a whisper, while silently lifting the pig trough off my father.

My father raised his head, half-expecting a welcoming committee of machine-gun toting SS. Instead, he saw Ignaz, by himself and pointing proudly to the building I now know as *57 Kristein Strasse*.[1] They had gone around to the back, out of sight of the street running past the house. Ignaz helped my father off the cart.

My father again. 'He took me inside, to the attic in their barn, and I waited there until Saturday night.'

That's it. That's all my father said. That's the way he told the story at our Seder that night in 2001, and that's the way he always told it. Again he was leaving out detail. Again, I didn't ask for more.

---

1 At the time, the building's address was 11 Kristein. It was changed in the post-war years as the neighborhood grew.

And, I eventually learned, his description wasn't quite right, either. Later he would hide in an attic in their barn. But not that first night.

Between Peter Kammerstätter's interview with Barbara Friedmann, and conversations and emails exchanges I've had while researching my father's year in Austria, here is a more complete picture of his first few days and nights at the Friedmanns'.

Ignaz led my father into a ground-floor room in the south end of the house where the Friedmanns kept a few farm animals. Barbara was there, waiting. Together they guided my father to a back corner of the room, away from the entrance, where he found an extra thick mat of hay covering the floor, and a cozy oversized quilt to keep warm.

Actually the Friedmanns had two adjacent rooms like this, their floors covered in hay and straw, with a single door in the back of the house leading to the first of the two rooms. The rooms were known as a *Kuhstall*, literally a cowshed, and at the time were very common in homes in the area. The Friedmanns kept a few cows in the rooms, along with an alternating menagerie of pigs, chickens, sheep and goats. And now they were keeping my father there as well.

My father was so overpoweringly overjoyed by his rescue by the Friedmanns that, entering the *Kuhstall*, he paced up and down for a few moments, pumping his fists like the excited teenager he was and exclaiming in whispers as loud as he dared, 'I'm alive! I'm alive!' Just minutes earlier he had been an escaped prisoner on the run, where at any instant he could have been spotted, captured, and killed. No more. Now his reward for having taken yet another huge gamble was a soft bed of hay in a solidly-built home where he'd be fed and cared for. It was nearly too much to believe.

My father knew how extraordinarily lucky he was, yet again. As he fell asleep in his new bed of hay, covered by the Friedmanns' comfortable quilt, he felt completely different than when he had knocked on the old woman's door. This evening he had the familiar sensation of being a kid back in Dej, at a sleep-over in a friend's barn. He smiled to himself. No doubt, things were looking good for him right then.

But it wouldn't last.

Chapter 54

The Sugar Factory

The route of the 34-mile death march from KZ Mauthausen to KZ Gunskirchen is well known. Leaving Mauthausen, my father and the other *KZlers* marched downhill to the Danube, took a bridge across the river, and skirted the eastern border of Enns. At the southeastern corner of town they turned west. That's where my father escaped the first time, at the *Steyrer Strasse–Ennser Strasse* intersection. *Ennser Strasse* was actually a short segment of an important military highway route stretching from one end of Austria to the other, called the B1 – B for *Bundestrasse*, or Federal Highway. Starting in the east in Vienna, the B1 ran through Enns on its way to Linz, Hitler's self-declared home town, twelve miles west. Today in Enns the B1 segment west of the *Steyrer–Ennser* intersection is called *Doktor Renner Strasse*.[1]

After finding the scene of the first escape and gendarmerie station, my plan now is to identify, with Angelika's help, the precise spot where my father went to the side of the road to die, where instead of dying he gave himself a chance to live. To find it, as with the first escape my father's story yielded four clues.

First, I know he reached his limit of exhaustion soon after the *Steyrer–Ennser* crossroads, though he never said *how soon* he hit empty. He never said how much further he walked beyond the intersection, not in time or distance. I doubt he even knew, that's how far gone he was by then. But thinking back on his tone and cadence as he told this story at the Seder table, I guess he'd lasted less than an hour. So at most, moving slowly he walked two more miles.

---

1 Hitler wasn't born in Linz, though he grew up there. And the B1 was renamed for Dr. Karl Renner, the Austrian Chancellor after both World Wars I and II.

219

Second, this escape took place next to – in my father's words – a 'woods, some trees.' There are no forests in the area, so more likely he was referring to a small stand or grove.

Third, a path ran from the shoulder of the road where he was nearly shot, into those trees.

Fourth, the spot where he escaped must be near the Friedmann home, because the couple were on foot when they met him just after sunrise on April 17, 1945, as was Barbara when she returned later that morning with food.

We return to Angelika's Citroen in the Enns town square after seeing the jail. We say good-bye to Dr. Harreither, who has museum business to attend to. But Dietmar Heck joins us, effortlessly folding his long frame into the back seat.

Angelika starts the car to get the air conditioning running and then announces she has something interesting to tell me about the route. 'There were no groups of trees on the road your father marched on from *Steyrer Strasse* until he reached to the old sugar factory.'

Predictably, she has found a way to narrow down our choice of locations quickly. No trees, no escape, I think to myself. But I don't know what she is referring to. 'What old sugar factory?'

Angelika asks Dietmar to hand her the papers piled next to him on the back seat. She thumbs through them until locating a Google Earth image she'd printed on legal-size paper. The image shows three miles of the death march route, starting with the *Steyrer-Ennser* intersection, and continuing west on the old B1, now *Doktor Renner Strasse*.

'A big Nazi sugar factory was here,' she says, pointing. 'It was destroyed after the war.'

Angelika's finger rests on a large greyish-white blot on the picture covering one-quarter of a mile of the north side of *Doktor Renner Strasse*. I recognize it, having seen the same blot on my computer in my office when I'd studied the area around the Friedmann home. But I thought it was a giant parking lot belonging to nearby industrial buildings.

'On this road,' Angelika continues, pointing to the B1/*Doktor Renner Strasse*, 'there are only two places where there are trees. Here, before the old sugar factory,' she moves her finger a short distance, 'and here, after the old sugar factory.'

'Can I have this for a second?' I ask, and Angelika gives me the printout so I can see it better in the sunlight pouring through her car windows. Clearly visible are two large collections of trees and grass, one the marchers would have reached immediately before, and one right after, the white blot that was once a sugar factory.

The trees are in deep shades of green, in sharp relief against the white of the old sugar factory grounds. I measure the first set of trees to be a mile and a quarter from where my father escaped the first time, the second set of trees another quarter of a mile along. That fits perfectly with what I am assuming about his endurance. Also clear is there are no other tree groves along this segment of the route as he marched from the intersection where he escaped the first time. Just these two.

I ask an obvious question. 'Do you think this road changed much since the war?'

'No. I researched this,' Angelika says definitively. 'All the buildings on the road are old, many even from before the war. I am sure this is how it looked in those years, too.' Then she points to a spot one quarter of a mile south of *Doktor Renner Strasse*. 'Here is where the Friedmanns lived, on *Kristein Strasse*.'

She is pointing both to the Friedmanns' house, the lowercase-h, which I recognize, and to a thin line, *Kristein Strasse*, snaking up from the Friedmann house to B1/*Doktor Renner Strasse*. The two streets meet at a T-junction on the former sugar plant's western boundary, exactly at the second set of trees. Distances from both the *Steyrer* intersection and the Friedmanns' home are small enough so that either corner of the old sugar plant could have been where my father went to the side of the road.

What I don't yet know is whether I will find a path at either.

Angelika puts her car in gear, and as we drive she fills me in about Dietmar. His father and Ignaz Friedmann were friends. Dietmar was around five years old when the war ended but later he worked as an apprentice to Ignaz as a bricklayer. He has brought with him a couple of receipts for work done by Ignaz's company. As Angelika speaks she cues him, and he hands them to me. I stare at Ignaz's signature. It is precise and orderly, as I'm sure he was.

A few short minutes later we pull over to the shoulder of *Doktor Renner Strasse* at the eastern corner of what had been the sugar factory. My father came upon these trees first as he marched. Hardly able to contain myself, I have my door open before the wheels stop rolling.

Dietmar remains in the car while Angelika gets me oriented. 'Your father and the other marchers would have walked on this side of the B1,' she says, referring to the north side, where we are standing. She takes a moment as a truck rumbles by. 'Across the street important SS officers lived in the houses just there.'

The mid-sized homes across from us, on the south side of the two-lane *Doktor Renner Strasse*, are well maintained and painted like so many of the buildings here dating from that era, in muted pastels. I easily imagine them being the homes of Nazis and their families during the war. We are half a mile from the Friedmann home. The risk the Friedmanns took, hiding my father this close to the Reich's nastiest men, is even greater than I realized until now. It is breathtaking.

Looking again at the trees on my side of the street, I notice a white three-story apartment building behind them. It is small, closer in size to a very large home. Angelika tells me it was built in the 1920s, so it was here during the war. It would have been impossible for my father to miss. It was, of course, on the Google Earth photos, but I couldn't tell what sort of building it was, or how completely it dominated the immediate area. Stepping a few yards to the west, I see a second, nearly identical three-story apartment building behind the first, this one painted light brown. Looking around, I see no path into the trees, though there is a road leading to both homes.

That settles it for me, and I tell Angelika. 'My father would never have escaped into these trees here.' I explain that he would have been running towards an apartment house he could see from the B1. He would have known doing so was as suicidal as sitting on the side of the road. Besides, if he had escaped here, he would have mentioned the apartment house in his story. And if he'd escaped down the road that passed both apartment houses, he would have called it a *road*, not a *path*. He knew the difference. This isn't the spot.

Angelika takes me at my word, and we return to her car. Hopefully the second site, the trees on the opposite side of the former sugar factory, will prove to be the right one.

Chapter 55

261st Regiment of the 65th Infantry Division: 156 Miles Away

In the spring of 1945, the 1.3 million men of the Twelfth Army Group comprised the largest and most powerful military force ever assembled in the 170-year history of the U.S. Army. It was commanded by 52-year-old West Point graduate General Omar Bradley, who'd missed action in World War I, but had earned his battle stripes in this one, in 1943, commanding troops in North Africa. During the Normandy invasion he was in charge of all U.S. ground forces. Third Army's 350,000 troops were part of Twelfth Army Group, and General Bradley was Patton's boss.

On Tuesday morning, April 17, 1945, while Barbara and Ignaz Friedmann were concocting their plan to rescue my father, General Bradley was issuing detailed orders for the units under his command to advance rapidly through Germany and link up with the Russians, who were simultaneously driving west towards them. Patton devoted the remainder of that day to positioning his corps and divisions to execute Bradley's battle plan.

The next day Patton ordered the entire 65th Infantry Division to advance. With the 259th, 260th and 261st Regiments now working together, they were trucked sixty-five miles south, to Bamberg, Germany, which by then was behind American lines. Over the next two days the division fought its way another forty-six miles southeast, capturing the town of Trautmannshofen. On Saturday, April 21, while the 260th and 261st Regiments held their ground, the 259th engaged in one of its biggest battles of the war in the town of Neumarkt, six miles southwest of Trautmannshofen.

That same Saturday, Barbara and Ignaz Friedmann were faced with a problem. They had a good friend, a local gendarme – not the one my father had encountered – who often came by the house to hear overseas broadcasts on the Friedmanns' illegal short-wave radio (the more I learned about Barbara and Ignaz, the more heroic they became). The Friedmanns had confided in the gendarme about my father's presence in their home. The officer came over that morning to warn the Friedmanns to move my dad out of the in-house barn, the *Kuhstall*. The fighting was getting very close, he said, and the risk of discovery was climbing steadily. The gendarme reminded them, as if they needed reminding, that if they were caught with my father, they'd be killed. They had to figure out what to do with him.

The 261st Regiment of the 65th division was now 156 miles from Enns.

Chapter 56

The Little Path

We drive a quarter of mile west on the B1/*Doktor Renner Strasse*. Angelika swings her car across the road and parks in the lot of a furniture store on the south side that is closed for the weekend. Exactly as I saw on Angelika's Google Earth image, the north side of the street is busy with trees and thick brush. Walking across the *Strasse*, my spine is tingling. I have a feeling about this. As if confirming my instinct, Dietmar is out of the car and with us this time.

Standing on the north shoulder of *Doktor Renner Strasse*, I study the mess of trees and bushes in front of me. I am facing north, the two-lane blacktop at my back. Angelika and Dietmar hover nearby, silently. Occasionally a car zooms by close behind me, but I am concentrating too hard to care. I want to take in everything I see, because I have an inexplicable but definite sense that everything I see, my father saw as well, in the gloomy late afternoon half-light of April 16, 1945.

I am exactly halfway between a road bridge ten feet to my left, and a cement wall ten feet to my right. The bridge traverses a small stream and is tiny. Except for the metal railing and grey cement roadway rather than black tar, a driver on *Doktor Renner Strasse* might not even notice traveling over it.

The wall on my right is set back ten feet from the road. It looks decades old, and continues eastward along the *Strasse*, away from me, for the entire length of the sugar factory property. Where the wall begins, ten feet from me, a chain-link fence runs from the wall, north into the brush. Within the corner created by the wall and the fence are the grounds of the old sugar factory.

I wonder if the wall was here in the mid-1940s, or if it was built later. If it wasn't here, then my father could have escaped anywhere between me, and 100 yards east of me, where the trees and bushes end. But if the wall had been here when my father marched by, then he could *only* have escaped right here, in the twenty-foot gap between the end of the cement wall and the start of the tiny bridge.

I need to find someone who knows the history of this wall. And I need to find a path here.

I turn to Angelika and Dietmar for help, suggesting that perhaps the mayor, who so helpfully provided the old map we'd used earlier, might be able to assist again? The two engage in an animated conversation in German. Angelika fills me in.

'Dietmar doesn't remember a path, or the wall, but he was a very young boy during the war, and he lived on the other side of town, near your hotel. He has a friend of his family that lives just here, very close to *Kristein Strasse*. His name is *Herr* Fisher. He is old now, but he is in contact, and the friend knew the Friedmanns a little also. He may know everything, so maybe we don't need to ask the mayor. Dietmar said he will telephone the friend to ask him to come to here.'

I say it would be great if he could join us, and ask how old, 'old now' is.

'Ninety,' Angelika says, as if it was just a number.

Dietmar makes the call, and a few minutes later Mr. Fisher, *Herr* Fisher, appears. Watching him cross the road at nearly a jog to miss cars whizzing by, he looks like no ninety-year-old man I've ever met. If Angelika had said he was sixty, I'd have believed her. People don't seem to age in this town. He is short and stocky, with thick glasses and equally thick grey hair, and wearing a bright multi-colored sweater. I'd probably be wearing a sweater in the heat of this afternoon, too, if I were ninety. His grip is firm and he smiles brightly as we are introduced.

Angelika, Dietmar and *Herr* Fisher launch into a spirited conversation. I understand none of it, of course, though I hear the word *Bahnhof* once or twice. *Herr* Fisher points towards the brush excitedly a number of times. Then Dietmar breaks away from the other two, takes long strides to the start of the bushes to the right of where I stand, and turns to face me.

'Jack!' he bellows, just like in the town square. Facing me, he swings his long arms in unison. Then he turns to face the brush, and repeats the arm-swinging gesture. I look at Angelika, who is grinning broadly, then to Dietmar's back. I turn my palms up, in question. I am missing something.

'*Der kleine pfad*,' Dietmar booms out over his shoulder. And then he says more, including *Bahnhof* again.

'The little path,' Angelika translates and points. 'It is just there. During the war a path was there where he is showing you with his arms. It was a shortcut to the train station for Enns, one mile from here, behind the sugar factory.'

Moving to join Dietmar, my breathing quickens as I peer into the foliage in front of him. At first I see only the trees and brush. And then slowly, like a dream resolving into reality, I make out slightly less growth in front of me. And then it becomes unmistakable. The path, or what I can see of it, what remains of it, wanders north away from me, keeping a few feet from the chain-link fence. The more I look, the clearer it becomes, until I don't know how I missed it the first time.

Remaining focused, I have one more question. 'How about the wall? How long has it been here?'

Angelika has already asked *Herr* Fisher. '*Herr* Fisher says the wall was built after the war ended, but during the war there was a wooden fence here with sharp wire. It was instead of the cement wall.'

Wood and barbed wire is the same as a cement wall. Both were impenetrable to my eighty-pound father.

This is it. Everything fits: the road, the trees, the distance from the first escape, the proximity to the Friedmanns' home. The fence and bridge mean it could only have been within these twenty feet. The path means it had to be right where I am standing.

I've found it.

This is exactly, precisely, within *inches* of where my father went to the side of the road, had a pistol jammed into the back of his neck, and expected to die.

A direct line connects what happened on this spot, with me. That rainy afternoon, if the SS man had been quicker on the trigger, if my father hadn't charged down the path, if the Friedmanns hadn't come by, I would not be standing here. I can't see clearly, my eyes have misted over. I don't dare speak for fear I will lose it. I am overwhelmed by the importance of what happened here. I am hitting the same sensory overload I experienced yesterday at the *Sanitätslager*, and maybe worse. There is suddenly so much to contemplate.

In the late afternoon of April 16, 1945, my father stumbled to the side of the road and sat down expecting to die, right here.

A Hungarian-born Nazi *Storm trooper* pulled his pistol out of his holster and prepared to shoot my father in the back of his neck, right here.

And because the Nazi didn't pull the trigger, I am now standing, right here.

The importance of this spot cannot be overstated. Some might know the place where their father or mother died. This is the place where my father *lived*. This is where he gave himself a new chance for life. The *Steyrer–Ennser* intersection is a place like this, too, but it is big and wide and not exactly the same now as it was in 1945. Plus, Dad was recaptured.

Not so of where I am standing.

If my father had gone to the side of the road just ten feet earlier, or ten feet later, he wouldn't have seen the path. Maybe less, maybe five feet to either side and he would have missed it. Five feet was the difference between living and dying, because he would certainly have died had he returned to marching down the B1. Can there be any doubt this was another example of his extraordinary luck? Or perhaps, another example of something more than luck?

I take a deep breath. Peering down the overgrown trail that was once a commonly-used shortcut to the train station, I am desperate to know where my father got the courage to run down here. Where did it come from? How in the name of heaven did he have the guts to do this?

If I knew where he had gotten it from, if I knew how he'd pulled this off, I might then know if I, too, have that courage. Could I have looked around, seen that, for a tiny sliver of a moment in time I was not being watched by rifle-toting storm troopers, and bolted down this path, run for all I was worth, saved my own life?

I remain standing here, cars motoring by, the sun shining intently, and let the questions sink in for a very long while.

Chapter 57

Excuse

Wednesday, Thursday and Friday passed comfortably for my father in the *Kuhstall*. He spent the days resting in his hay and straw bed, eating every few hours and feeling his strength slowly returning. He was as cautious about his food intake as he'd been on the cold November night the KZ Gusen I *Revier* had been emptied, when the prisoners in the latrine barracks had been given unlimited quantities of soup. Barbara Friedmann would have fed him whatever he desired, but he asked mostly for garlic bread in small portions, raising his intake slowly as he felt his body tolerate it better. The Friedmanns also put salves and ointments on his cuts and boils, so that they could finally begin healing properly. Every bite of food, every day of rest, every drop of ointment, was a step closer to recovering the young man he had once been.

Resting there must have been an otherworldly experience for my father. On Monday of that week he had been a *KZler*, a prisoner of the Nazis, starting his day like all his other horrific days in KZ Mauthausen, with no expectation that anything would ever change until he died. On Tuesday he had been a man on the run, a starving, weakened fugitive who could be discovered in his hiding place and killed at any moment. And now, here he was at the Friedmanns, a free man, eating whatever he wanted, sleeping as much as he cared, and finally healing. It was all so incredible, but he didn't dwell on it much because it was too new, the shock of change had not yet worn off.

And because he feared it could be taken from him.

My father, at the Seder table. 'It was my fourth day with the Friedmanns,' he said. 'Ignaz came to tell me that fighting between the Americans and Germans is getting very close, and he was required to put up SS soldiers to sleep in his house. It was like we had to do at my house in Dej. He said he was not happy about it, but he had to obey the order. He said he would have to move me to another hiding place.'

Obviously my father couldn't remain where he was while German soldiers, SS storm troopers no less, were living in the house. I didn't know at the Seder table in 2001, but I now know his situation was even worse, even scarier than he'd said.

Ignaz had lied to my father. SS soldiers were not coming to sleep at the Friedmanns' house.

They were already there.

SS troops had been living in the Friedmanns' house for months.

Just like in Dej, months earlier the Friedmanns had been ordered to billet German troops, in their case front-line SS combat soldiers. To comply, Ignaz, the master brick mason, constructed a bedroom for them in his house's second floor, and built a separate entrance exclusively for their use. That entrance was one of the two doors at the southern end of the front of the house. The other southern door led to the *Kuhstall* – and my father. I assume the SS didn't have a key to that door.

The-SS-are-coming story was just an excuse Barbara and Ignaz had concocted that morning, after the warning from their short-wave-radio co-listener and friend, the gendarme. They wanted my father to sense their urgency, and to buy in to the importance of moving from his comfortable spot in the *Kuhstall*.

Keeping an illegal short-wave radio in their house was nothing compared with this. The Friedmanns, those incredibly brave people, had brought my father to their house – and kept him there – literally under the noses of the Nazis' best soldiers. As far as I know, my father never learned about this. He had never read Peter Kammerstätter's account, and he had never been in touch with Mauthausen Memorial staff, so he had no way of knowing the real reason he had to leave the house that day.[1] He only knew what Ignaz had told him that afternoon. And until my trip to Austria, that's all I knew, as well. When I heard about the SS living in the Friedmanns' house, it floored me. I remain stunned by it.

I understand why the Friedmanns never told my father that SS men were living right above him – it would have freaked him out as surely as it did me when I heard it. But why use it as a reason that

---

1 There is no record at KZ Mauthausen or KZ Gusen of my father's visit in 1997. He didn't contact anyone, nor is there even a record of him signing a visitor book. There is no way he could have known about the SS troops in the house.

Saturday? Why not simply tell my father he now needed to leave the house? They didn't have to give him a reason.

I think the Friedmanns were showing how taken they were with my father. They cared about him. They cared about how he felt, and they wanted him to be emotionally comfortable with the need to leave the shelter of the *Kuhstall*.

All their efforts on behalf of my father raises the question, *Why*? Why did they risk their lives to rescue him? Why did they work so hard to keep him fed and safe, and care for his emotional well-being in addition to his physical needs? What was in it for them?

I know no obvious answer. But I have a theory, derived by discarding reasons that don't fit.

For instance, they didn't have a son who'd died in the war, a son whose presence my father was replacing. That would not be unheard of, and even understandable on some level. The Friedmanns' only child, their son Ignaz Jr., was living in their home during my father's stay. He was eleven years old at the time, and was never told about my father hiding in their *Kuhstall* and barn – not during the war, and not after, either. He only learned about what his parents did for my father from relatives, long after the war ended. I understand the reason for keeping Ignaz Jr. in the dark *during* the war. Eleven is not the age to be told secrets that could kill your parents. But I can't explain him not being told *after* the war.

The Friedmanns were not from Czechoslovakia, and had no known connection to it, so Barbara's remark on the path, about having relatives there, wasn't why they'd saved him, either. They tried hard, but Mauthausen Memorial historians could find no connection between the Friedmanns and that country. Clearly Barbara was trying to make my father feel at ease that first morning.

So I end up with one final possible reason – the most altruistic reason of all. They rescued my father because they were good people. They saw someone in need – in a dire, life-threatening need – and they did the right thing. *That* is why they saved my father.

Back at the Seder, I asked, 'Did Ignaz tell you how close the Russians and the Americans were right then?'

'Yes, I remember very clearly. He said the Americans were only 150 miles away to the west, and the Russians were already in Vienna, which was less than a hundred miles to the east'

My father's liberators were closing in. 'What was he going to do with you?'

'He told me he and Barbara had a plan where to put me.'

Chapter 58

The House

After soaking up all I can feel from the foot of the path, from the spot where my father nearly died, Angelika, Dietmar, *Herr* Fisher, and I cross the B1/*Doktor Renner Strasse* and walk together down *Kristein Strasse* to the Friedmann house. As I suspected from the Google Earth image, the street is very narrow, really a one-lane paved path more suitable for a horse and cart than for an automobile. It's not far, only a quarter of a mile, so Angelika has left her car in the furniture store lot. At the second intersection along, we say goodbye to *Herr* Fisher, who saunters away with his youthful stride.

Then, as we are walking, an angular roofline appears through trees, just ahead of us.

I stop. That's the Friedmann house.

Even without seeing the number, I know it is the house whose stucco façade I saw in the photos I'd been emailed. This is the house where my father stayed after miraculously encountering the Friedmanns. This house, I know, is as much a part of me as it was a part of my father.

I soon collect myself and continue walking, catching up to Angelika and Dietmar.

Now standing in front of the house, its steeply sloped roof makes it appear taller than I expected. The white paint on the window frames is chipped in places, and the small plot of grass in front needs cutting. The door near the north end, its color not black or brown, but somewhere in between, has the number *57* in white on a square blue plate above the doorframe. The front door, most likely. The two other doors I saw in the photos, near the southern end, are smaller. They are the doors leading to the *Kuhstall* and the SS troopers' upstairs bedrooms. I hear the soft gurgling of a small stream behind me. Turning around, it is obscured by thick brush, but I know it is the *Kristeinerbach*.

Looking past the house brings into view the vast farmlands to the east that I saw on Google Earth. Though the Friedmanns were not farmers, they lived among lush fields which stretch away from me to as far as I can see. Trees dot the scene.

I am suddenly aware of the staccato sounds of hammering coming from the back. I wonder how long I've been hearing it. We walk around the house's southern end and into the yard within the inside of the lowercase-h, as I characterized the picture I saw on my office computer. A man around my age is leaning a ladder against the house. Long-limbed and lean, with greying hair but a dark mustache, he wears a leather tool belt over his jeans and a t-shirt marked with sweat from laboring in the afternoon heat. Angelika asks if he is Mr. Hofer. Saying that indeed he is, he walks over and we shake hands all around. He was expecting us. Angelika had arranged it.

Mr. Hofer explains, in German, that he rents part of the home and he's lived there for a few years. The interior of the house was remodeled and divided into two units before he moved in. He is currently the only tenant.

My father had never been inside the family living quarters of the Friedmann house, so the remodel means little to me. I would have nothing to compare it to. But I hope the old in-house barn, the *Kuhstall*, is still intact. The backyard door to that space is near where we are standing, and Mr. Hofer opens it with a key. We all step inside.

The *Kuhstall* runs nearly the width of the house, twenty-five feet, and is square. It is divided near its center by a thick structural support beam holding up the house's second floor. It is now used for storage, old furniture, old flower pots, old stuff. It smells musty, and if I stretch my imagination, maybe of animals, too. The greyish-green walls need repainting. The floor is brick and cement – without animals here, there's no need for a covering of hay. Four worn metal hitching posts running through the room's center define where the cows or goats or sheep would have been. The home remodel clearly hadn't extended this far. An interior door leads to a second room, a second *Kuhstall*. A door from that room leads to a small bathroom and the remainder of the house.

Back in the first *Kuhstall*, standing by the support beam and taking it in, I'm unhappy the room is now used to store somebody's junk. It seems almost heretical to me. I try ignoring what it's become, and instead imagine it as my father must have seen it. This is where he had his first taste of freedom, his first indication that maybe he would survive the war. But the rubbish and broken furniture piled haphazardly throughout is getting in my way, sucking the sanctity out of this room. Perhaps I am not focusing properly. Perhaps I've seen too much on this trip already.

After another minute sorting through my thoughts, I look at Angelika and shrug almost imperceptibly. My gesture says, 'I'm ready to go back outside.'

She understands, and leads the way out of the *Kuhstall* and into the back yard, to the grass within the lowercase-h. After being hidden for the first four days in the *Kuhstall*, the Friedmanns eventually moved my father to an attic in their barn. His memory was right about that, only his timing was off. Now I see that the short vertical part of the 'h' across from the *Kuhstall* door is a barn – I assume it is *the* barn of my father's story. It is made of brick and wood, covered in chipping brown stucco, and features two sets of large wooden double-doors facing the courtyard, that is, facing the inside of the 'h.'

The short horizontal part of the 'h' connecting the house with the barn is a real, operating cowshed, unlike the *Kuhstall* in the house where the family den might have been. I walk inside and discover the floor thickly cushioned with hay, and the interior filled with animals – a few chickens, a pig, and a pair of goats. But while it is attached to the barn on one side, it is not attached to the house on the other. This surprises me. The Google Earth photo was deceiving. The gap between this real cowshed and the house was filled by a stand-alone structure, like a portico, loosely attached to both the cowshed, and the house. The overhead photo made it look like a single contiguous lowercase-h-shaped building, but it wasn't. It is two separate structures. And when my father was here, I'm certain this portico wasn't.

One pair of the barn's twin doors are open, and we step in. The floor is dirt, and the peaked roof twenty feet over my head is in need of repair, holes in it letting in rays of light. Dust floating in the rays twinkle like glitter. There is clearly no attic. That's odd, there is supposed to be one here.

In the weak light, I spy stairs to my left. They creak and groan loudly with each step as I climb, but at the top I am rewarded with a view of a deep, windowless but roomy opening lit the same way as the barn, by light sneaking in through holes in the roof. This space is directly above the functioning cowshed, the horizontal part of the house's 'h.'

Stepping into the opening, I stand under the highest part of the roof, which slopes steeply down on either side of me. I try an electric switch near the stairs, and am bathed in the harsh light of a bare bulb hanging near my head. The space is cluttered by support beams, their wood an aged deep brown. The floor is wood, as well, and dressed in a thick coating of dust. There are no windows, so it would have been as dark in here as, say, a 'transport' cattle car. *This* must have been the other place where my father had hid – he would have gotten here through the barn, as I did, so his description, 'the attic in the barn,' is close enough.

I look around for a sign of my father's presence, his initials or 'Dave was here' carved into the wood, something to that effect, but I find nothing except markings from the mill that had cut the two-by-fours when this was built in the 1930s. I can't say why, but this feels genuine, this feels like I can detect my father's presence, like he absolutely was here. I've been having those feelings since yesterday, and each time they have been right. I am feeling them now. Maybe a piece of him remains here. Maybe a piece of my father remains in all the places he'd been. Only in the *Kuhstall* I didn't feel anything, yet I know he was there. It must have been all the junk scattered about.

I sit down in the dust. I have the intense sense I am in my father's personal space. I feel I am intruding, like when, as a kid, I went into my parents' bedroom to watch their black-and-white TV when they weren't home. I absorb the feeling of this attic, the sense of warmth and safety it gives me, and that it must surely have projected to my father. He must have had an incredibly positive experience here. I feel it in my bones.

And so I sit, thinking of nothing, but feeling my father all around me. It is a happy feeling, and I know that hiding here, he was, too. After a short while, I return to the stairs, careful not to disturb anything. Then I turn around for a long last look, turn off the light, and descend.

Chapter 59

Lost

The Friedmanns owned a barn in one of the farm fields surrounding their house. They used it to store straw and hay for the animals they kept in their *Kuhstall* and in the real cowshed attached to the barn across from their house. That Saturday afternoon, Ignaz told my father he and Barbara decided the barn in the field would be a perfect hiding place for him. It was close by and easy to walk to.

'You'll be safe,' Ignaz promised sincerely. He said he would come by daily with food and news of the fighting.

My father believed Ignaz. The Friedmanns had been both good and generous to him, and this seemed to be more of the same. He didn't want them getting into trouble for saving him. He would do whatever was necessary.

A few hours past nightfall, Ignaz returned to the *Kuhstall*, this time with Barbara. My father was ready. He wore the jacket he'd taken from the dead marcher, and a pair of shoes belonging to Ignaz. The three walked together outside.

'Jeckeleh, they gave me a good, warm blanket, and a sack with seven or eight potatoes, in case Ignaz had to miss a day of bringing me food. Then they told me how to find the barn.'

'It must have been scary,' I suggested.

'It was not so terrible. But I kept remembering while I was walking to the barn something my mother, may she rest in peace, used to say to us at home. She used to say, "Be wary of Saturday nights."' My father chuckled. 'Be wary of Saturday nights. Can't you imagine? I am walking through fields in Austria in the darkest black at night and this is what I'm thinking!' That smile came on.

Less than one year earlier, my father had been living in his parents' house and telling them what time he'd be home in the evening. Now he was making one of the most important journeys of his young life on the one night of the week his mother always warned him about.

'Then what?' I asked.

'Then what? Then I got lost.'

Incredible. Like most of my father's story, I already knew what he was going to say in answer to my next question, but I asked it anyway. 'How did you get lost?'

My father gave me the same response as he did each time I asked this. And I asked it often, because it was such an important turn of events.

'How did I get lost? I got lost.' He shrugged, tipped his head, lifted his eyebrows, and offered a weak smile.

He was saying, how does anyone get lost? A wrong turn, a missed turn, a misheard direction. I knew this was all the detail I was going to get, and I bet it's also all the detail he ever remembered.

One thing I never wondered about: whether the Friedmanns had misled him. Not a chance. They wouldn't have sent him out to their field hoping he'd get lost. There isn't a rational reason in the world why they would have done that. My father either misheard part of the directions, or forgot what he'd been told. When I've asked for directions, how many times have I forgotten if the next turn was a left or a right? And I'm healthy, well fed, and speaking my native language. My father was a starving teenager following instructions given to him in the language of his mortal enemy, in hostile country, stepping into total darkness wearing the clothes of a dead man, in wartime, with a blackout in effect and barely a half moon in the sky, and with his mom's admonition about Saturday nights bouncing around his head. He was leaving a warm and comfortable sanctuary that he had grown accustomed to over the past four days, and stepping into a complete void. He was probably disoriented by the turn of events, and scared silly. It's eminently reasonable to believe he made a wrong turn.

No matter how it happened, my father was now thoroughly lost. The air chilled him. Nights in Enns in April 1945 were not yet warm. He walked in what he thought was the right direction. No barn. Maybe he hadn't gone far enough? He walked a little further, then turned around. Looking back towards the direction he'd come from, he couldn't make out anything, it was too dark. His palms were sweating so much that he had trouble holding the sack with his potatoes. He stopped to wrap himself in the blanket, he picked a new direction, walked a few feet, and paused again. He heard nothing, and he saw nothing. He took more steps. Now he heard running water, like a brook or stream, the sound of water coursing over stones.

He made his way towards the sound, until the grass under his feet changed to dirt. He halted again. Directly in front of him was a stream. He knelt and put a hand gingerly in the water. It was cold, and when he licked the water off his fingers, it tasted clean. He looked to his left and right and above, and in the dim light saw that he was in a protected enclosure. There were thick vines all around him, though not much brush yet, as the leaves hadn't had their season.

The ground under him was earth, as smooth as a table top, as if it had been flattened by machine, but my father knew this was not man-made. He was, remarkably, in a natural shelter, with an unlimited supply of water at hand. He sat down and took a deep, long breath.

His luck had held yet again.

Except he had no idea where he was. And neither did the Friedmanns.

Chapter 60

The Fields

It is outrageously unbelievable to me that my father got lost that Saturday night. He knew the war was almost over. He had expected a short, easy walk to the Friedmanns' storage barn, where he would make himself comfortable for a few days. His horrible year was nearly over.

And suddenly his life was in danger again.

Whenever I heard my father tell about getting lost on his way to the Friedmanns' barn, I assumed what happened that night was forever lost to history. Especially when he'd admit to me he had no idea *how* he'd gotten lost. But from my first glimpse of the Friedmann house on Google Earth on my office computer, I realized there might be a way to retrace my father's steps. And I figured that if I could discover *how* he got lost, I might even be able to locate *where* he found shelter for himself.

Visualizing my father's choices that night, it turns out there were only two places where he could have made a wrong turn.

First, when my father left the *Kuhstall* in the house and stepped onto *Kristein Strasse*, he had a choice: left or right. Right led north, towards the B1, the street he had marched on and escaped from, one quarter of a mile away. The B1 was an important military artery, and since sound travels particularly well at night, he probably would have been able to hear army traffic rumbling by. The road had been quiet the night he had escaped, but the fighting was now much closer, and so the road was probably busy twenty-four hours a day. Since there were only a few houses in the hamlet of Kristein in those years, it's even possible he would have been able to see the B1. Combining that he might have been able to hear and see the main road, with how unlikely getting the *first* turn wrong

241

would have been, I'm sure my father did this correctly. He went left, towards the south.

The second left-right choice was fifty yards south of the Friedmann house on *Kristein Strasse*, at the Y-intersection I identified on Google Earth. This one is in the middle of the fields, and I can't reason through my father's choices. I need to walk it.

Leaving the Friedmanns' yard, I walk south on *Kristein Strasse*. Angelika and Dietmar are a few steps behind me, while Mr. Hofer goes back to his hammering. I focus on how my father might have been feeling and on what he might have been thinking – besides his mother's heads-up about Saturday nights. I find that putting myself in my father's shoes isn't easy – it is sunny and warm out, rather than dark and cool as it was that night.

Reaching the Y-intersection, directly in front of me is a pale-green two story house with a small black Volkswagen in the driveway.

Should I turn left? Or right?

I turn left, to the southeast.

In front of me are picturesque farm fields, green and yellow carpets of grains. They are the same fields I saw a few minutes ago from the southern side of the Friedmann home. I begin walking, and after seventy yards or so I come across a barn on my left.

'This barn never belonged to the Friedmanns,' Angelika says as I near it. She'd already checked it out. I walk up to it anyway. Constructed of dark wood, pitted and splintered, it is sturdy and old. It had passed the brutal test of Austrian winters better than the KZ Mauthausen barracks. It highlights for me how rough the winters here are.

Before coming to Austria, I'd seen this barn on Google Earth. Intriguingly, the image also revealed long white scars on the ground nearby, footprints left by other barns now long gone. Likely they had been here during the war, and I'm certain that if the Friedmanns had sent my father to one of them, he'd have found the right one – *if* he'd turned left. I mention this to Angelika, and she acknowledges that I could be right.

But my father didn't see a barn. So I have to assume he hadn't gone left.

If he had gone right at the Y-intersection, were there barns in that direction, as well?

I retrace my steps. Passing Angelika and Dietmar, and then the Y-intersection, I continue southwest, as if I had initially made the right turn. Next to the house with the Volkswagen is a two-story rectangular structure, painted brown. It looks more like a small factory building than a barn, and anyway it appears too new to have been here during the war. I keep walking.

Just past the brown structure the path becomes a rutted dirt track, ideally suited for a 4x4 jeep. Trees and bushes on the right side of the track grow twenty feet into the air and cantilever over my head. Near the end of the track, trees on my left reach up to meet the growth on my right, forming a canopy. I keep walking under the canopy until the track ends and I step into the open. I have been walking for only two minutes since the Y-intersection, a distance of probably 150 yards. Taking a few more steps, before me are more beautiful broad fields.

I admire the peacefulness of the scene for a moment, and then come back to why I am here. Turning around, I see the path I just took, with its cantilevered-bush-tree canopy. There is a triangle-shaped grass field to the left of it. Beyond the grass field is a wall of vines and trees.

A woman who isn't a day under eighty years old walks towards us. Angelika and Dietmar stop her. Small, almost frail, and dressed for cooler weather than we are having, she lives nearby and is out for her daily stroll. The woman volunteers that she and her husband have lived in the neighborhood since the 1950s. She recalls the Friedmanns but didn't know them well, so she offers us nothing about them. She remembers barns on the other side of the Y-intersection, and none on this side. Most importantly, she confirms for us that very little has changed since she'd move in. Only a few more houses here and there, especially in the hamlet. The track, the brush, and the fields have not changed in decades. We thank her for her help and she resumes her strolling.

I take stock. I now know that when my father reached the Y-intersection after leaving the Friedmanns' house, if he had gone left, he would have quickly found barns, and presumably *the* storage barn Ignaz had sent him to. But if he had gone right, he'd have found no barns, only a rough track that ends in farm fields. No doubt about it for me: my father had gone to the right.

So I have now figured out, with as much certainty as is possible, *where* my father had gotten lost. But I still don't know *how* he'd gotten lost. When he went right, exited the canopied path, reached the fields, and saw no barns, why didn't he turn around and retrace his steps? He hadn't gone very far. Why didn't he walk back to the Y-intersection and then continue southeast towards the barns I knew were there? It seemed pretty easy to do. Or – perhaps even easier – why didn't he just walk back to the Friedmanns and admit he'd gotten lost?

The answer had to lie in what my father could or couldn't see in the utter darkness of a wartime Austrian night. If I am going to fully answer this question, if I am going to definitively discover *how* he got lost, I have to return at night, when it's dark. *I have to.* I won't be able to duplicate my father's mood, his fear, his nervousness that night, but I can reproduce what he saw. It is the only way to *really* know how he got lost.

I tell Angelika I intend to return after sunset, and explain why. Checking the weather app on my phone, sunset is around 7:30pm, so it will be dark by nine. I ask her to join me. She politely declines, saying she has dinner plans with her husband Kurt. Studying her earnest face, I don't believe her, but I don't press the point. I think she is giving me space, the way she's expertly done since we met. Since yesterday she has intuitively known when I needed room to absorb what I was seeing and feeling. She must feel she can't contribute anything to tonight.

'I'll tell you what I learn,' I offer, and she says she knows I will. I am grateful for her understanding.

Before I leave the fields that afternoon, I have one last thing to find.

When my father got lost that Saturday night, he ended up by a stream. It was unquestionably the *Kristeinerbach*, which flows past the Friedmanns' house. There are no other streams within a mile of the house, and I am completely certain my father didn't walk a mile that night. I want to see where the stream is in relation to me now, in relation to where my father might have been when he realized he was lost. I need this knowledge for when I return in the evening.

After meandering past the Friedmanns' house, the *Kristeinerbach* makes a sharp right at the same Y-intersection where I'd made the right to walk southwest along the 4x4 track. The stream runs northwest for around a hundred yards, and then it turns almost due south. That divergence between the southwest track and the northwest stream creates a triangle-shaped gap that is filled by the grass field I saw to the left of the 4x4 track's tall vegetation.

I walk from the track to the wall of trees and vines. They are twenty paces away. Reaching them, I discover they guard the near bank of the *Kristeinerbach*, which was otherwise not visible to me. But now standing by the stream, its waters gurgling past me, I am stymied. Did my father know it was here? Why did he head towards it and not, for instance, in the opposite direction, deeper into the field? Again, I need the darkness to figure this out.

I will be back tonight.

Angelika drives me back to my hotel, which is coincidentally near Dietmar's home. I shake hands vigorously with Dietmar, thanking him for coming with us and helping answer my questions. Then I hug Angelika for a long moment. I tell her she has made possible a journey I could not have imagined when I first saw my father's photo on the internet. In fact I couldn't have even imagined it in the Chinese restaurant the day before. That journey is not over, not by a long shot. She knows that. We promise to stay in touch. I will have many more questions, and I trust her to help me find the answers, just as she did before, and during, this trip.

Chapter 61

The Stream

Settling into the natural shelter by the stream, my father must have felt like the loneliest person in the universe, a feeling that, by now, might have been familiar to him. He knew he was completely lost. He figured he would never find the barn in the dark, and he dared not try finding it during the day. The farm fields around him were actively worked by the local farmers. And for all he knew, kids, or troops, or families walked the roads and paths crisscrossing the fields. Just because the Friedmanns were willing to harbor an escaped KZ Mauthausen prisoner didn't mean their neighbors would be so agreeable. He had no plan, no thoughts about what to do next, so he stayed put.

'I wasn't worried,' my father said to me. 'I had the sack with potatoes, I had water from the stream, I had on warm clothes, and I had the heavy blanket.'

What he didn't say, but what I learned when I walked into the fields by the Friedmann home, was that he also had a roof of sorts over his head. In sum, he had about as much as he'd ever had since his first day in Auschwitz, and so he had enough to last a short while.

Of course, he also had his monumental *Will*, that will to live no matter what he faced.

And finally, he had hope. He figured the Friedmanns would check on their storage barn the next morning, find him missing, and search for him. He had no way of knowing how long he'd have to stay in his new shelter, but he didn't expect it to be long. Until the Friedmanns found him, he'd remain right where he was.

My father remained right where he was for seven and a half days.

It boggles my mind when I consider that. While he had plenty of water, the potatoes couldn't have lasted more than two days, three at the most. He wouldn't have rationed his eating, because he never would have expected to be there very long. My father said it drizzled and rained for much of that week. Though his shelter kept him mostly dry, the bad weather kept people out of the fields, including the Friedmanns.

He had lived through the Dej ghetto, through the Birkenau selection process, through the Kastenhof granite mine and Stone Crusher *Kommando*, and through the *Bahnhof* infirmary ward. He had escaped twice, and had been captured once. Patton's Third Army was 156 miles away, an eighty-five minute drive at *Autobahn* speeds, and now he was lost? A couple of weeks remaining in the war, and he was going to die in a field, alone? The injustice of that was astounding.

Yet that's exactly the situation he found himself in.

'I was not going to die there,' my father stated to me. 'I was going to wait for as long as I had to wait until the Friedmanns found me. Water I had. I got a little hungry but that was nothing new for me. It was not so terrible.'

Seven or eight potatoes for seven days and he was only a *little* hungry? Is this really how he felt, 'not so terrible?' Or is it how he remembered it? Or once again, is it how he wanted me to see it? No matter the reason, he weakened as the days dragged on.

I was curious whether a person could survive for seven days with just seven or eight potatoes but unlimited water. It wasn't that I didn't believe my father. But this was yet one more incredible story in a string of incredible stories. I have friends who are doctors, but their expertise doesn't extend to this, so I turned to the internet, which made researching the question easy. The answer, I discovered, was definitely yes. The potatoes equaled between two and three days of his daily caloric intake in KZ Mauthausen. So he'd really endured 'only' five days by the stream with no food. Plus, for the past four days he'd been eating better than in the camps, garlic bread and whatever else Barbara prepared for him, so he had some calories stored up. Most importantly, his access to unlimited clean water multiplied his chances of survival. The week in the field was difficult, but well within my father's capability, even at that point.

That eighth day, Sunday, April 29, dawned bright and clear. My father said it was the first nice morning since the previous Sunday. He lay still. For the past two days he'd not expended any energy to move, except to reach water from the stream flowing next to him. He assumed he'd been forgotten about, abandoned, so he sat in his filth, just waiting to die, because there was nothing left for him to do.

Then he heard rustling in the grass. He'd been discovered.

Someone was approaching.

Chapter 62

261st Infantry Regiment.
121 Miles Away

To reach Enns, Austria, the 65th Infantry Division had to get cross the Danube River. At 1,700 miles, it is the second longest river in Europe, behind only the Volga River, 600 miles longer. It is such a formidable natural obstacle to armies that it served, for a time, as the northern border of the Roman Empire.

The Danube originates in southwestern Germany. First flowing northeast, at the German town of Regensburg it changes direction to flow southeast, coursing through Linz, and skirting Mauthausen and Enns. Ten miles from Enns it turns due east.

Patton was not going to let the Danube River slow his army's advance. He chose the small town of Kapfelberg, eight miles southwest of Regensburg, as the point that Third Army would cross that major waterway, and he honored the 65th Infantry Division by ordering it to lead the assault. At 2:00am on the morning of April 26, 1945, the 260th and 261st Regiments of the 65th, fighting side by side, crossed the Danube under cover of darkness in small boats.

German resistance on the far bank of the river was as heavy as anything the 261st had ever faced. Even in late April, 1945, the Wehrmacht was not ready to capitulate. The regiment got ashore on the east bank and fought its way slowly towards the day's objective, the German spa town of Bad Abbach, one mile to the east. Behind them, combat engineers struggled, under intense artillery fire, to build a Treadway Bridge across the river so reinforcements could get across easily.[1] At 9pm that night the bridge was opened, and troops and tanks poured across to support the 261st Regiment's soldiers heavily engaged on the eastern side.

---

1 A Treadway Bridge is, essentially, a series of rectangular inflatable rafts lined up side to side to support a makeshift roadway placed over the rafts.

Fighting around Bad Abbach continued for two days, until Friday, April 28, when the last of Nazi resistance was defeated. From then until Monday, May 1, the men of the 261st rested and reequipped, preparing for their last major push of the war. They were 121 miles from Enns. They would jump off shortly after my father discovered who, or what, was rustling in the grass.

Chapter 63

Miracle

Back at my hotel, I feel worn out, both mentally and physically, even more than when I checked in late the afternoon before. I am too amped up for a nap, too nervous about whether this evening will reveal to me the secret of how my father got lost. A short run, I decide, would let me gather my thoughts, clear my head, and prepare for one last big emotional push. Though I no longer run marathons, I still enjoy going for an occasional light jog. I change into shorts and t-shirt, and head out.

This part of Enns is flat, with homes and lo-rise apartment buildings scattered between small factories, train tracks, and farm fields. I run easily, planning to keep my heart rate up and my head empty. But my head refuses to cooperate. I think about all I saw the past two days, and marvel at how much I've learned. The places I visited – KZ Mauthausen, KZ Gusen, the Wiener-Graben and Kastenhof quarries, the stone crusher buildings, the *Steyrer–Ennser* intersection, the dusty side of the B1, the Friedmann home and barn – made me appreciate my father's survival so much more. My father's life was changed forever by each of these places. Each took something from him, or gave him something. Now I feel I need a descriptive word for my father's survival that exceeds *amazing*, or *incredible*, or *remarkable*, because those words are overused and wholly insufficient. I ponder what the right word might be.

Long before I'd written my first email to Mauthausen Memorial, their staff knew of my father from Peter Kammerstätter's unpublished manuscript. As a successful escapee, my father was a minor celebrity among them, and even among the town's leaders. That's why he was on the concentration camp website, it's why the mayor had assisted Angelika in her research of the intersection where he escaped the first time, and it's why Dr. Harreither and Dietmar Heck were so eager to meet me and help. One of their own, a citizen of their town, had helped a young Jew, an enemy and victim of the Nazis, to survive the war, and they were rightfully proud of the Friedmanns. My father had presented a very rare opportunity for someone in the shadow of KZ Mauthausen to do the right thing, and the Friedmanns had jumped at the chance.

More than a string of facts, Angelika told me she, and others at Mauthausen Memorial who now knew my father's complete story thanks to our email correspondence, considered his survival a series of six separate miracles. She could name them, in chronological order. One, his transfer from Gusen II to Gusen I, where his odds of living were significantly better. Two, being moved out of the *Bahnhof* infirmary ward, where he was sent to die. Three, his first escape and the SS boys not killing him. Four, encountering the sympathetic gendarme who returned him to KZ Mauthausen. Five, his second escape and then being found by the Friedmanns. And six, surviving after he'd gotten lost that Saturday night.

And so *miracle*, I decide, is the appropriate descriptive word I am seeking.

But that immediately brings up the biggest question nagging at me since my conversation with my cousin Vivi: if my father's survival was such a miracle, why didn't he tell me he was coming back here in 1997? Why wasn't he so proud of his survival that he would have jumped at the chance to be here with me? *What was he afraid of?*

As I run through the outskirts of the town whose citizens saved my father's life, I realize his own words, words I'd heard dozens of times, answer this question for me. It was that phrase he used at the Seder table in 2001 when telling me about the SS guards murdering the *KZlers* who'd elected not to go on the death march. It's the phrase he used whenever he told me, or anyone, of the worst of his experiences.

'You should never know.'

It was never just something he said that came out of his mouth to fill dead air.

It is what he was afraid of.

My father always used 'you should never know' when describing something particularly bad or difficult. Then he'd go on, telling me just a small amount, just a hint, of what it was I 'should never know.' He didn't ever want me knowing the worst of anything in life, and especially of this year of his life, of the year he'd spent in the camps. It was important to him that I knew his story of survival and escape. But he wanted me knowing only the highlights, the good stuff, the parts that made him feel proud or strong or smart. He wanted me knowing just enough to appreciate what he'd pulled off.

Perhaps in my father's mind I didn't need to know how he got from the Mauthausen town train station to the concentration camp; I didn't need to know how he 'made the ground spotless,' after the latrine barrel spill; and maybe he really was in the horrifically unsanitary *Zeltlager*, the tent camp erected in 1945 to handle the overflow of Jews. To him, I didn't need to know the worst.

But if I had come with him to KZ Mauthausen and KZ Gusen, then I 'would know' the worst, because by the Nazi's own rating system nothing was worse than KZ Mauthausen and KZ Gusen. *That's* what he was afraid of. He was afraid of me knowing. By not telling me of his trip and not inviting me to join him, he was protecting me from truly knowing the horrors he experienced. He was keeping me from walking in places where I would perhaps see what he saw, smell what he smelled, feel what he felt, *know what he knew*.

As I turn around on my run and head back to the hotel, I consider that 'you should never know' also meant *my father* should never have to fully remember. With those four words, he was throwing up his own internal mental roadblock so his mind would never have to go there again. He spent a year there, he went back once, and that was it. Done. He wasn't going there again, not physically, and not in his head, either. When he said 'you should never know,' he was stopping himself from remembering anything more than the bare facts. He wasn't going to think about it for a second longer than necessary to relate the story.

No doubt this was one of his most important survival mechanisms. His ability to bury these emotions kept him sane in the camps, enabling him to live every day that year with hope that the nightmare might end before he died. And then, after the war, after the nightmare finally did end, those buried emotions needed to stay there, out of sight, so he could live in the world again, live among people who would *truly* never know what he knew. But he was a natural storyteller, and he had quite a story to tell. So he told it, but he made it light, humorous, without much detail, and with almost no emotion.

This, I think, is how my father coped. This is how he got himself out of bed every morning.

Perhaps another reason he didn't tell me about his trip, another fear he had, is he didn't want me to see him as anything other than the strong, tough, ('give 'em a *zets* in the face') man he had always been in my eyes. He knew it would be an emotionally difficult, even gut-wrenching trip, and he wanted to do it alone. He was *Dad*, a man who had survived the unsurvivable and who had escaped twice from the Nazis. I think he didn't want me to see that under his *Dad* veneer, beneath the surface, he was human, that during that horrible year he was no more than a frightened kid living by his wits and relying on miracles to get from day to day. He probably figured he'd cry. I had only seen him cry once before, the day his friend Yishai Lovinger called, after my mother died. Maybe he didn't want me to see him cry again.

That toughness was partly a generational thing. The Greatest Generation, as the newsman Tom Brokaw famously named them, had expectations of behavior we now know were unrealistic and unhealthy. Men didn't cry, men sucked it up, men were men, and my father was a made member of that tribe.

I think the image in his mind of what a father should be derived not only from his peers in his Greatest Generation, but also from his own father, an Austro-Hungarian cavalry soldier, a prisoner of war, and a successful businessman. My grandfather must have presented to his children a nearly unattainable ideal. My father no doubt tried to come close. It may never have occurred to him that surviving a year in the worst concentration camp in the Reich, and then escaping, was a great accomplishment, not – in his mind – compared to the accomplishments of his own father. So in that context, the last thing he would have wanted was for me to see him weak. I think he needed to behave in a manner that his generation thought right, and that my grandfather would have approved of. I am pretty sure I show my children that I'm vulnerable, that I make mistakes, that I cry, that I can be hurt. But I can't be certain.

Which was the bigger reason my father didn't tell me about his trip back here – that 'I should never know,' or that I shouldn't see him as anything less than the *Dad* he wanted me to see? I'm not sure. But I'm not sure it matters, either. I finally get it. I finally understand. He had his own personal reasons for not taking me here, or even telling me he was going. And he loved me still.

As I near the hotel and the end of the jog, one quick thought makes me almost shout with joy when it pops into my head. 'Luxury way.' I know nothing about my father's return trip to KZ Mauthausen in 1997. But whether he'd flown coach or first class, if he'd stayed in a pension like the Hotel Romer or something higher end, if he'd rented a small Honda or a Range Rover SUV, his return trip was, relative to that first trip in June 1944, in a 'luxury way.'

My grandmother had been right. I wish I could have known her.

After my run, I return to the Italian restaurant I ate in the night before, in the Enns town square. It is bustling with diners. Sitting inside this time, I relax a bit while watching them. The few I overhear are speaking German, and none appear to be tourists. Presumably they are locals, and I fight the urge to tell them all where I am heading after finishing my dinner. I want to tell them all about the importance of one special family from this town – that without this family, without these fellow townspeople, I would not be on this earth. I say nothing, though.

It's dark when I pay my bill. I make a quick stop at a gas station to buy a flashlight, figuring I might need it. Soon I am back at the Friedmanns', parking just past their house. It's early September, and yet there's already a coolness to the evening air. I can only imagine how chilly an April evening must have felt. But my father never complained of being cold when he told his story, so I assume he must have had enough clothing. That, or yet again he had been holding back on the worst details of what he went through.

I glance up at the sky. There are no stars. In a lucky coincidence, though there is a full moon, its light barely penetrates the thin cloud cover that has blown in since this afternoon. It is no brighter out now than when my father walked under a half-moon that fateful Saturday night, April 21, 1945. And as it rained much of that week, it is possible he walked under cloud cover that obscured the moon entirely. This truly will be as close as I can come to what my father saw that night.

I roll my shoulders once to loosen them, and head towards the Y-intersection on *Kristein Strasse* south of the Friedmann house. Turning left at the fork, I quickly reach the barn I saw earlier this afternoon. It isn't easy to spot in the darkness, but there is enough moonlight filtering through the clouds that I see and sense a hulking structure before me. As I did once already this long day, I conclude with certainty that if my father had gone left at the fork, he would have found the barn he sought. He couldn't have missed it.

I turn and walk in the opposite direction.

Chapter 64

261st Infantry Regiment. 11 Miles Away

In April 1945, with Germany close to capitulation, General Eisenhower and his Russian counterpart agreed that the Enns River, a north-south waterway forming the town of Enns' eastern border, would serve as the dividing line between their armies – the U.S. wouldn't advance further east, and the Russians wouldn't go further west.[1]

After a short breather, on May 1, the 261st Regiment began closing the gap between its hard-won position on the eastern bank of the Danube, and the Enns River 121 miles away. What the regiment wouldn't know until it started moving, was whether the German Army would continue defending its territory, and especially the rivers blocking the regiment's route to Enns.

Beginning that morning, the 261st, this time with the 259th Regiment on its shoulder, crossed the Isar River in Platting, Germany. Though some die-hard SS units harassed the Americans, the regiments passed through the town quickly and safely. The next day they reached Passau, where a few weeks later my father would begin his long recuperation. The Second Battalion of the 261st (regiments are made up of battalions) crossed the Inns River and secured Passau after hard but brief fighting against more SS troopers.

Eight miles to the south, the First Battalion of the 261st became stuck in the town of Neuhaus when the bridge over the Inns River was blown up just as the battalion arrived. Not wanting to wait for a Treadway Bridge to be built, over the night of May 2 the battalion crossed the river in boats 'requisitioned' from locals and seized the town of Scharding.

---

1 This is why, after his discharge from the Kohlbruck Klinik in 1946, my father's train was required to stop in Enns on its way to Romania and Hungary.

After consolidating their territorial gains around Scharding, on May 3, the 261st Regiment mounted trucks and drove forty miles to Linz, Austria. Meeting little resistance along the way, by noon on Saturday, May 5, 1945, the regiment had overrun the city of 200,000 people where Hitler had spent most of his youth. Waiting till darkness, they then got on the B1, heading east.

The 261st Infantry Regiment of the 65th Infantry Division was now eleven miles from Barbara and Ignaz Friedmann's home, a fifteen-minute drive keeping to the speed limit.

Chapter 65

How

Walking west, I pass the Y-intersection and the driveway with the black Volkswagen. I reach the 4x4 track bordered by the tall growth, though I feel it more than I see it because the darkness on the track is nearly total. When I reach the canopy produced by the growth on my right cantilevering into the trees on my left, light doesn't penetrate at all, and I cannot see a thing as I walk. I take each step over the pockmarked ground cautiously.

Emerging into the clearing I see, barely, the fields that I know are there. Half a mile from me, beyond the fields, I note car headlights moving rapidly from my left to right, and right to left. Later I learn the cars are on an elevated section of the A1, an east-west trans-Austrian *Autobahn* built after the war to replace the B1. I hadn't noticed the highway when I was here with Angelika and Dietmar earlier in the day.

I take a dozen steps into the fields. The rutted track has given way to smooth grass underfoot, like walking on a lawn, or a ball field. Turning about-face to the direction I came from, I get a jolt. I see a dark mass, a wall where I should have seen trees and the path's cantilevering vegetation. The wall is wide and devoid of color, and I can't tell how far it is from me. I can't tell what it's made of, though I assume it's partially the cantilevering growth and trees. But what else is it made of? Where did it suddenly materialize from? I can't see the 4x4 track I just stepped off. I can't see the opening in the vegetation I'd walked through, even though I'd just emerged from it. All I see is this wall. It is fantastically disorienting.

I stand still for a moment, letting my eyes adjust further to the little moonlight sneaking through. Now I hear the cars on the A1 behind me because of how well sound travels at night. But I still see nothing except that dark wall of vegetation. Where did the path go? I turn around to recover my bearings. The fields are a bit easier to see now that my eyes have grown accustomed to the darkness. And there again is the A1 in the middle distance, though I remind myself that the highway didn't exist during the war.

Turning around once more to the direction I just came from, I still see nothing except that wall. *How did I get so lost so quickly?*

And then it hits me. If I can see nothing, neither could my father. If I feel lost now, imagine how lost *he* must have felt.

If my father had gone right at the fork that Saturday night, he would have hit the 4x4 track, come out into this field two minutes later, and walked a few yards into it to see where a barn might be.

Just as I did.

Failing to spot anything, he would have turned around and seen exactly what I see now: a dark wall of vegetation. Without the advantage of having been here this afternoon, I might have really been lost. My father was a skeleton with a sack of potatoes and a blanket: I bet his heart was coming out of his chest.

Did he panic? I think not. Even though at that moment his entire world was at stake, my father probably tried to figure things out calmly. Maybe I still have him on a pedestal, but that's what I think. I try doing the same.

I walk towards the dark wall, presumably the direction I just came from. As I draw closer, I slip down a short embankment. It's not steep, just a few feet of angled ground. I briefly wonder why I hadn't spotted it this afternoon. I guess when I could see well it didn't register with me as significant. I feel the manicured grass under my feet change to tall and uncut, soaking my shoes and pants legs. It is dew already forming. It is so dark in front of me, all I see is blackness.

I check behind me, and now I've lost sight of the wide expanse of fields and the A1. Something has blocked it. Surprisingly, I truly feel lost, even though I know I'm not really.

I keep walking forward. Five yards. Ten. I stop to listen. Still nothing but the occasional car far behind me, and now soft rustling of brush from a light breeze that has picked up. Even the birds are silent tonight. Five more steps, and I detect another sound. Low, bubbling, murmuring. Water. The *Kristeinerbach.* I tread carefully, not wanting to fall in.

A few steps more, and the grass ends. I bend down and run my hand along the ground. It feels like dirt. Smoothed dirt. I close my eyes so they'll adjust further to the dim light and count to twenty before opening them again. Now I make out the stream right in front of me, down a foot or so. But I still can't see much else.

Tired of the mystery, I turn on my new flashlight.

Pointing it in the direction I've come from, the powerful beam reveals I entirely missed the 4x4 track. I walked right past it, near the cantilevered trees, and as I did, I lost sight of the A1 – it was blocked by the trees. Slipping down that short embankment – which turns out to be about half my height – hid the fields past the track. In the other direction, I figure out that the dark wall was a combination of the cantilevering vegetation covering that track, merging with the line of trees and vines on the bank of the stream. I saw that same wall of trees and vines during the day. But in the afternoon sunlight I could distinguish distances. Tonight, in this deep darkness, I cannot, and so even though they are yards apart from each other, to my eyes they created a single long wall.

Shining the light around me, up and down, left and right, I see that I am standing in a natural hollow created by a gap within the trees and vines. The space is seven feet in length running along the stream, and three feet wide. Above me I see leaves, tree limbs, and thick knots of vines. A natural canopy envelopes me. Water flows next to me. The ground beneath me is dry dirt. There is protection from rain. It is safe.

It is more than safe. It is perfect.

Chapter 66

Why

I hear rustling again. Spinning around, I see nothing. I suddenly can't catch my breath. I drop down on one knee. I know, without a doubt, *this* is where my father stayed when he got lost. By coming to the Friedmann home at night and duplicating what he might have done that Saturday night, April 21, 1945, I found not only *how* my father got lost, but *where* he waited by the stream for someone to save him. I walked right smack into it, as he must have done that night.

My father spent a week here, alone except for eight potatoes and a blanket. I can't help myself, but I am wondering if I could have done this. Could I have spent a week lying here while people lived and worked nearby who hated me for no other reason than the religion I was born into, who might have killed me if they'd found me?

It is then, exactly at this moment, that I realize why I have so many unanswered questions about the details of my father's fateful year in the camps. I know why I never asked the questions I should have asked him, why I never dug deeper to learn what he'd been through here.

I know now what I am afraid of.

As the stream gurgles and the branches rustle, I know I never asked those questions because I didn't want to know the answers. The more answers I'd have known, the more amazing, *miraculous* actually, my father's achievement of survival would have been, the greater my burden, the harder it would have been to live up to what he'd accomplished, to what he'd pulled off. So far it's been a losing game for me, seeking tests that equal what I knew before this trip, about what my father survived. Imagine how much harder it is going to be *now,* with all the dark new detail I've learned here yesterday and today.

That's why I never asked the deep, probing questions I should have asked when he told his story at the Seder in 2001, and every time before then. That's why I had never made a trip here on my own, to see where he'd been, to see what he'd lived through. It would have increased the weight I feel being the son of a man who had, in my mind, done the impossible, a man I considered invincible.

But now, by this stream that saved my father's life, I am okay knowing the answers. Now I am glad I came here.

Not before tonight. But now.

Now I want to know everything I can learn about my father's year in the camps, his escapes, and his rescue.

I lower myself from my knee and sit on the smooth dirt.

Sitting in this naturally protected spot where I have no doubt Dad had been, I know it doesn't matter how much detail I learn: matching my father is impossible. As I figured out last night at dinner, nothing I do, no test I contrive for myself, no ski run, no aerobatics maneuver, no cycling or running speed or distance, nothing comes close to what my father accomplished by merely remaining alive. Nothing I *ever* do will equate to loading and pushing mine wagons at the stone crusher from morning till night, to enduring numbing starvation for months on end, to waking every day to the horizon-less hopelessness my father conquered. He will forever own the record in my family for physical accomplishment and mental toughness, and I don't need to match it. Instead, I need to be proud of him and let him have his seat at the top of that pyramid.

I look up at the vines overhead shielding me from the moonlight. Studying them, I know I need to be satisfied with my life, with its successes and failures and seized moments and missed chances. I have three beautiful children who are well on their way to being anything they choose. While I've lost my marriage, I have the time to find a new love.

What about the anger? On this trip anger seems to be lurking in me not far from the surface. Even just sitting here now, anger has been welling up over the indignity of my father having had to spend a week here by this stream. It has risen before since landing in Munich. Why should my father, or anyone, have had to load and push mine wagons until they were dead? Why did the white haired old woman call the SS on him? Why is someone living in the *Jourhaus*? Why are Gusens I and II now middle-class housing? Why are some of Gusen I's granite walls still standing?

Given all that I've seen, the anger might be perfectly understandable, but I will still have to master it. At least now I acknowledge it's there. Until this evening I couldn't say that.

My father can help. His life contained so many lessons for me, many of them wrapped up in his simple phrases. But one single, important lesson stands above them all: no matter how tough things are, no matter how difficult they may get, they are 'not so terrible,' and they are 'no big deal,' because 'life beats the alternative.'

So why now? Why am *I* here this night? Why had I contacted the Mauthausen Memorial staff after my cousin Vivi had alerted me to my father's picture on their website? Though it really took a while after that morning in 2007, why had I finally boarded a plane and come to this natural cover by a stream where my father had certainly been?

It is because I was ready. Until this trip, I had not been ready for the lessons my father's past could teach me. Now I am. Though I miss him terribly, his passing is long enough ago that his accomplishments no longer loom over me like … like the granite walls of Kastenhof or Wiener-Graben. I can see myself as separate from him, and my accomplishments – whatever they may be – as separate from his survival of the worst place in the world. I don't have to compare the things I do to the things he did. I see his for what they are, and now, at last, I see mine for what they are.

I sit here, the water gently coursing by me, a breeze filtering through the vines. I found what I had come to find, and I'd also found what I had not expected to find. I bend my head and let the tears flow.

Chapter 67

Found

The rustling in the grass grew louder. My father turned his head to the sound, and was face to face with its source: the Friedmanns' little dog. When the dog made eye contact with my father, it began yapping with the energy of a crazed Rottweiler. Maybe it recognized him, or maybe it was repulsed by his smell, but soon Barbara Friedmann came along to investigate.

She saw my father and froze. 'Dave! We thought you had run off!' Her eyes were wide in shock and remorse.

My father took a breath. 'No,' he said hoarsely, 'I couldn't find the barn.' He added a smile to make Barbara feel better.

'I'm so sorry!' She was nearly in tears as she knelt beside him and fixed the blanket covering him. 'I will come back quickly with some food. You must be so hungry!'

Barbara returned just minutes later with garlic bread and fresh clean water. She told him she couldn't move him until darkness, when no one would see them, but she and Ignaz would return and take him to the attic in the barn next to the house. The SS were still living in their home, but with fighting so close, they hadn't been around in a few days. She'd brought a change of clothes, and my father said he'd be cleaned up by the time they returned. The stream that kept him alive would help him with that, too.

After nightfall Barbara returned with Ignaz and a hand-drawn cart. My father got on, they covered him in case they ran into anyone on the path, and they wheeled him back to their home. The trip from my father's hiding place to their house was ridiculously short. On a straight line he was less than 200 yards from their front door. If there had been no foliage around the *Kristeinerbach*, he would have been able to *see* their house from his spot on the stream bank. It was crazy, how close he had been, but he was safe now and that's all that mattered.

Ignaz helped my father up the barn's stairs and into the attic space I had been in that afternoon, the one above the real cowshed. Finally he was in the *attic in the barn*. Ignaz was profusely apologetic, taking responsibility for not escorting my father to the barn in the field in the first place eight days earlier. My father put him at ease, saying, predictably, that it was no big deal. Soon he was comfortably ensconced on a bed of hay, in clean clothes, and with water and food.

Until my trip to Austria, I never understood why the Friedmanns hadn't taken my father to the storage barn that Saturday night, instead of sending him out alone. Now that I had walked their property, it was clear to me why. They feared getting caught with him. They feared being seen with him on *Kristein Strasse*, or on the path to the storage barn. Although in my mind they are heroes, I also recognize they had understandable limits to the risks they were willing to take.

My father spent nearly a week in that attic. Each day, as promised, either Ignaz or Barbara brought him food and water. Each day he got stronger, not only recovering from his week in the field, but starting to gain weight again.

At our Seder table late in the evening, my father's face glowed with what he was about to tell me. He cleared his throat. 'It was in the morning of May 4 or May 5, I don't remember. Ignaz came running up the steps to the attic.' My father needed to catch his breath. He was back there again, perhaps as excited now as he was that day. 'He was yelling "*Die Amerikaner sind da! Die Amerikaner sind da!*' 'Der Krieg is vorbei!*" The Americans are here! The war is over!' Then my father lowered his voice. 'Yes, Jeckeleh, it was true, the war was finally over.' My father exhaled deeply, and then beamed his best smile of the night at me.

At 10:30 the night before – according to regimental records it was Saturday, May 5 – American troops of the 261st Regiment, 65th Infantry Division, U.S. Third Army, drove past the *Kristein Strasse* intersection on the B1 on their way to the Enns River, where, fifteen minutes later they halted and bivouacked. They had taken the town without firing a shot.

It was so transparently clear at our Seder table how *miraculous* this felt, how incredibly happy and lucky and alive my father felt right then. He continued the story. 'Ignaz took me into his house, and gave me a bathroom to wash myself up properly. When I was ready to go, he met me with Barbara on their doorstep. I thanked them both. Really, what they did for me was something special.

Then I told them that I wasn't really from Czechoslovakia. I told them that I was a Jew.'

'They didn't know?'

'No, I said to them I was a Czech. I never told them anything different.'

'Did that matter to them?'

'Barbara said to me that they didn't care.' Then he paused for an instant. 'But I'll tell you the truth. For many years I didn't believe them.'

'Why, Dad? What did they say when you told them?'

'Barbara said she had watched thousands of marchers go by on the road near her house, and she knew by this time that only Jews were on the "transports." She thought maybe I was a Jew from Czechoslovakia, but she said it didn't matter where I was from. She wanted to help me. She thought it was terrible what the Nazis were doing. She wanted them to leave Austria already.'

'So why didn't you believe her?'

'Because Ignaz just stood there while she was speaking. He didn't say not one word.'

That was interesting. I suppose his own father would not have stood quietly while his wife, my grandmother, did the talking. My father had taken Ignaz's silence as an expression of his true feelings.

'Maybe,' I offered, 'he was content with Barbara doing the talking. It's not unheard of that the wife speaks for the husband.' I was being serious, but my father chuckled at that one. I thought perhaps he was remembering Mom.

'Yes, Jeckeleh, that's what I've been thinking this year. Maybe I misunderstood why he was so quiet. Maybe since that first day I was always wrong about him.'

I didn't know that evening, but I learned later that Ignaz's quiet was just who he was. He was a simple, principled man. He was an Austrian patriot, with views and opinions, but he didn't broadcast them, he kept them to himself. He did the same thing on the Enns train platform eighteen months later, being quiet and undemonstrative. Barbara might have been the effusive one, the alpha in the family. That's why I knew with certainty that Ignaz's silence was not an indication of anti-Semitism, of regret at saving my father's life.

I wonder now about all those years of my father thinking the Friedmanns would not have saved his life if they'd known he was Jewish. I had a feeling it pointed to something much bigger. Both behaviors – my father thinking the Friedmanns wouldn't have rescued him if they'd known he was Jewish, and his leaving out the worst parts of his story – were of a piece. Both, I decided, were his way of downplaying his own self-worth. With the Friedmanns, he thought if they knew he was a Jew, they'd consider him not worth saving. For himself, what he'd done that entire year was 'no big deal.'

I think this degrading of his own value, of his self-worth, wasn't modesty: it was another part of his post-war survival mechanism. Once he learned the magnitude of the destruction the Nazis inflicted on the Jews, once he learned the Jews lost six million souls while he'd lost four brothers and sisters and all their kids and his mother, and yet he survived, this is how he remained a functioning human being. This is how he stayed sane. He needed to believe he wasn't anything special, that surviving the Stone Crusher *Kommando* wasn't anything special, that escaping twice from death marches wasn't anything special, and that he, *as a Jew*, certainly wasn't special enough for the Friedmanns to save.

And now finally, he was beginning to think he was worthy. The first step was acknowledging that the Friedmanns would have saved him even if he'd said he was a Jew that first morning on the path.

Uncharacteristically, I probed my father's thinking. 'Dad, why the new view?'

My father just smiled and shrugged.

We were not going to go deeper, not that night. Perhaps it was his impending surgery. Perhaps he was taking inventory of his life and figured it was time to reconsider some long-held beliefs. But he wouldn't say, and I didn't ask further.

And so on the morning of May 6, 1945, my father and his rescuers, the Friedmanns, parted ways. The Friedmanns pointed my father towards American soldiers patrolling the B1, and off he went.

'This time I followed the directions,' Dad said, 'and I reached to the main road where I saw American tanks on the shoulder. I came up to the first U.S. soldier, he was sitting on a tank smoking a cigarette. So I asked him, "*Sprichst du Deutsch?*" Do you speak German? I'm sick, I told him. I hadn't met Mommy yet, so I couldn't talk to him in English.' The twinkle in my father's eye, his left eye, was sparkling brilliantly.

Many American soldiers spoke German, either because they'd hailed from families with German heritage, or because they'd picked it up in combat. This soldier spoke the language well enough.

Dad went on. 'He said to me in German, "Go into town, it's a mile that way,"' and held out his arm to show me the way. This was my welcome to freedom.'

270

Though my father was disappointed he wasn't offered a ride into town, he was alive and he was free, and so he happily followed the soldier's arm pointing him east down the B1. He'd walked so far, so often, that another mile wasn't going to kill him. Literally.

My father soon found himself in the Enns town square. He'd been here one month earlier, in the custody of two juvenile Hungarian SS troopers who could have killed him but didn't. He'd been here in the charge of a local gendarme who gave him a plate of eggs and let him sleep comfortably in a jail cell. And now he was back as a free man. He could hear that train his mother told him to expect. It was pulling into the station.

The square was bustling with military activity, soldiers moving every which way, jeeps crossing left and right with drivers running noisily through their gears, orders being shouted. My father spotted the jail where he'd spent the night one month earlier, now with a huge Red Cross flag flying above its entrance. He walked towards it, and, suddenly, not quite there but completely out of breath and strength, he stopped and lay down on the ground. He could walk no further. He had gone far enough.

Dad's vision locked on to a young medic, Red Cross symbols on his helmet and his left arm. The medic must have felt eyes on him because he turned, saw my father looking at him, and trotted over. The man knelt and leaned over Dad. Their eyes met. The American put his hand gently on my father's boney chest and smiled.

'I got you,' he said.

Epilogue

After being found by a medic from the 261st Regiment, my father was sent first to a local hospital in Neinhausen, Austria. Following a few days of emergency care he was transferred to the Kohlbruck Clinic, in Passau, Germany. He spent eighteen months in Kohlbruck, recovering from tuberculosis, pneumonia, dysentery, typhus, jaundice, and a nearly deadly bout of peritonitis. When he was finally released eighteen months later, he returned to his home town of Dej by train, reuniting with his sister Rosie and brothers Villi and Isadore. It was on that trip that Dad met Ignaz Friedmann at the Enns *Bahnhof* to thank him, leaving the photo with him that Barbara later passed on to Peter Kammerstätter.

While the three brothers and sister earned a good living running the family soap factory, to my father Dej didn't feel like home any more, not after all that had happened to him. He wanted to move to Israel and make a new life for himself there. It was a thought he had been entertaining since his pre-war days in Bnei Akiva, the Zionist youth group. In 1947, he finagled a visa by pretending to be the son of an orthodox family whose son had already emigrated. The authorities never caught on, my father landed in Haifa, and so once again he had gotten away with something.

One thing my father didn't get away with was the surgery in July 2001 to repair his failing mitral valve. On a Friday morning early that month, he went under anesthesia in a New York City hospital operating room. He fell into a coma during the operation and died eight days later, one day after his seventy-sixth birthday. The odds had finally caught up with him. Incredibly, the man I'd always believed was indestructible, who couldn't be killed by the Nazis or by two heart attacks, died on an operating table.

The Friedmanns went on with their lives. They never had other children. From what Mauthausen Memorial staff could learn, they apparently told none of their neighbors, and only a few of their close relatives, about saving my father's life.

Author's Note

While researching this book, I often came across inconsistencies. Some were small, some bigger. Dates didn't always line up. Did my father walk into the Enns town square after the Americans liberated the town on May 5, or the next day, May 6? Was my father 'transported' from Birkenau to KZ Mauthausen on June 10, 1944, or June 11? I know the exact date he arrived at Birkenau, and I know exactly six days later he checked into KZ Mauthausen, because both dates were stamped by the Nazis on his *Häftlings-Personal-Karte*, his Prisoner Personnel Card. And from his story I know he spent at least two nights in Birkenau and three nights on the train. The rest is a guess. Even researching Patton's Third Army, I found accounts, 'official' and otherwise, to be off between them by a day or so.

In the end, the accuracy of a day or an afternoon is not as important as the fact that these things all happened, and they happened the way I described them.

A curious inconsistency is in the story of my father meeting the Friedmanns. Barbara Friedmann told Peter Kammerstätter she was alone when she'd encountered my father on the path to the train station. My father says she was with Ignaz. Also, my father tells the story of them first seeing him on the side of the path feigning death, and later running into them on the path. Barbara never told Peter Kammerstatter that feigning-death anecdote. Instead, she said their first meeting was when they ran into each other on the path. Barbara has been described to me as very strong-willed, or more bluntly, as the one who wore the pants in the family. Perhaps she wanted sole credit for rescuing my father, and maybe she was embarrassed that they couldn't tell whether my father had been alive. We obviously will never know whose story is right, but I wrote it the way my father always told it.

Besides, the details of that morning don't change what happened next – details that both versions agree on. Barbara brought my father food, later that night Ignaz took him back to their house, and he stayed with them until the end of the war. And so I am here.

Although it was my hope that the places I saw in Austria would forever remain exactly as they looked during my trip, it was not to be. While KZ Mauthausen is tended by The Mauthausen Memorial and unlikely to ever change, and while the areas around Gusen and the first escape intersection are already built up and so unlikely to change much more, the second escape intersection has recently been redeveloped. The brush, trees, chain-link fence, and cement wall are gone, replaced by a manicured field. The intersection now looks nothing like the one I stood on with Mr. Fisher, Dietmar Heck and Angelika Schlackl that sunny afternoon and, by following my father's story, discovered where he sat down on the side of the road to die.

This book would not have been possible without the assistance of the dedicated staff at the Mauthausen Memorial. I hesitate to name names for fear of leaving someone out, but I must single out Angelika. She is immensely knowledgeable and insightful, and was hugely helpful in my efforts to learn all I could about my father's time in the camps in Austria. I am especially grateful to Joseph Olshan, whose world-class editing skills steered me through crucial midcourse corrections that put the manuscript on its final trajectory. I'm greatly indebted to my publisher, Martin Mace of Frontline, for taking on this book and guiding me to the finish line and beyond. Finally, I must thank my children, Sam, Rachel and Lauren, for their help with the manuscript, and especially for their love and support. It is partly for them and their generation that I wrote it, so they would know exactly what their grandfather survived, know the unspeakable horrors man can inflict on others, know that the limit of human endurance is far beyond what they might have ever considered, and know that a piece of their grandfather is within each of them.

Jack J. Hersch
New York, NY

Index